Herbert Hoover in front
of Hoover Tower

THE LIBRARY OF THE HOOVER INSTITUTION ON WAR, REVOLUTION AND PEACE

EDITED BY PETER DUIGNAN

FOREWORD BY W. GLENN CAMPBELL

HOOVER INSTITUTION   STANFORD UNIVERSITY

Endpaper map courtesy of *San Jose Mercury News*

Hoover Press Publication 316

Copyright 1985 by the Board of Trustees of the
    Leland Stanford Junior University

First Printing, 1985
Manufactured in the United States of America
89 88 87 86 85   9 8 7 6 5 4 3 2

Library of Congress Cataloging in Publication Data
Main entry under title:

The Library of the Hoover Institution on War,
    Revolution, and Peace.

    Bibliography: p.
    1. World politics—20th century—Library
resources—California—Stanford.   2. Hoover
Institution on War, Revolution, and Peace.
I. Duignan, Peter.   II. Hoover Institution on
War, Revolution, and Peace.
Z6204.L62 1985   [D443]   026.3   85-838
ISBN 0-8179-8161-6
ISBN 0-8179-8162-4 (pbk.)

Design by P. Kelley Baker

CONTENTS

FOREWORD

Since its founding in 1919, the Hoover Institution on War, Revolution and Peace at Stanford University has become an international center of documentation and research on problems of political, social, and economic change in the twentieth century. Thousands of students and scholars from the United States and abroad have used its resources and facilities, advancing knowledge and learning as well as contributing to the attainment and preservation of freedom and peace with honor.

The worldwide coverage of the Institution's collections gives them special value in this period when so many problems are international in scope. While each of the area collections (Western Europe, Eastern Europe and the Soviet Union, Africa, East Asia, Latin America, and the Middle East) is in itself outstanding, the distinguishing feature of the Institution lies in its housing under one roof for convenient study the records of the major upheavals of the contemporary world. These great collections offer an opportunity to concentrate on one area or to undertake comparative studies on critical subjects relating to two or more areas or to study important problems in a global perspective.

Many experts consider the Institution's holdings on the Russian and Chinese revolutions and the growth and spread of communism throughout the world to be the premier collections in these fields in the free world. The Hoover Institution contains one of the most extensive records on Hitler and the Nazi movement as well as on Mussolini and fascism. It is a place where scholars can document such diverse but important twentieth-century events as the story of Vichy France, the French Fifth Republic, the rise of the Chinese Communists, underground movements in Africa and Asia, the turbulent history of the Middle East, the postwar German and Japanese economic recoveries, or the development of the Western Alliance. Several country collections—on the USSR, Germany, Poland, China, Japan, Cuba, and

South Africa—are unequaled in their fields; many of the Institution's documents are the only copies in existence.

But the Hoover Institution is more than a group of collections for the study of revolutionary movements such as communism and fascism. It serves not only the currently attractive fields of scholarship—Soviet, African, and East Asian studies—but also more fundamental and seemingly prosaic areas of research. Besides its internationally distinguished resident research staff, more than a thousand scholars and students come each year to do the conscientious work that advances the frontiers of learning. As a result, the Institution has become a world-renowned center for investigating international affairs and many other aspects and problems of the twentieth century, such as colonialism, decolonization, the North-South debate, disarmament, the arms race, women's movements, and all aspects of U.S. domestic policies.

The primary focus of the Institution's program is the problem of securing and maintaining peace. This is in keeping with the expressed aim of its founder, who at the dedication of the Tower building on June 20, 1941, stated:

> The purpose of this Institution is to promote peace. Its records
> stand as a challenge to those who promote war. They should
> attract those who search for peace.

We are concerned primarily with promoting basic research and documentary studies—studies that provide the foundation upon which new knowledge is built. But we are concerned with living issues and, hence, with dynamic rather than static research. The object of the Institution's research program is, therefore, to investigate topics where the collections are particularly strong and to promote studies whose findings can make important contributions to national policy. Finally, our approach is multidisciplinary. The research staff includes historians, economists, sociologists, demographers, and political scientists, as well as persons broadly trained and experienced in international law and the social sciences in general.

W. Glenn Campbell
Director
Hoover Institution on War, Revolution and Peace

PART I

THE HOOVER INSTITUTION

1 | ORIGIN AND GROWTH

Peter Duignan
Senior Fellow

While crossing the North Sea late in 1914, Herbert Hoover read and was impressed by the comments of Andrew D. White, president of Cornell University, on the difficulties he faced in studying the French Revolution because of the disappearance of contemporary documents and fugitive materials. Mr. Hoover resolved not to let this happen to the records of World War I; the idea of a collection of contemporary materials on the war became a reality, initially as a result of his personal enterprise and later as a cooperative effort with Stanford faculty, friends, and assistants throughout Europe.

The Commission for Relief in Belgium (CRB), which Mr. Hoover organized and directed, was without precedent in international history; a British diplomat once described it as "a piratical state organized for benevolence." The purpose of the commission was to aid and protect the civilians of Belgium and northern France living behind German lines. In carrying out its work, the commission performed the functions and enjoyed the privileges of a national state. It had its own flag; it made contracts and informal treaties with governments; its ships were granted special exemptions; its officials enjoyed extensive powers and immunities. The commission was both an international body under the patronage of neutral states and a private organization to which the belligerent powers entrusted responsibilities no single government or public body could carry out.

When Mr. Hoover returned from Europe in 1917 to become United States food administrator, he extended the collecting of documents in this country and abroad through many agencies of the Allied governments. Opportunities for gathering data increased greatly after his return to Europe in 1918 as director general of relief for the Allied and associated powers and an executive of the Supreme Economic Council. For expert aid in these collecting activities, Mr. Hoover turned to his alma mater, Stanford University. He offered $50,000 to Dr. Ray Lyman Wilbur, president of the University and a longtime friend, "for an historical collection on the Great War," if a suitable commission were organized and sent to Paris to gather the records. Professor E. D. Adams of Stanford's Department of History was chosen to go to Europe and direct a group of young scholars released from military service by General Pershing.

These "historical sleuths" enjoyed exceptional opportunities. Wartime restrictions and censorship had ended, and most governments, old or new, were well-disposed toward the United States and especially toward anyone connected with Mr. Hoover's widespread humanitarian activities. Professor Adams set up headquarters in Paris and dispatched his young scholars to every corner of Europe. Dr. Adams and his main collaborators, historians Dr. Ralph H. Lutz and Dr. Frank A. Golder, laid the foundations for much of the present collection by acquiring previously unobtainable government documents and material on the various revolutions of 1917–1919 and on the new states established by the Peace Conference. The Latin American Collection also originated in 1919 with delegation propaganda collected at the Paris Peace Conference.

The friendly relations between the American Relief Administration (ARA) and central and local governments, private organizations, and individuals in the states of Central and Eastern Europe, from Finland in the north to Turkey and Greece in the south, greatly aided their collecting efforts.

The original grant was soon exhausted, and Mr. Hoover made an additional $100,000 available. As a result, by 1921 the Hoover War Collection of Stanford University contained close to 80,000 items.

The collection grew so rapidly that it could no longer be designated a "special collection" within the University Library; it became, in fact, a library in its own right. In 1922, the University administration named it the "Hoover War Library" and assigned an entire wing of the University Library to house it.

By taking the initiative in 1919 in bringing together documents on political, economic, and social developments leading to the outbreak of World War I, as well as

Professors Ralph H. Lutz and E. D. Adams beside the first shipment of documents to the Hoover War Collection in 1921

materials on all aspects of the war and its aftermath, Mr. Hoover entered a field that had been neglected in the United States. The records gathered between 1919 and 1922 put the Hoover Institution twenty years ahead of any other American center of learning.

Collecting trips were the major method used to build up the library and to broaden its scope beyond being the depository for the CRB and ARA archives. The men who did most of the traveling and collecting were Adams, Golder, and Lutz. Adams was the first to undertake an acquisitions trip. In 1919 he initiated collecting for the library, and then in 1922 and 1924 he renewed European contacts and obtained pledges for collections. Since Adams was in poor health, Golder became the great traveler-collector. He laid the bases for the Central and Eastern European collections between 1920 and 1922 and visited the Soviet Union in 1925 and 1927.

THE INTERWAR PERIOD

When the ARA undertook to feed millions of famine-stricken Russian children in 1921, Professor Golder joined the organization's team in Russia and was able to acquire excellent materials dealing with modern Russia. Although frequently followed by the Cheka, the first communist secret police, Golder calmly went about his task of gathering records of the last days of Tsarist Russia, the short-lived Provisional Government, and early post-revolutionary years. He acquired some 25,000 volumes and over 60,000 pamphlets, government documents, periodicals, and newspapers. Besides obtaining important records from Central Europe, the Baltic states, Turkey, and the then-independent nations of the Caucasus, Golder laid the basis for the collections on Imperial, Revolutionary, and Soviet Russia, which today are among the major resources of the Institution.

During his travels to Europe, Professor Golder renewed old contacts and established new ones in many countries in order to ensure a steady delivery of publications. But this tremendous flow of research literature to Stanford posed a new problem: cataloging and listing this material to make it available to interested scholars and students. A small staff under the direction of Miss Nina Almond, the librarian of the Hoover War Library, was set to work, and, with the help of G. T. Clark, the University librarian, the material was gradually processed.

Dr. Frank A. Golder, who directed a group of young scholars in gathering records of World War I and its aftermath

As Golder built the collection on Imperial and Soviet Russia, Professor Ralph H. Lutz laid the foundation for the German and Central European collections. Crossing and recrossing Western and Central Europe, Lutz gathered material on the German revolution of 1918, the Paris Peace Conference, economic reconstruction, the reparations question, the occupation of the Ruhr, and the rise of left- and right-wing organizations. As a result, the Institution now has priceless documents on the interwar period in Central Europe, especially on the rise of the Nazi Party.

Professors Adams, Lutz, and Golder thus not only secured material on the war of 1914–1918 but also, by broadening the collecting purposes of the library, acquired valuable records on the revolutionary movements that swept through Central and Eastern Europe and the Soviet Union as a result of the war.

In the early 1930s, when the triumph of National Socialism in Germany heralded another crisis in world affairs, the Board of Directors of the Hoover War Library adopted a new definition of the purposes of the library and initiated collecting on a broader scale. "The Hoover War Library is a collection of materials for research in the causes, conduct, and results of the World War, the peace settlements, and the principal national and international problems of the period of reconstruction."

This policy was firmly established and consistently maintained until the outbreak of World War II. The library covered practically all European countries and all revolutionary movements. The Soviet Union received special attention, as did fascist Italy and Nazi Germany, but the activities of the League of Nations and the efforts of Great Britain and France to secure peace and prosperity in Europe were not neglected.

The library acquired materials concerning events in Latin America, Asia, the Middle East, and Africa only when those events were relevant to its major emphasis. For example, interest in the League of Nations led the staff to secure reports of the African and Middle East mandates. Combined with records from the British, Belgian, and German governments, these League of Nations mandate reports and other government documents formed the nucleus of an African collection. Similarly, materials from the Paris Peace Conference on the liquidation of the Ottoman Empire, the League of Nations mandates in Asia Minor, and reports of the mandate-trustees were the basis for an excellent collection on the modern Middle East.

The scope of the Hoover War Library had certainly extended much beyond subjects connected with World War I and Hoover's relief activities. The peace settlements of 1919–1925 and the various peace movements of the 1920s and 1930s became a major field of interest; the vast holdings on revolutionary movements, particularly in Germany, Italy, and Russia, made the library a leading center for the study of social, political, and economic change in the twentieth century. To house the collections and to provide office space for the large staff of scholars and visiting researchers, a new building was erected. This building, known as the Hoover Tower, was dedicated on June 20, 1941.

In 1938 the name of the library had been changed to the Hoover Library on War, Revolution and Peace due to the growth of the collections. The designation was changed again in 1947 to the Hoover Institute and Library on War, Revolution and Peace to reflect the growing importance of the research programs. The present name—Hoover Institution on War, Revolution and Peace—was adopted in 1956.

FROM WORLD WAR II TO THE PRESENT

A small dossier of military material had been purchased from the widow of a French brigadier general. It contained a complete set of French military maps of North Africa. At the time of the landing of Gen. Mark Clark in North Africa in November 1942, these were the only maps available. The United States Army found them of immense value, and they undoubtedly saved many lives.

The outbreak of hostilities in Europe found the Institution's directors prepared. In 1939, Professor Lutz visited agents in Europe and left funds to be used in the event of war. The old established network of friends in France and Belgium was alerted to collect important documents. In 1941, as a result of the war against Japan, the Far East became a major field of collecting interest.

During the war, students and scholars shared the Institution's facilities with uniformed men in search of data needed by the United States armed forces and various governmental departments and agencies. Many documents, maps, newspapers, and special collections originally acquired for research to promote peace were now intensively used to help secure military victory. The Institution organized a Civil Affairs Training School to prepare army officers for occupation duties in Europe, a Civil Communications Intelligence School to train censorship officers for Japan, and a School for Naval Administration. In addition, a radio station to monitor enemy broadcasts and a clandestine radio transmitter beamed to the Philippines also operated from the Hoover Tower.

During the war, collecting activities were greatly increased and preparations were made to extend collecting to areas in Europe and Asia that would be opened after the termination of hostilities. Herbert Hoover, through his friends and former associates, was able to provide considerable funds for these expanded collecting activities once the war ended. A Hoover Library mission in Europe attached to the official group from the Library of Congress was able to ship to Stanford more than 200 crates of materials from most of the countries involved in the war. Only Russia and the Soviet-occupied areas remained closed to the collectors. In Belgium and France, old friends of the Hoover Library renewed their collecting activities. Many Stanford students, faculty members, and alumni who had served in the armed forces also contributed valuable material acquired during their service at various fronts. For example, Maj. Lee Telesco, a Stanford graduate who was a leader of Filipino guerrilla forces, sent the Institution a large collection on the Japanese occupation, including a complete set of the journals of the Japanese military government in the Philippines.

Soon after the Japanese signed the surrender pact aboard the USS *Missouri*, members of the Stanford University Alumni Association of Tokyo made plans to collect documents that would shed light on the movements and forces within Japan that had plunged the nation into war. In November 1945 with the permission of the Supreme Commander for the Allied Powers, a Tokyo Office of the Hoover Institution was established under the direction of Yoshio Higashiuchi, a member of the Stanford University class of 1937, and under the informal supervision of Col. Hubert G. Schenck, then chief, Natural Resources Section, General Headquarters, Supreme Commander for the Allied Powers. Schenck was a professor at Stanford on military leave.

In 1946 President Truman appointed Mr. Hoover to coordinate world efforts to meet the great famine that followed World War II. He visited 39 countries and acquired many valuable documents. Chiang Kai-shek's government gave important materials on the Nationalists' war against the Communists, and an old friend of Mr. Hoover's, T'ang Shao-yi, twice prime minister of the Chinese Republic, contributed important records of earlier revolutionary actions. Representatives were also appointed to collect materials in China. The result of their work was a particularly fine collection on political and economic developments in that country since the founding of the Chinese Republic in 1911. As a result of Mr. Hoover's visit to Japan in 1946, the United States Army formally recognized the Tokyo Office, and collecting activities were intensified.

The collapse of the totalitarian governments in Italy and Germany offered an opportunity for gathering books, periodicals, and archives documenting their history. Special representatives were dispatched to Europe to seek materials on the conduct of the war, resistance movements, refugee problems, psychological warfare, and related subjects.

One of the most striking finds was the diary of nazi propaganda chief Joseph Goebbels, a revealing account of the activities of Hitler's inner circle. This diary was presented to Mr. Hoover when he visited Berlin in 1946. Many other rare wartime records were secured by Mr. Hoover on trips to Europe in 1947, 1954, and 1958.

Quick thinking on the part of Hoover agents in Belgium brought the Institution a complete record of German propaganda and occupation directives. Institution committee members were the first to arrive after the Germans evacuated their headquarters, leaving all their records behind them.

Mr. Hoover himself figured in one dramatic episode that brought the Institution rare files from the Polish underground. During a government-sponsored reception in Warsaw in 1946, six bound volumes were thrust into Mr. Hoover's hands by Deputy Premier Stanisław Mikołajczyk, who explained: "We have been asked to give you a memento of your visit to Poland. This is mine." The Polish leader realized that with the Iron Curtain falling rapidly around his country, he would have few chances to deliver these documents to the free world. A year later, he fled Poland.

As a result of these activities, the flow of materials in the first five postwar years more than doubled the prewar holdings of the Hoover Institute and Library on War, Revolution and Peace. Research activities based on materials in the Hoover Library, which had begun in the late 1920s with research programs on the German and Russian revolutions and had been abandoned for lack of funds during the Depression,

A German-born American soldier, Sgt. E. J. Cramer, who attended the Civil Affairs Training School at the Hoover Institution during the early part of the war, remembered the library when he found bound volumes of the complete file of the rabidly anti-Semitic Der Stürmer *on a visit to Julius Streicher's former country home soon after Germany's defeat. This vivid record of nazi thought is now a part of the Hoover Institution's extensive collection on the Hitler regime in Germany.*

In Vienna, a Hoover Institution agent located a rare wartime file of the newspaper Pester Lloyd. *He bought it from a servant girl, who had received it as part-payment on a delinquent bill from a penniless journalist.*

were revived. During the years of this high tide of incoming materials, new area collections on China, Japan, the Near East, Indonesia, and Pakistan were added to the library. Although the first three developed into major area collections, the latter two were limited to material in Western languages only. As a consequence of this expansion, the staff increased considerably.

By 1950, the area collections were served by six area curators and several area assistants. In this process, the library developed the concept of area and subject curators. Today many university libraries have created similar positions in imitation of the Hoover curatorial area and subject specialists. Also, the traditional concern of Hoover curators with collecting the documents of contemporary history has been adopted by some research libraries.

The new collection on China was of particular interest to students and scholars. Dr. Mary Wright, curator of the Chinese Collection, who with her husband, Arthur, had collected much of the material upon release from a Japanese prison camp in China, initiated and directed the preparation, by Miss Chao Kuo-chung, of a survey of materials held by the Hoover Library relating to communism in China during the years 1927–1934. This was the first bibliographical aid to the excellent collection on communism in China, which, in 1948 when this survey was completed, was not yet fully cataloged.

The Belgian-American Educational Foundation had been active since 1920, when it was created by former associates of the Commission for Relief in Belgium, an American WWI organization headed by Herbert Hoover. In prewar times, this foundation aided in the Hoover Library's acquisition of Belgian materials. Some of its members, at great personal risk, continued collecting activities during the German occupation of 1940–1944 and eagerly renewed their broad acquisition activities after the cessation of hostilities. In 1950 the foundation published an "inventory" of the 39 large crates of collected material that reached the Hoover Library.

The Tokyo Office of the Hoover Institute and Library, as noted earlier, was formed by Japanese alumni of Stanford University who decided documentation should be gathered "which would shed light on the movements and forces within Japan which had plunged the nation into total war and complete defeat." They decided to place these documents in the Hoover Library, and thus began the combined efforts of the Tokyo group and the Hoover Library administration that led to the creation of the collection on modern Japan.

In the middle and late 1950s, financial difficulties forced the Institution to curtail its collecting and research activities (although during this time Mrs. Ruth Perry did establish the African Collection). After 1960, however, when Dr. W. Glenn Campbell became the director, the annual acquisitions and research budgets began to increase substantially, with striking results. The research program was revitalized with four senior appointments, a Hoover publications department was started, and a fellowship program was initiated. The African Collection was strengthened by the appointment of a full-time curator, who in one year purchased thousands of volumes and entered subscriptions to 38 newspapers and 250 magazines. Among the unique items acquired were issues of the South African communist newspaper, *Guardian*, and copies of other publications by radical and revolutionary groups. The microfilming of the Confidential Prints of the British Foreign Office and Colonial Office, which deal with Africa since 1870, gave the Institution the most valuable single collection of documents on African affairs in the United States.

This expansion into the African field did not lead to neglect of the other collections. Notable acquisitions in Western European documentation during those years included the resources of the Allied Commission for Austria during the period

W. Glenn Campbell,
Director of the Hoover Institution

1945–1955; the stenographic protocols of the congresses of the French Mouvement Républicain Populaire, 1945–1962; a microfilm copy of the NSDAP Hauptarchiv, the main historical archives of the Nazi Party; and the papers of Louis Loucheur (1872–1931), onetime French minister of war, armaments, and reconstruction.

Documents on the Third International included the unpublished memoirs and papers of some former communist leaders, such as Henri Barbé, a member of the Presidium of the Comintern (1928–1930), and Albert Vassart, representative of the French Communist Party to the Comintern (1934–1935).

In 1960 the Honorable Chen Cheng, vice-president of the Republic of China, permitted the Hoover Institution to microfilm some 1,170 documents on the Kiangsi Soviet (1931–1934). At the time this collection was the most important file of Chinese Communist Party (CCP) records in a Western library. In addition, 150 Chinese communist publications relating to the 1945–1949 period were microfilmed in Taipei. These unique records, issued for use only within the CCP, contain a wealth of data on events during the communist struggle for power.

Hundreds of gifts enrich the collections each year. One of the more important ones was the extensive collection of books, pamphlets, and files on the Far East and communism of Mr. Alfred Kohlberg, a longtime student of Chinese affairs.

In 1962 systematic collecting on Latin America resumed after interruptions in the 1940s and 1950s. In addition to Cuba, seven countries received primary attention: Argentina, Bolivia, Brazil, Chile, Colombia, Mexico, and Venezuela.

During most of the 1950s and the early 1960s, Witold S. Sworakowski was both associate director and curator of the Eastern Europe and Soviet Union Collection. In 1962, Karol Maichel replaced him as curator. Professor Sworakowski was one of the greatest collectors and bibliographers in the history of the Hoover Institution. Perhaps his most impressive feat was obtaining Boris Nicolaevsky's library on European socialist revolutionary movements—notably communism—in the face of intense competition from Harvard, Columbia, and Indiana universities. Ranging from 1901 to the 1960s, the Nicolaevsky Collection includes more than 20,000 books and other publications, plus scores of archives, manuscripts, and letters. In the collection are papers of Trotsky and Bukharin, letters of Lenin, Zinoviev, and Andreev, and a recently discovered collection of over one hundred items of correspondence between Trotsky and his son. Professor Sworakowski obtained not only the collection, but the collectors—Nicolaevsky and his assistant, Anna Bourguina.

Sworakowski's collecting genius did not cover just Eastern Europe and the Soviet Union; he bought or received as gifts numerous archives on Western Europe, Turkey, and the United States. For example, the Raymond Moley Collection on the New Deal "Brain Trust" period was brought to Hoover thanks to Sworakowski. Sworakowski retired in 1969 and died in 1979. Dr. Richard Staar replaced him as associate director for library and archival operations; he served in that position until 1981, when he became U.S. ambassador to the Mutual and Balanced Force Reduction negotiations in Vienna, Austria.

The 1960s and the early 1970s were a troubled period in Stanford's history. The Hoover Institution, in common with other organizations, had to cope with bitter hostility from militants and suffered physical damage as well as much abuse from radical faculty and students.

Nevertheless, the Hoover grew in a remarkable fashion during this period. In just over one decade, its income rose sixfold (from $389,686 in academic year 1959–60 to $2,393,402 in 1971–72). The physical plant also expanded; in 1967, the Lou Henry Hoover Building opened its doors. The gubernatorial papers of Ronald Reagan came in 1975, followed by the papers from his 1976 and 1980 presidential

First printing of the 1848 Communist Manifesto. This copy is held by no other American library and is one of the few to exist anywhere in the world. A typographical error on the last page identifies it as a first printing.

Ronald Reagan's biographical sketch, handwritten on misprinted stationery, which the president used as scratch paper (ca. 1966)

campaigns and the papers from the 1980–81 presidential transition teams. Relations with Stanford University grew closer through joint appointments between the Hoover Institution and several academic departments; Hoover curators also served as curators for corresponding programs in the university library system.

During 1969–1972 G. K. Hall and Company of Boston completed the filming and publication, in 88 volumes, of the Hoover Institution's entire library catalog. Publication of the catalog reduced the need to compile special bibliographies of Hoover's rare holdings and bibliographical publications were reduced after that time.

The filming of the card catalog of the Institution by G. K. Hall was in part also a safekeeping measure. During the period of student hostility in the late 1960s, the card catalog of the University Library suffered severe damages when honey and red ink were poured over drawers and cards were ripped out.

A new Hoover collection begun in 1969 covered national, regional, and local publications of the various movements and coalitions known collectively as the "New Left."

In 1971, moreover, the Hoover Institution began a program of National and Peace fellowships offering gifted young scholars an opportunity to spend a year at the Hoover to do research, free from teaching or administrative duties. These fellowships, as well as a concurrent program of Public Affairs fellowships, have brought many young scholars to Hoover. (By the end of 1984, almost 190 fellows had been appointed.) Their work has resulted in many new publications in fields of special interest to the Institution—history, politics, and economics, for example. The program also resulted in more intangible gains, in new friendships and new academic bonds between Hoover and other academic institutions and governmental agencies.

The Institution's general research program expanded rapidly during this crucial decade and became the leading program of its kind on the campus and one of the largest and most wide-ranging research programs in the United States. Major projects included the *Yearbook on International Communist Affairs* (first published as an annual in 1967) and publications derived from a series of major conferences. Devoted to such topics as Marxism and the Modern World, the Revolutionary Internationals, 1864–1943, Marxist Ideology in the Contemporary World: Its Appeals and Paradoxes, and Fifty Years of Communism in Russia, the conferences involved the participation of leading Hoover scholars such as Milorad Drachkovitch, Sidney Hook, and the late Bertram Wolfe and also of distinguished guests such as the late Max Hayward and Leonard Schapiro, Lewis S. Feuer, Raymond L. Garthoff, and men and women of similar caliber. Soviet studies at Stanford were further enriched in 1967 when the *Russian Review*, a leading scholarly quarterly nearly thirty years old, came under the Hoover's sponsorship, where it remained until 1983. Other Hoover publications were numerous in scope and kind; they include, for instance, completing republication (from 1967 by Hoover Press) of Stalin's *Collected Works*, whose publication had been discontinued in the Soviet Union as a result of the de-Stalinization campaign.

In addition to stressing issues concerned with Marxism, the Institution also paid special attention to the study of colonialism in Africa. Senior fellows Peter Duignan and L. H. Gann became responsible for the largest extant research project on the subject. This resulted in the publication of the five-volume *Colonialism in Africa* (Cambridge University Press, 1969–1975), and of many related works, including a new Colonial Studies Series to which outside scholars contributed extensively. The Hoover Institution has played a leading part in bibliographical research on Africa in the United States since 1960. (See Chapter 12 for a survey of this work.)

In 1969 the Institution initiated a consortium of fifteen Western colleges and universities designed to coordinate acquisitions policies. The Hoover was to be the central library for international studies in the western United States. Unfortunately the consortium failed to secure foundation support and ceased to operate in the mid-1970s. Yet the concept was a farsighted one and has now become a reality through computer networking. The library also served historical scholarship by expanding its archival collections.

In addition to its extensive foreign area studies program with research and publications on Western Europe, East Asia, Africa, the Middle East, Latin America, East Asia, and the Soviet bloc, the Hoover Institution in 1971 initiated a Domestic Studies Program. Such a program had always been intended by the founder, and research on domestic affairs had been carried out throughout the Institution's history. With the participation of scholars such as senior fellows Thomas G. Moore (the coordinator of the program), Rita Ricardo-Campbell, and Martin Anderson, the program, from the early 1970s onward, began to equal in scope the International Studies Program, thereby rendering a valuable service to scholarship and to the study of public policy, as well as to the training of future academic leaders and the formulation of economic policies.

The library had equally expanded its operations. By 1970, its collections had reached the one million–volume mark, and thereafter continued to grow steadily to about one and a half million in 1984. By this time, the library contained the most extensive collections on modern China and the Soviet Union to be found in the Western world, as well as impressive resources on almost every major region except the Indian subcontinent and Southeast Asia, which remained outside the library's sphere of operations. Hoover curators, archivists, and librarians continued to deal with a large and varied body of manuscripts, archives, books, serials, and ephemeral publications in a great variety of languages. (The 65 librarians and curators among them were able to cope with some 35 foreign languages for the purpose of conducting research and operating the library.)

The late 1970s and the early 1980s witnessed a further period of expansion, as impressive as the growth experienced in any preceding period. The budget for 1983–84 anticipated an annual expenditure of $9.3 million, a fourfold increase over the 1971–72 figure, achieved at a time when many other American academic institutions had to wrestle with financial difficulties. The bulk of this income derives from individual, foundation, and corporate gifts (41 percent) and from endowment income (24 percent). About 30 percent came from Stanford University; almost no funds came from the federal government. The Hoover Institution, thus, has achieved a degree of financial independence exceptional among the institutions associated with Stanford.

In 1978, the Herbert Hoover Memorial complex was completed. The sole federal memorial to the former president and a valuable addition to Stanford as a whole, the complex consists of a group of handsomely designed buildings, well integrated with existing facilities, and plays an important role on campus. (See Chapter 2 for details on the Memorial buildings.)

Successful fundraising enabled the Institution to expand its staff. In 1983, an important addition was made to the library: Dr. John B. Dunlop was appointed associate director for the library and archives. A Middle East bibliographer (Edward Jajko) and a conservation officer (Judith Fortson-Jones) were also added. By 1984, the Institution provided office space for 75 librarians, archivists, and support staff and nearly a hundred scholars engaged in full-time research. Academicians associated with Hoover included five Nobel laureates and 32 members of the American Academy of Arts and Sciences, the American Association for the Advancement of Science, the National Academy of Sciences, the National Academy of Education, and the American Philosophical Society.

At the same time, the number of research projects under way had grown enormously, as had the scope of topics under consideration. Coordinated by Peter Duignan, the International Studies Program was supporting more than 220 authors by the end of 1984. The diversity of themes was enormous, with one feature in common: the program aimed at concentrating on issues of vital importance to the United States. The Hoover had also inaugurated a National Security Studies Program directed by Dr. Dennis L. Bark. The Hoover Institution Press has published many cooperative policy studies (for instance, Peter Duignan and Alvin Rabushka, eds., *The United States in the 1980s*; Dennis L. Bark, ed., *To Promote Peace: U.S. Foreign Policy in the Mid-1980s*; John H. Moore, ed., *To Promote Prosperity: U.S. Domestic Policy in the Mid-1980s*). In addition, Hoover has developed a major series on U.S. foreign policy. Major conferences have dealt with subjects as different as nationalities and the Soviet future, the Pacific Basin, arms control, and East-West trade.

The Domestic Studies Program, working in association with four Nobel laureates (Milton Friedman, George J. Stigler, Friedrich A. Hayek, and Kenneth Arrow), continued under the guidance of Thomas G. Moore. The program concentrated on three primary subjects: regulation and deregulation; government taxing and spending; and income redistribution and welfare programs. By the end of 1983, the Domestic Studies Program was supporting forty scholars working on these and related themes. Between them, the International and Domestic Studies programs had produced a substantial body of publications. By the end of 1984, the Hoover Institution Press alone had turned out over 390 titles. In addition, there was an equally impressive number of books and articles published by present and former Hoover fellows and associates with other university or commercial presses, or in learned journals.

From its modest start under Herbert Hoover during World War I, the Institution has grown steadily, and today it stands as one of the world's leading research libraries for advanced study of the problems of political, social, and economic change in the twentieth century.

2 | THE LIBRARY AND ARCHIVES

John B. Dunlop

Associate Director for Library and Archival Operations

The Hoover Institution is a specialized library (containing as of mid-1984 some 1.5 million volumes, 42,000 reels of microfilm, and 25,000 serial titles with subscriptions to over 3,000 current newspapers and journals), an archival depository housing over 3,700 collections, and a center devoted to advanced interdisciplinary study on twentieth-century domestic and international affairs. Its unique collections comprise priceless books, documents, and other research materials crucial to the study of social, cultural, philosophical, economic, and political change in the twentieth century.

PLANT AND OPERATIONS

The Institution has one of the finest physical complexes in the United States. Reading rooms, exhibit areas, library and archival stacks, conference and seminar rooms, and offices for staff and scholars are included in the nearly 520,000 square feet of space in the complex. The 32 million items constituting the archival collections are kept under controlled climate conditions.

More than 3,000 items from the collections, including Russian art and artifacts, items pertaining to the lives of former President and Mrs. Hoover, and paintings and art objects from throughout the world, are on display at any one time at locations throughout the Institution. Exhibits in the Tower rotunda and the archival pavilion are rotated twice yearly. Each year more than 50,000 visitors view these exhibits, which are prepared by the curatorial and archival staff.

The collections housed in the Tower and the Lou Henry Hoover buildings are accessible Monday through Saturday; the archives are open Monday through Friday. No fee is charged for the use of materials, but users are required to register. During academic year 1982–83, scholars from 35 states and 28 foreign countries registered to use the collections.

The Hoover Institution participates in the Research Libraries Information Network (RLIN) of the Research Libraries Group, Inc. (RLG), a consortium of 26 of the nation's major universities and research institutions. This program affords library users on-line access to bibliographic data from all RLG members.

John B. Dunlop,
Associate Director
for Library and Archives

ADMINISTRATIVE STRUCTURE

Since its founding, the Institution has had five directors: Dr. E. D. Adams, chairman of the directors from 1920 to 1925; Dr. Ralph H. Lutz, chairman from 1925 to 1944; Dr. Harold H. Fisher, chairman from 1944 to 1952; Dr. C. Easton Rothwell, director from 1952 to 1959; and the present director, Dr. W. Glenn Campbell, who assumed the post on January 1, 1960. Dr. Campbell subsequently guided the Institution to its present position of national and international prominence. The associate director for library and archival operations, John B. Dunlop, a specialist in Russian and Soviet history, politics, and culture, has general responsibility for the operations, maintenance, development, and conservation of the library and archives of the Institution. The associate director represents the Hoover Institution in university-wide library affairs and is a member of Stanford University's library council.

The four major administrative subunits of the library and archives are (1) the acquisitions, cataloging, and conservation departments, supervised by assistant director for technical services Joseph Kladko; (2) reference, circulation, interlibrary loan, photography, and serials records, supervised by head of readers' services David Heron; (3) the archives, supervised by archivist Charles Palm; and (4) five curatorial areas—Africa and the Middle East, Central and Western Europe, East Asia, Eastern Europe and the Soviet Union, and Latin and North America—each headed by a scholar-curator or bibliographer-curator.

The curator of the African and Middle Eastern collections is senior fellow Peter Duignan, who is assisted by deputy curators Lewis Gann (also a senior fellow) and Karen Fung and by Middle East bibliographer Edward Jajko. Curator Agnes Peterson heads the Central and West European collections. Senior fellow Ramon Myers directs the East Asian Collection, assisted by deputy curators Emiko Moffitt and Mark Tam and by research fellow Fu-Mei Chen. Senior research fellow Robert Conquest, assisted by deputy curator Joseph Dwyer, oversees the Soviet and East European collections, and Joseph Bingaman serves as curator of the Latin and North American collections.

The assistant director for technical services, the head of readers' services, the archivist, and the area curators report to the associate director. As of mid-1984, the staff of the Hoover Library and Archives numbered 75 persons.

Robert Conquest, Curator, East European Collection

FINANCES

The total budget of the Hoover Institution for academic year 1983–84 was $9.3 million. Of this, university funds accounting for approximately 30 percent of the total provide much of the support for the Hoover Library and Archives and for the general administration of the Institution. These funds are used to purchase books, periodicals, and additions to the archival collections, to pay the salaries and benefits of the library and archives staff, and to help cover other expenses of the library and archives. The last category includes, for example, the costs borne by the Institution for its membership in and use of RLIN, which makes the collections accessible to scholars throughout the nation. University funds account for slightly less than 80 percent of direct library and archival costs. The balance is covered by gifts to the Hoover Institution and income from the Institution's endowment.

In 1982–83, the library and archives accounted for approximately 36 percent of the Hoover Institution budget. Research in both domestic and international studies accounted for about 49 percent. The remaining expenditures were divided equally between administrative and publications costs.

The Hoover Tower   THE BUILDINGS

The Tower of the Hoover Institution, which contains the major part of the library collections, is Stanford University's most famous and prominent landmark. It was completed in June 1941. Designed by San Francisco architect Arthur Brown, Jr., the Tower rises 285 feet above the campus. From basement to dome, it has 23 levels and a total of 75,000 square feet of floor space.

Hoover Tower and Lou Henry Hoover Building

De Basily Room

The entrance to the Tower leads into a spacious rotunda. On the south side is an exhibit room commemorating Mr. Hoover's illustrious career; opposite, in the Lou Henry Hoover Room, are art objects that belonged to Mrs. Hoover and mementos of her work in peace and humanitarian organizations. In the rotunda are exhibits of library materials and the desk of the student Guide Service, which welcomes visitors to the campus and gives them directions, information, and tours of the Tower observation platform.

Above the structure surrounding the base, which contains library reading rooms, work areas, exhibit rooms, and offices, there are seventeen stack levels, three floors of offices, including that of the director, and an observation platform. The observation platform houses a 35-bell carillon—a gift from the Belgian-American Education Foundation. The carillon was exhibited at the 1939 New York World's Fair on its way from Belgium to the Hoover Institution. The carillon is played from a clavier on the floor below (which also contains an automatic mechanical player with notes set on a drum like that of a giant music box). Professor James B. Angell, Stanford's carillonneur, reports that it is the only one of its kind in use in the United States.

In the basement of the Tower are the Current Periodicals and Newspaper Room, Research Reading Room, a public photocopying service, and a microfilm reading room, as well as several offices for staff members, visiting scholars, and university staff.

The second floor contains the main reading room and circulation desk for the Western-language collections, offices and work areas for the library staff, desks for visiting scholars, and rooms for the library's catalog and the National Union Catalog.

Each floor of the Tower is approximately 50-feet square, and the stack floors are filled with floor-to-ceiling metal shelving. The stack areas are air-conditioned to maintain constant temperature and humidity.

The Lou Henry Hoover Building

Mr. Hoover lived two months beyond his ninetieth birthday on August 10, 1964, and had the satisfaction of knowing that his friends—beginning with a $750,000 challenge grant from the Scaife family—had assembled in honor of his ninetieth anniversary a fund sufficient not only to add a new building to the Hoover Institution's establishment, but to provide a substantial endowment to further the aims and purposes of the Institution.

He asked that the new building, for which ground was broken in the summer of 1966, be named for his wife, Lou Henry Hoover. Architect Charles Luckman of Los Angeles designed a four-story building, with two floors above ground and two basement levels containing bookstacks for East Asian–language books and for all the library's newspapers. Its 60,000 square feet provided the East Asian Collection not only with stack space, but also with a comfortable reading room and work space, as well as 36 offices for staff and researchers.

The Lou Henry Hoover Building was dedicated on October 9, 1967, as were the Milbank and de Basily rooms in the Tower building. Stanford President J. E. Wallace Sterling, one of the dedication speakers, described the importance of the new building to the development of the Hoover Library:

> Since World War II, the collections have grown greatly. Increasing numbers of scholars from this country and from overseas have come to explore and use the library's resources.
>
> With this growth, the Tower building in its turn needed help. And this help has now been provided by the new building which is dedicated today in memory of Mrs. Hoover and in honor of the ideals which she personified.

Pavilion and Herbert Hoover Memorial Building

Tower Reading Room with senior Library
staff (standing, l. to r.) David W. Heron,
Judith Fortson-Jones, Joseph Kladko;
(seated, l. to r.) Galena Dotsenko, Riva
Richards, Ellen Leung

Within the Lou Henry Hoover Building, the East Asian Collection has had space
to develop into one of the most important Asian-language libraries in America, and
the offices, classroom, and seminar rooms have made the building an important facil-
ity for the development of the whole university. Various university area-study committees and Hoover scholars occupy the second floor of the building.

The Herbert Hoover Federal Memorial Buildings

Late in 1974, not long after the hundredth anniversary of Herbert Hoover's birth
in West Branch, Iowa, Senator Mark Hatfield of Oregon introduced a bill in the Senate authorizing construction of a new building on the Stanford campus, an addition
to the Hoover Institution, as a national memorial to Herbert Hoover, thirty-first
president of the United States. The bill was also sponsored by Senator Alan Cranston
and cosponsored by Majority Leader Mike Mansfield, Minority Leader Hugh Scott,
and Senators Goldwater, Kennedy, McGovern, Brock, and Tunney; House supporters
were Speaker Thomas O'Neill, Minority Leader John Rhodes, and several western
representatives including area congressmen Paul McCloskey and Charles Gubser.
Both houses of Congress approved this legislation, which appropriated $7 million in
a grant to be matched by private funds. President Gerald Ford signed it into law January 2, 1975. In the following months architect Ernest J. Kump, advised by representatives of the Hoover Institution and Stanford University, planned a 102,000 square
foot building to stand with the Lou Henry Hoover Building east of the Tower.
Ground was broken in July 1976, and the Herbert Hoover Memorial Building was
dedicated on July 20, 1978.

The exterior of the new building is similar to that of the Lou Henry Hoover building—tall, arching columns, dark glass windows, and red tile roof. The two buildings
form a quadrangle, its center a sunken courtyard around a fountain; to east and west
of this courtyard, on the main floor level, are two smaller glass and redwood buildings.

The three top floors of the memorial building provide private offices for research,
seminar and conference rooms, and a small working library. On the first or podium
level, two seminar rooms are named for their donors, the DeWitt and Lila Acheson

Archives Reading Room with deputy archivist Robert Hessen, archivist Charles G. Palm, and former archivists Milorad M. Drachkovitch (senior fellow) and Rita Ricardo-Campbell (senior fellow)

Wallace Room and the Frank O. Prior Room. The conference room is named the Kathryn and Charles Kendrick Memorial Room. The second floor, its construction and furnishing substantially supported by grants from the Pew Memorial Trust and the J. N. Pew, Jr. Charitable Trust, is headquarters for the Center for Domestic Studies. The seminar room on this floor is named the Dudley Swim Memorial Room. The third-floor research facilities are named in honor of Anthony John Bittson (Ivan Bydzan).

The smaller building nearest the Hoover Tower is an exhibit pavilion open to the public. Just outside is a working sundial on a granite mining core inscribed "Herbert Hoover, 1874–1964; Engineer–Humanitarian–Statesman–Public Servant–Author." Exhibits in the pavilion are drawn from the resources of the Institution's vast archival holdings. Changed periodically, the exhibits deal with such topics as the U.S. presidency or twentieth-century revolutionary and peace movements throughout the world. Many of the items displayed are unique and include examples from the large poster collection of the Hoover Institution, as well as medals, diaries, and letters.

Below the exhibit hall and connecting at the courtyard level to the Tower and main memorial building is the Archives Reading Room. It is open to all qualified students and scholars.

The John Stauffer Memorial Auditorium is across the courtyard directly opposite the Archives Reading Room. It is used for conferences, seminars, and larger meetings. The mezzanine level of the auditorium is named the John A. McCarthy Memorial Room and is the senior commons meeting room for scholars at the Institution and visiting scholars.

Extending under the entire memorial complex is a huge stack area of 33,500 square feet with specially controlled constant levels of temperature and humidity. Initially equipped with about 25,000 linear feet of shelves, the area has a capacity for more than 51,000 linear feet, or ten miles, of shelf space. Here are stored the entire archives, the unpublished primary source materials that comprise one of the largest and richest private archival collections in the United States.

The architect for the new buildings was again Ernest J. Kump of Ernest J. Kump Associates, which became during the course of the construction, Sprankle, Lynd & Sprague of Palo Alto. Dale Sprankle was principal-in-charge. The sundial and its memorial inscriptions were designed by Ernest Born of San Francisco, and the exhibit room cases were designed and built by Formetics, a Palo Alto firm. The hand-carved wood door to the exhibit pavilion was designed and executed by Stan Dann, woodcarver, of Oakland. Fred H. Dilg of Palo Alto was consultant on interiors, and the SWA Group of Sausalito designed the landscaping. Rita Ricardo-Campbell, senior fellow, was the principal Hoover Institution staff member concerned with the exterior and interior design and shared with Associate Director Darrell M. Trent the task of overseeing planning and construction. The contractor was Dickman Construction, Inc., of Mountain View, California.

3 | USE OF INSTITUTION RESOURCES

Peter Duignan
Sara and Ira Lilick Curator

Within the concrete and steel walls of the Hoover Tower are stored countless irreplaceable documents. But the Hoover Institution is more than a library. It is also a research center for the study of war, revolution, and peace on a global scale; as such it has been used by the Institution's own staff and by students and scholars from all over the world.

STAFF RESEARCH   In 1927, Stanford University received a research grant from the Rockefeller Foundation, part of which was made available to the Hoover Institution for research on revolutionary movements in Russia and Germany during and after World War I. Two special research groups were organized to exploit the Institution's unique collections: the Institute for Research on the German Revolution, headed by Professor Ralph H. Lutz; and the Russian Revolution Institute, headed by Professor Frank A. Golder and, after his death in 1929, by Professor Harold H. Fisher. In creating the Russian Revolution Institute, Professor Golder pioneered American studies of the Soviet Union. Only after World War II did other American universities establish such centers.

In 1936, a grant of $55,500 from the American Relief Administration made possible a steady flow of publications containing the results of the work of the Russian and German institutes. Several volumes of documentary studies by Stanford doctoral candidates and visiting scholars based on Hoover Institution materials were also published.

During the years 1948–1951 the Hoover Institution undertook a broad study entitled Revolution and the Development of International Relations (known as the RADIR project), for which the Carnegie Corporation provided a grant of $202,000. The outcome of this project was seventeen volumes published in the Hoover Institute Studies Series.

The Institution initiated a new research and publication program in 1956. Three major studies were undertaken: one on the 1917 Provisional Government of Russia;

The Premier of Russia's 1917 Provisional Government, Alexander Kerensky (right), contributed firsthand knowledge to editing of the Institution's three-volume documentary study of his government. Here he confers with Witold Sworakowski, former Assistant Director.

one on France during the German occupation; and one on the Soviet Union as a treaty partner. The first result of this program was *La Vie de la France sous l'occupation (1940–44)*, a three-volume work published in 1957. The Soviet Union project produced two volumes: *A Calendar of Soviet Treaties, 1917–1957*, published in 1959; and *Theory, Law, and Policy of Soviet Treaties*, published in 1962.

The project on the Russian Provisional Government resulted in a three-volume collection of over 1,400 translated documents, which was published in December 1961. The former prime minister of the Provisional Government, Alexander F. Kerensky, and Dr. Robert P. Browder, professor of history at the University of Colorado, compiled and edited these volumes. This major study provides the necessary documentary material for a reappraisal of the events in Russia that led to the overthrow of the Provisional Government and the establishment of the first communist state. The aspirations and actions of the government, its administrative problems, and the activities and opinions of its supporters and critics are all thoroughly examined. Official documents, correspondence, memoirs, unpublished manuscripts, and contemporary press reports are included. Because of the absence of such a reference work during the preceding forty years, Soviet writers were able to distort the history of this crucial period.

Since 1926, the Institution has published over 390 books and monographs. Bibliographies and scholarly works constantly call attention to the great importance of these publications, especially the documentary studies. For example, Ambassador George Kennan in his book, *Soviet Foreign Policy*, acknowledged special indebtedness to authors of the Hoover Institution, "whose services generally to the study of recent Russian history no scholar can mention without a sense of warmest appreciation" and for the Institution's "excellent and highly useful documentary survey, *Soviet Russia and the West*."

The current research program is varied and extensive (over 280 projects as of mid-1984). The International Studies Program, coordinated by senior fellow Peter Duignan, concentrates on issues of vital importance to the United States in the fields of national security, foreign policy, geopolitics and area studies, publishing an average of twelve volumes a year through the Hoover Press. The major series include the *Yearbook on International Communist Affairs*, Ruling Communist Party Histories, Latin American Politics, and International Studies. Among topics covered are Hispanics in the United States, politics in Western Europe, the peace movement in Europe, and Japanese defense.

The Domestic Studies Program sponsors research on social, political, and, in particular, economic policies. Founded in 1972, the expanded program has received wide recognition as a center for multidisciplinary scholarly research in public policy issues. The program focuses on regulation and deregulation, government fiscal policies, and income redistribution and welfare programs. (For a description of the research program of the Institution, see Chapter 1.)

USE BY THE SCHOLARLY COMMUNITY

Many scholars from outside the Hoover Institution have benefited from using its resources. Stanford graduate students and faculty have made the most extensive use of the collections, and the number of undergraduates using the library is increasing.

Many of Stanford University's international studies programs are based wholly or in part on Hoover material. With the teaching and research programs of Stanford and other universities turning more and more toward international and area studies, the Hoover Institution will render increasing service to the academic community.

Researchers come here not only from all over the United States but also from abroad. Among the foreign institutions represented during 1983, for example, by scholars studying at the Institution were Oxford, Cambridge, London, and Glasgow universities (Great Britain); Wakayama, Hokkaido, and Tokyo universities (Japan); University of Siena (Italy); University of Ankara (Turkey); Warsaw University (Poland); Australian National University (Canberra); National Taiwan University (Taipei); University of British Columbia (Vancouver); Queen's University (Kingston, Ontario); Hebrew University (Jerusalem); King Saud University (Saudia Arabia); Academia Sinica (Beijing); University of Genoa (Italy); Addis Ababa University (Ethiopia); Catholic University of Lublin (Poland); University of Toronto (Canada); University of Auckland (New Zealand); University of Malaya; National University of Singapore; University of Paris; Max Planck Institute (Berlin); National Archives (Damascus, Syria); University of Cape Town (South Africa); University of Hong Kong; Centre National de la Recherche (Paris); University of Amsterdam; and Institute of Technology (Beijing).

Scholars and students are free to publish anything they wish from the unrestricted and uncopyrighted documents and materials in the Hoover Library and are requested only to mention their source.

Through the interlibrary loan and photoduplication services, the Institution's holdings are made available to researchers unable to visit the Stanford campus. Use by other research centers is increasing rapidly.

Much of Hoover's unique material has been microfilmed by the Institution and is available on 35 mm film. Important journals, newspapers, documents, monographs, series, and serials are continually being filmed to meet the needs of the academic community. (See *Hoover Institution Microfilms Catalog*, 1976.)

These are but a few of the ways in which Institution materials have met national and international needs. Numerous publications have resulted from the use of these documents, and the prefaces of books and monographs from commercial, government, and university presses in this country and abroad acknowledge the use of Hoover materials and thank the staff for its services.

FELLOWSHIP PROGRAMS

Each year hundreds of graduate students and scholars travel at their own expense to the Hoover Institution. Given the present urgency of developing area specialists, research in British, French, or American studies is often ignored. The Institution seeks to encourage and assist scholars in all fields and thereby contribute as fully as possible to enlightening the public about the great issues of our times. At present the Hoover has programs for National, Peace, Public Affairs fellows and visiting scholars.

OTHER SERVICES

Since World War II, the United States government has made extensive use of Hoover facilities. Because the collections in political and economic affairs frequently provide materials not available elsewhere in the country, federal departments have entrusted the Institution with special research projects.

The collections are used by such agencies as the Department of State, the Central Intelligence Agency, the Department of Justice, the Federal Bureau of Investigation, and the military services. Congressional committees, congressmen, and senators also request information or documents available only at the Institution. The microfilming of rare books and other materials for the research organizations of federal agencies has become a routine job for the Institution's staff.

Another field of public service has been assistance to public schools and civic organizations that request speakers or materials for programs on international relations or foreign countries.

Many hundreds of foreign visitors—political and trade union leaders, government officials, businessmen, and journalists—come to the Institution every year. The government and foundation administrators who sponsor these trips have often commented on the favorable impression of the United States foreign dignitaries have carried away after visiting the Hoover Institution.

In these ways—by research, publications, fellowships, reference assistance, and public service—the Institution carries out its functions of collecting the living documents of international affairs, organizing and making them available for use, fostering their utilization by qualified persons, and encouraging and aiding the spread of knowledge.

HOW TO USE THE
COLLECTIONS

The library and archives of the Hoover Institution are open to anyone who needs them, without fee. Full public access was one of Mr. Hoover's founding stipulations, and it makes the Hoover Library more accessible than most campus libraries. The collections, however, contain much that is rare or fragile; the major part of the Hoover Institution's research resources must be used within the Institution's reading rooms. For the same reason the seventeen floors of the Tower's book stacks and the stacks of the Hoover Institution Archives are closed except to staff members.

USE OF THE WESTERN
AND MIDDLE EAST
COLLECTIONS

All visitors must register at the Circulation Desk, in the central foyer of the Hoover Tower. Those engaged in extended research may be assigned study tables or carrels on the first floor or on the ground floor of the Tower. Books listed in the catalog—the card catalog off the central foyer, the book catalog published by G. K. Hall (1969–1977), or (for books acquired since 1976) in SOCRATES, the Stanford Library on-line catalog in the Stanford Computer Center—can be obtained by presenting call cards at the Circulation Desk. The reference librarians in the Tower Reading Room can assist with the catalog or with other approaches to the library's collections.

Stanford faculty, staff, and graduate students may borrow circulating books for a month, Stanford undergraduates and faculty or staff dependents for two weeks. University of California faculty, staff, and students with Cooperative Program identification cards have the same privileges as their Stanford counterparts.

Other visitors may use books only within the library building and must return them before the end of the day. Visitors with assigned desks or carrels may charge books for use there without time limit; all materials are subject to recall after two weeks. Books marked FOR USE IN THE LIBRARY ONLY may not be removed from the building. Those marked REFERENCE BOOK, VAULT COPY, FOR REFERENCE, or REFERENCE SHELF must be used in the Tower Reading Room, unless a reference librarian authorizes their use elsewhere.

Microforms—microfilm and microfiche—of many periodicals and some books are available from the Circulation Desk. The catalog shows which microform format is used. Reading machines are available in the microfilm room and the Tower Reading Room. Current periodicals are to be found in the north corner of the Tower ground floor. The current serial record files are at the desk, and current newspapers in the adjacent newspaper room.

CHINESE-, KOREAN-, AND JAPANESE-LANGUAGE MATERIAL

The East Asian Collection is housed in the Lou Henry Hoover Building, and the registration procedure for readers at the East Asian Circulation Desk is identical to that in the Tower. Borrowing privileges in the East Asian Collection are somewhat different from those in the Tower: faculty members may borrow books for three months. Students (both graduate and undergraduate), Stanford staff members, and long-term visitors may borrow circulating books for a month. Book borrowings are renewable, but all materials are subject to recall after two weeks. Short-term visitors must use materials in the East Asian Reading Room. The East Asian catalog is printed in both Asian and roman characters, as is the adjacent Serials Record file. Reference librarians are available for assistance in using the collections and the catalog. Recent entries are available on-line in the Research Libraries Group computer catalog, both in roman and in Asian characters.

THE HOOVER INSTITUTION ARCHIVES

The archival and manuscript collections in the Hoover Institution Archives, entered from the courtyard level of the Herbert Hoover Memorial Building, can be consulted by any reader who presents the required identification and completes and signs an archives registration form.

All archival materials must be used in the Archives Reading Room. For the protection of these unique collections, no personal property may be taken into the reading room except for pencils, ballpoint pens, typewriters, and reference books. A coatrack and lockers are provided for storage of other personal possessions. Food and drink are forbidden in the archives, as they are in the other reading rooms at the Hoover Institution.

LIBRARY AND
ARCHIVES HOURS   Hours of service for the Hoover Institution Library and Archives are:

Library (Tower and East Asian Collection)
    Monday–Friday   8:00 A.M. to 5:00 P.M.
    Saturday   9:00 A.M. to 1:00 P.M.
Archives
    Monday–Friday   8:15 A.M. to 4:45 P.M.

The archives is closed Saturday, and both the library and archives are closed on Sundays and holidays.

PART II

THE
COLLECTIONS

In the ceremonies opening the Hoover Tower on June 20, 1941, former President Herbert Hoover dedicated the building to the promotion of peace. "Its records," he noted, "stand as a challenge to those who promote war. They should attract those who search for peace."

These words express Mr. Hoover's ideals regarding the Hoover Institution's collecting and research efforts. They guided the Institution until Mr. Hoover's death in 1964, and they remain the fundamental principles underlying the policies and programs of the Institution. The Institution's name, its library holdings, and the history of its development reflect its focus on peace and the prevention of war.

The Institution began in 1919 with the effort to document the causes and consequences of World War I. The interest in war—not only its military aspects but also its political, economic, and social aspects, as well as the modern strategy and the history of wars and battles—has persisted as a major direction for the collections. Nuclear war and arms limitations have become an important area of the Institution's collecting programs. Propaganda, psychological warfare, and the means of controlling people and public opinion, both in war and peace, have long concerned the Institution.

A second area of permanent interest is revolution. This embraces all of the most important revolutionary movements of this century—nationalism, colonialism, decolonization, liberation movements, socialism, communism, and fascism.

The third area of great significance is peace. This encompasses diplomatic, economic, and cultural relations and the organization of peace through international administration and law. In addition to the many formal organizations devoted to peace, the numerous peace movements that sprang up in Europe in the 1980s are actively covered.

The Hoover buildings house millions of items. Major categories are government documents and archives, books and pamphlets, newspapers, publications of private organizations, posters, maps, films, manuscripts and archives, and special collections of underground and guerrilla movements, and political and trade union ephemera. Perhaps only the Library of Congress and the New York Public Library are comparable to the Hoover Library in the varieties of materials collected, many of which most libraries refuse to acquire, as well as in its methods of acquisition and its sources of materials. The Hoover's methods include collecting trips, exchanges, gifts, letters of introduction, personal contacts and agents, purchase, the promise of protective handling and security, and an active solicitation program using agents, staff, students, and faculty.

Through collecting trips, the Hoover curators have borne the primary responsibility for acquisitions. But bookdealers and government officials have also been important. Government officials receive letters asking for their papers and libraries. So do scholars, politicians, military officers, and intellectual elites. Private collectors have also been a good source. These collectors usually gather materials on the spot as a hobby or for family histories. Stanford faculty and students became highly productive collectors from 1930 on. And Stanford alumni have provided access to unique materials. But for Stanford faculty, student, and alumni help, the Hoover Library would not have so broad a coverage or so many unique collections.

4 THE RUSSIAN, SOVIET, AND EAST EUROPEAN COLLECTION

Joseph D. Dwyer
Deputy Curator

Joseph D. Dwyer,
Deputy Curator,
East European Collection

The Russian/Soviet and East European Collection at the Hoover Institution is one of the world's great scholarly resources for the study of the modern history of Eastern European states, especially Imperial Russia and the Soviet Union. The library and archives endeavor to gather and preserve primary and secondary documentation on recent political, historical, and ideological developments within this geographical area, as well as on the international affairs and intrabloc relations of these countries. In addition, the collection includes materials on one country not ruled by a communist government, namely Greece.

The collection emphasizes the twentieth century or, in the case of the East European countries, their history since achieving independence during the World War I era. However, background material from the late nineteenth century and, in the case of Russia, from the mid-nineteenth century, also forms part of the collection.

In accordance with the Hoover Institution's dedication to the study of war, revolution, and peace, the collection is concerned primarily with the history, ideology, politics, and international relations of the various countries. To some extent the collection covers economics, demography, law, geography, and the humanities.

As of mid-1984 the collection consisted of more than 400,000 volumes of books and pamphlets, some 7,000 periodical titles, and over 2,000 files of newspapers. In round figures, the sizes of the various national collections within the Eastern European area are shown in the accompanying table.

Country	Monographs (volumes)	Periodicals (titles)	Newspapers (titles)
Albania	1,500	21	15
Baltic states	6,000	500	100
Bulgaria	10,000	100	41
Czechoslovakia	26,000	300	150
Greece	3,500	115	45
Hungary	14,000	200	42

Country	Monographs (volumes)	Periodicals (titles)	Newspapers (titles)
Poland	39,000	1,500	270
Romania	13,000	60	50
Russia	275,000	4,000	1,200
Ukraine	6,000	250	80
Yugoslavia	20,000	350	180
Total	414,000	7,396	2,173

Additionally, the archives of the Hoover Institution holds nearly a thousand manuscript collections dealing specifically with Eastern Europe and the Soviet Union. These personal papers and organizational records include rare and prized materials.

The collection serves pertinent teaching and research programs at Stanford University and the worldwide community of scholars working in this field.

The holdings of the Hoover Institution Library and those of the main library of Stanford University complement each other. Although slower in developing until the early 1960s, the Stanford University Library has built a remarkable Slavic collection of nearly 250,000 volumes since then. During that period, the growth of the Hoover and Stanford collections has been closely coordinated. The Hoover's strength in twentieth-century history, politics, and other social sciences is matched by Stanford's strengths in the humanities and pre-twentieth-century history and social sciences. The Stanford University Library has especially outstanding holdings of Slavic serials, including microforms. The cooperation between the two libraries will continue in the future. The two libraries' network of exchange agreements with other libraries ensures that together both will be able to satisfy most needs and services.

HISTORICAL DEVELOPMENT

The collecting of Russian and East European materials began in 1919 when, on Herbert Hoover's initiative, Professor E. D. Adams of Stanford's Department of History went to Paris to gather documentation on World War I and the Peace Conference. He contacted all East European delegations, those representing existing states as well as those representing groups with claims for statehood. Most delegates were cooperative, and the large amount of material they provided formed the basis of the Hoover War Library, as it was then called. Particularly detailed documentation was obtained for Russia, Poland, Czechoslovakia, Romania, and Yugoslavia.

The first material on Russia came from members of the Russian Political Conference, in which two prominent politicians, Vasiliĭ Maklakov and Sergeĭ Sazonov, played leading roles. In September 1920, Professor Frank Golder, a specialist on Russian history who had lived in Russia before and during World War I, was sent to Eastern Europe as a roving acquisitions agent for the Hoover Library. He and Professor Harold H. Fisher, a member of the American Relief Administration, acquired books, pamphlets, periodicals, newspapers, and archival collections dealing with Russia and its former provinces of Estonia, Latvia, Lithuania, Finland, Ukraine, and Poland. An additional trip by Golder to the then-independent Caucasian states produced still further documentation.

While in Russia, Golder came across a complete 200-volume collection of tsarist laws. He also purchased 145 volumes of eighteenth-century Russian diplomatic correspondence.

Golder obtained the greatest quantities of published matter concerning Russia when he participated in the American Relief Administration mission to Soviet Russia between late 1921 and mid-1923. With funds provided by Herbert Hoover, he acquired some 25,000 volumes and over 60,000 pamphlets, government documents, periodicals, and newspapers. Quite fortunately, he had the assistance of Anatoliĭ

Lunacharskiĭ, an old Russian student friend of his who had become the Soviet people's commissar for education. Along with the documentation gathered previously, these acquisitions from Russia served as a solid foundation for the further development of the Hoover Institution Library's collection.

Since the 1920s, the collection has been systematically expanded. Gaps that emerged during World War II and in the late Stalin period, when acquisitions from the Soviet Union were limited, have been filled in with original materials or microfilms. Since the survey of the Russian/Soviet Collection by Witold Sworakowski in 1954 (see Chapter 12), it has grown more than fivefold.

Like the Russian Collection, the Polish Collection was begun early in 1919, when Professor E. D. Adams contacted the Polish delegation to the Paris Peace Conference. He obtained the collection's first books and pamphlets on Poland and was assured that the government in Warsaw would be glad to contribute more material to the library. Acting on this promise, Professor Ralph H. Lutz, also a member of the Adams team, visited Warsaw in September 1919 and received the full cooperation of the Polish government. He also contacted a prominent publisher and bookdealer, Dr. Stanisław Arct, who helped to select and locate important library and archival materials and, until World War II, served as the honorary curator of the Polish Collection and contributed greatly to its quality and growth.

Acquisition of materials on Poland has continued steadily since these beginnings in 1919. During a trip to Warsaw in 1939, Professor Lutz left $500 with Arct to secure acquisitions in Poland should war break out and direct contact be cut off. This foresight on the part of the director of the Hoover Library paid off after the termination of hostilities when Arct delivered a considerable amount of wartime material, mostly unique clandestine publications and items issued by the German occupiers.

After World War II, collecting activities in Poland were renewed and, despite some difficulties in the 1950s, have developed satisfactorily. No other library in the United States has a similar record of consistency in collecting such materials on Poland.

Collecting activities similar to those described for Russia and Poland have been carried out for most countries of Eastern Europe. For example, the Romanian Collection also had its origins during the 1919 Paris Peace Conference where Adams contacted the Romanian delegation. This produced fairly good coverage of Romania's affairs during World War I. Professor Golder visited Bucharest two years later, obtained additional material, and established contact with the prominent Romanian historian, Nicolae Iorga, who gave his support to library acquisitions in Bucharest. For some time the leading Romanian bookdealer of the interwar period, Cartea Românească, sent selections of current publications. In 1939, Gardner Richardson visited Bucharest and attempted to improve bookdealer services and to make arrangements for acquisitions in case of war or other interruption of direct contact. This arrangement was successful, and after the war a large number of publications were delivered. Acquisitions from Romania ceased completely during the years of the cold war. Only in the mid-1960s were acquisitions and exchanges renewed.

Comparable efforts have resulted in the development of sizable and valuable collections for Czechoslovakia, Hungary, Yugoslavia, and Albania.

The magnificent accomplishment that this collection represents is due to the work of many scholars who have directed the acquisitions effort. Apart from Professors Frank Golder, E. D. Adams, Ralph H. Lutz, and Harold Fisher, who laid the foundations in the early years after World War I, the appointment of area specialists as curators for the various collections guaranteed good selection and organization of the material on a high scholarly level. In 1924, Dimitry M. Krassovsky, a Russian-trained lawyer and a graduate in library science from Berkeley, became the first curator of the

Alexander Kerensky, who served as prime minister of Russia during the brief rule of the Provisional Government in 1917, came to the Hoover Institution in 1956 to head a project devoted to editing and documenting the official records of that period. He was surprised to find how many of these documents—most of which he last saw in the tempestuous days of 1917 when the Provisional Government was struggling to survive the Bolshevik attacks—were preserved at the Institution.

collection. Former tsarist general N. N. Golovine became acquisitions agent in Europe. Both men, particularly Krassovsky, contributed substantially to the growth and quality of the collection. Witold S. Sworakowski, first as curator, then as associate director of the Institution, became one of the great collection developers. He was followed as curator by Karol Maichel, Wayne S. Vucinich, Robert Wesson, and Robert Conquest.

RUSSIA/SOVIET UNION   The 287,000-volume Russian and Soviet Collection (including 12,000 volumes in the Baltic States and Ukrainian collections) is one of the most outstanding features of the Hoover Institution. Few libraries in the world can match its depth or quality. It covers history, politics, economic and social conditions, and many other topics for Imperial Russia after 1861, the period of the Provisional Government of 1917, the Bolshevik Revolution, the Civil War, and the Soviet period. In addition to monographs and pamphlets, the collection includes some 4,000 periodical titles and files of more than 1,200 newspapers. The publications of Russian political émigrés in Western Europe before and after the revolution are also well represented.

Pre-revolutionary Russia is well documented by a large collection of publications, many rare or even unique in the United States. There are particularly strong holdings on the rise of political parties in Russia, Imperial Russian diplomacy, revolutionary movements, land and peasant questions, economic development, Asiatic Russia and territorial expansion, the tsarist secret police ("Okhrana"), the "zemstvo" movement, the Russo-Japanese War, and Russia's participation in World War I.

Alexander Solzhenitsyn using the Hoover Institution's collection of Russian newspapers

Materials from the Okhrana (Imperial Russian secret police) archive. The photo album shows police snapshots of suspected Russian revolutionaries, including Leon Trotsky (upper right). The archives of the Paris office of the Okhrana were acquired by the Hoover Institution in 1926 from Basil Maklakoff, the last ambassador in Paris of the Russian Provisional Government. From 1883 to 1917 the Okhrana maintained a Paris office to spy on communist revolutionaries operating in Western Europe. The archives contain some 225,000 documents, including dossiers on Lenin, Trotsky, and Stalin; agents' reports; photographs; transcripts of intercepted letters (including some from Lenin); codes; arrest records; revolutionary literature; and other unique materials.

The Okhrana Archives, a "phantom file" of Russian secret police dossiers from 1895 to 1917, which the Communists thought were destroyed nearly sixty years ago, are in the Hoover Institution. The dossiers and other materials, a veritable "who's who" of the Russian revolutionary movement, were shipped secretly from Paris to Stanford University in 1926 by Vasiliĭ Maklakov, the last pre-communist Russian ambassador to Paris. He then signed a statement that he had burned the entire lot.

Because the truth would have placed his life in jeopardy, Maklakov stipulated in a contract with the Hoover Institution that the sixteen large wooden packing cases were to remain sealed until his death and the contents not shown to the public until at least three months thereafter.

Maklakov died in July 1957 in Switzerland at the age of 86. Hoover Institution scholars only then began to put the material in order.

Nearly complete documentation is available on Russian legislation, the dumas, and the first general census of 1897. The collection contains extensive files of pre-revolutionary periodicals and newspapers.

Primary sources for the period include the records of the Paris office of the "Okhrana"; the papers of Nicolas de Basily (Imperial Russian diplomat, personal attorney to Nicholas II, and drafter of Tsar Nicholas II's abdication document); the papers of A. O. Sapon'ko (chief of the Stenographic and Records Division of the Russian Duma); Iosif V. Gessen (Constitutional Democratic Party leader); Grand Duchess Kseniia Aleksandrovna (sister of Nicholas II); the records of several diplomatic posts in Germany; the papers of Sergeĭ D. Sazonov (Russian minister of foreign affairs, 1910–1916); the papers of Alexandre Tarsaïdze (dealing with the Romanov family); and the papers of Feliks V. Volkhovskiĭ (Socialist Revolutionary Party leader).

The Hoover collection on the 1917 revolutions, the Provisional Government, and the Civil War is probably the greatest such collection in the West. Documentation on the Provisional Government, including official gazettes, legislation, and ministerial publications, is quite complete. Research materials on the Civil War are enhanced by the Hoover Institution Archives, which possesses the records of White Army Generals Iudenich and Wrangel, materials dealing with Admiral Kolchak and General Denikin, and the papers of Gen. W. S. Graves of the American Expeditionary Forces in Siberia.

Holdings of Soviet periodicals dedicated to the history of the Civil War (*Proletarskaia revoliutsiia, Krasnaia letopis'*, and others) are supplemented by memoirs, studies, and documentary publications of émigrés (*Arkhiv russkoĭ revoliutsiĭ, Beloe delo*, and others). Developments in Siberia during the Civil War are excellently covered by several archival collections and copious printed material.

The largest part of the Russian and Soviet Collection pertains to the Soviet period. Subject areas especially well covered are the time of "war communism," 1918–1921; the terror and forced labor; antireligious activities; separatist movements and the nationality question; collectivization; economic planning; Soviet foreign policy; the Comintern; trade unions; the Russo-Finnish War of 1939–1940; the Soviet military; and all aspects of the Communist Party of the Soviet Union.

In the field of Soviet law and government, the holdings include the official all-union legislative gazette, *Sobranie zakonov i rasporiazheniĭ raboche-krest'ianskogo*

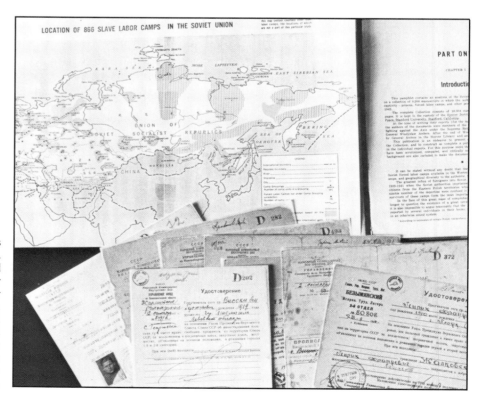

Samples from the collection of documents on Poles in the Soviet forced labor system. When the Soviet government released Polish prisoners from its forced labor camps during World War II, each prisoner was issued a release certificate. The Polish government-in-exile (London) collected some 43,000 of these certificates and interviewed about 9,000 prisoners. On the basis of the information in the certificates and interviews, the locations of and conditions in the Soviet gulags were exposed.

pravitel'stva SSSR, and the collections of laws of the Russian Socialist Federated Soviet Republic and several other republics. A file of the *Vedomosti* of the Supreme
Soviet is maintained, as are files of leading periodicals such as *Sovetskoe gosudarstvo
i pravo*, *Sotsialisticheskaia zakonnost'*, and *Sovetskaia iustitsiia*. The Institution possesses excellent materials on and by the Soviet Communist Party, including, for example, the stenographic minutes of all party congresses. Bolshevik materials on the
history of the party, as well as regional party publications, are abundantly represented. The prize items in this field are the early newspapers issued by Lenin, *Iskra*
and *Proletarii*, in the originals. In addition to a full run of the party's daily, *Pravda*,
the library has a wide range of other party journals and newspapers, almost all of
them in complete files. From many notable items only a few can be mentioned, such
as *Kommunist* (1924 to present), *Pod znamenem marksizma* (1922–1944), and *Par-
tiinaia zhizn'* (1946–1948, 1954 to present). To a large extent, the organs of regional
communist parties in the various constituent republics are also held.

One can also find in the library a complete run of the central Soviet government
organ, *Izvestiia*, covering 1918 to date and including well over 20,000 issues, as well
as the first organ of the Soviet secret police, *Ezhenedel'nik Chrezvychainykh Komisii*
(1918), and other rare periodicals.

More recently the library acquired through U.S. government intelligence channels
selected translated issues of *Voennaia mysl'*. This journal of military theory is distributed only among the higher ranks of the Soviet military.

The published material for the period of consolidated Soviet power (1922 to the
present) is complemented by superb holdings of primary documents. The archives
contains such collections as the papers of Boris I. Nicolaevsky (Russian Social Demo-
crat and writer), Vasilii A. Maklakov (ambassador of the Russian Provisional Government to France, 1917–1924), Sergei P. Mel'gunov (Russian historian), Pëtr B.
Struve (Russian historian and politician, minister of foreign affairs in the Wrangel
government), Mark V. Vishniak (Socialist Revolutionary Party leader), Sergei L. Voi-
tsekhovskii (Russian historian), Leon Volkov (lieutenant colonel, Soviet Air Force),
Nikolai V. Vol'skii (Russian revolutionary), and Bertram D. Wolfe (one of the leaders
of the American Communist Party, who spent time in the Soviet Union in the 1920s
as U.S. representative to the Comintern). Numerous Polish archival collections also
document events in the Soviet Union, especially during World War II. The Axelbank
Collection of 266 films records the history of twentieth-century Russia/Soviet Union
as well.

The Ukrainian Collection at the Hoover Institution originated from materials collected by Professor F. A. Golder in Russia and in Russia's borderlands in 1921. As an
agent for the Hoover War Library, Professor Golder's primary responsibility was to
secure materials from Russia (including Ukrainian lands and the Baltic states) dealing with the revolutionary period of 1917–1921 and with the newly emerging states
and their problems. Before coming to Stanford, Golder had in 1919 been the expert
on Ukrainian and Lithuanian affairs for the House Commission of historians preparing studies to be used by the American delegation at the Paris Peace Conference. His
collecting expertise is reflected in Ukrainian materials covering 1914–1921, the period of World War I and its aftermath. In the early 1940s, the holdings on this earlier
period were supplemented by the John Petrushevych Collection. This era, therefore,
is the best-documented period. Subsequently, the Ukrainian Collection was not systematically enlarged. Changes in occupying powers and territorial subdivisions, fre-
quent armed conflicts, and the resulting different rates of cultural, political, and
economic development always complicated the gathering of a good representative
collection.

At Riga, Latvia, on August 20, 1921, Soviet Russia and the American Relief Administration (ARA) signed an agreement that resulted in the extension of relief to Russia, ravaged by war and revolution. In two years, between 1921 and 1923, 11 million men, women, and children were fed, 15,000 hospitals were furnished with medical supplies, 7 million individuals received inoculations and vaccinations, and 8 million acres of land were sown with new seed.

The presence of the ARA in Russia offered the Hoover Institution a chance to begin collecting Russian materials. Stanford University professor Frank Golder was stationed with the ARA office in Moscow. He convinced the commissar of education, a former school friend, to give him one copy of every Soviet government report and issuance for the Hoover War Library, as it was then called. Golder argued successfully that this would ensure preservation of the materials in case their revolutionary regime were ever overthrown. This was the beginning of the Hoover Institution's Slavic collection.

Due to the Hoover Institution's interests in territorial questions, minorities, nationalist and revolutionary movements, and communism, however, the collection developed peripherally, through other major national collections. It presently includes some 6,000 monographs, about 250 periodical titles, and files of 80 newspapers. The Ukrainian Collection is supplemented primarily by the Russian and Polish collections and secondarily by the Austrian, Czech, Slovak, German, Hungarian, and Romanian collections.

Since 1978 the library has made a concerted effort to expand the collection and has filled in many gaps with original and microfilmed materials. It has paid particular attention to acquiring all possible dissident "samizdat" items and publications concerning nationalist and separatist movements among the Ukrainians.

Professors Golder and Fisher laid the foundation of the Baltic Collection in the 1920s while they were in the Baltic states as representatives of the American Relief Administration. In the 1930s, valuable materials, notably government documents from Estonia and Latvia, were added to the collection through exchanges arranged earlier by the two professors with the universities of Riga and Tartu. Later, Professor Malbone W. Graham of the University of California at Los Angeles added considerably to the collection by depositing his papers in the archives. In more recent years, the efforts of the Hoover Institution's late associate director, Witold S. Sworakowski, and Professor Edgar Anderson of San Jose State University are noteworthy. Professor Sworakowski, formerly a Polish diplomat stationed in the Baltic states, knew many exiled Baltic statesmen and secured several important archival collections from them. Professor Anderson has made available for microfilming numerous rare Latvian and Lithuanian publications and has been influential in securing Latvian archival materials. The Baltic Collection currently includes 6,000 volumes of monographs and pamphlets, some 500 periodical titles, and files of approximately 100 newspapers.

For the twentieth-century history of the Baltic states, since World War II incorporated into the Soviet Union as the Baltic republics, the archives holds such valuable sources as the records of the Latviešu Centrāla Komiteja (Latvian Central Committee, 1918–1948); and the papers of Jānis Lējiņš (member of the Latvian parliament, 1931–1940); Kaarel L. Pusta (Estonian diplomat, foreign minister of Estonia, 1924–1925); Voldemars Salnais (Latvian diplomat); and Eduardas Turauskas (Lithuanian diplomat, ambassador to Czechoslovakia, Yugoslavia, and Romania).

International organizations sponsored and directed by the Soviet Communist Party and the Soviet government are excellently documented in the library holdings. Since the period of war communism in Soviet Russia, these organizations have acted more or less openly as auxiliaries to Soviet foreign policy. The scholar studying relations between the Soviet Union and certain other countries from 1918 to 1943 must consider Communist International (Comintern) material in order to understand all aspects of these relations.

The congresses of the Communist International and the meetings of its Executive Committee are all available in stenographic reports. *Kommunisticheskiĭ internatsional*, its official organ, is available for the entire life of the organization (1919–1943) in four languages.

There is also fairly complete documentation covering the Red International of Labor Unions (Profintern) and ample materials on the Communist Information Bureau (Cominform).

Since the mid-1970s, the Soviet and East European Collection has made a major effort to collect and preserve all possible examples of clandestine, uncensored, private publishing initiatives in the Soviet Union known as "samizdat."

Drawing by Adam J., born 1928, from Stanislawow, an eyewitness of the 1939 Soviet invasion of Poland. Inscription on the drawing reads: "Bolsheviks are chasing the civilian population away from train cars in which they were deporting the Poles. . . This is the picture we saw from the cars."

Beginning in 1972, the Hoover Institution was designated as a depository for Soviet samizdat documents gathered and distributed by Radio Free Europe/Radio Liberty and later by Arkhiv Samizdata, an organization in Munich. Between 1972 and 1978, 30 volumes of the *Sobranie dokumentov samizdata* (Collection of samizdat documents) were produced. The individual volumes are devoted to various types of samizdat (specific serial titles, specific subjects, or the samizdat of specific Soviet ethnic or religious groups).

Since 1977, the *Sobranie dokumentov samizdata* has been kept up to date by means of the biweekly publication, *Materialy samizdata*, which reproduces documents newly received in the West. Hoover has a full set of *Sobranie dokumentov samizdata* and a complete, current run of the *Materialy samizdata*.

Additionally, the Soviet and East European Collection has two recent samizdat serial titles from Soviet Estonia and twelve titles from Soviet Lithuania amounting to some 140 issues.

THE POLISH COLLECTION

The Hoover Institution collection on Poland consists of some 39,000 volumes, approximately 1,500 serial titles, and 270 files of newspapers. The collection has been systematically built for more than sixty years and is probably the most comprehensive such gathering of materials outside of Poland.

The collection documents political, social, and economic changes, first on Polish soil occupied by the three partitioning powers (Austria, Germany, and Russia), then during World War I, the period of twenty years of interwar independence, World War II, and finally under the Polish People's Republic. Political parties, revolutionary movements, military matters, paramilitary organizations during the two wars, demography, minority questions, and Polish emigration are well covered. Documentation of developments since the outbreak of World War I is particularly broad and strong. An outstanding collection of posters, leaflets, and other fugitive materials from World War I and a fine collection of publications of the Polish underground movement during World War II are special attractions to scholars interested in Polish affairs. The collection contains an extensive file of official gazettes and other government documents from 1918 on.

The strongest areas of coverage for the pre-1939 period include Polish lands during World War I, the activities of the Polish delegation to the Paris Peace Conference, the Polish-Soviet War of 1919–1920, the 1920 plebiscites in Silesia and East Prussia, the Polish-Czech conflict over Cieszyń, and, particularly, Polish interwar political parties.

All major aspects of the conflict in and about Poland during World War II are abundantly documented, including the German invasion and occupation, underground resistance movements, the Home Army (Armia Krajowa), and the Warsaw Uprising. The library's collection of clandestine publications issued by the Poles during the nazi occupation is unique. Other aspects well covered are Polish-Soviet relations during the war, German war crimes in Poland, Polish prisoners in Soviet labor camps, the Polish government-in-exile in London, and the pro-Soviet Polish Committee of National Liberation in Moscow and its People's Army (Armia Ludowa).

For the post–World War II era, the library holds a vast amount of material supporting the study of the Polish People's Republic, its origins, and subsequent history. The collection is strong in government documents, parliamentary records, and statistics. One of the best-documented areas within the Polish Collection is the history of the Polish Communist Party from its inception through its rise to power after the war and its turbulent history since then. The library holds all published records of party congresses, plenums, and special commissions. The collection contains a complete file of the party's ideological periodical, *Nowe drogi*, from its beginning in 1947 to the present, as well as a complete file of the Central Committee's organ, *Trybuna ludu*, since 1949. All party publications on specialized subjects, particularly on economic planning and performance, can be found among the holdings. The library also acquires all publications concerning trade unions and the armed forces.

The collection is supported and made truly outstanding by the rich primary, unpublished sources in the Institution's archives. As of 1984, there were approximately 160 individual collections of personal papers and organizational documents dealing with Poland, amounting to well over a thousand linear feet of materials. Some of the most noteworthy collections are the records of the Polish government-in-exile in London during World War II (including records of the armed forces of the government-in-exile and records of its various ministries, such as the Ministry of the Interior and the Rada Narodowa); records of fifteen Polish diplomatic posts (including embassies in the Vatican, China, France, the United States, and the Soviet Union); the papers of Władysław Anders (commander in chief of Polish Forces in the USSR, and the 2nd Polish Corps in Italy—these records include documents for some 18,000 Poles interned in the Soviet Union at the beginning of World War II); the papers of Jan Fryling (counselor, Polish embassy in China); Adam Galiński (Polish resistance leader during World War II); Hugh S. Gibson, (U.S. ambassador to Poland, 1919–1924); Jan Karski (courier for the Polish government-in-exile); Stefan Korboński (member of the Polish government-in-exile); Stanisław Mikołajczyk (postwar pre-communist prime minister of Poland); Leon Mitkiewicz (onetime chief of intelligence, Polish Army); Ignacy Jan Paderewski (Polish statesman, musician, and premier); Valerian P. Platonov (Russian secretary of state for Polish affairs, 1864–1866); Alfred Poniński (Polish diplomat, counselor of the legation to the Soviet Union, 1926–1933); M. Z.

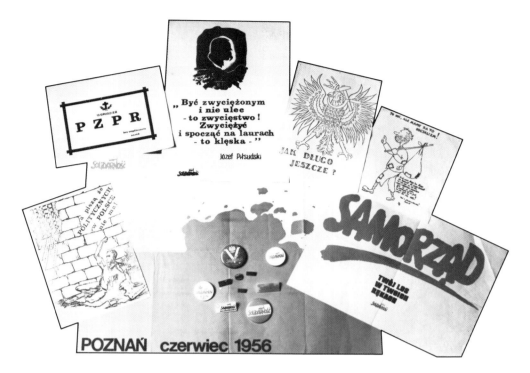

Posters and materials from the Polish Solidarity movement, 1980–1982

Rygor-Słowikowski (brigadier general, Polish Army during World War II); Henry Bancroft Smith (U.S. technical adviser and commercial attaché to Poland, 1919–1923); and August Zaleski (Polish foreign minister, 1926–1932, president of the Polish government-in-exile, 1947–1972). These sixteen collections give an indication of the wealth of the total holdings.

Recently the Hoover Institution has made a special effort to acquire dissident and uncensored publications to document the current turbulent period of Polish history.

Dissident publications began to appear in quantity in Poland in the late 1970s. The Hoover Institution began acquiring them in 1978. Originally these documents consisted of small numbers of serials and organizational materials issued by clandestine groups of intellectuals.

With the birth of the Solidarity movement in 1980, the flow of uncensored publications changed from a trickle to a flood. Nearly every local branch of Solidarity—in each city, town, factory, and university—began to publish a newsletter, an information bulletin, or some sort of serial. Through contacts in Poland and in Western Europe, as well as in the United States and Canada, the Hoover Institution has made, and is making, a concerted effort to obtain as many as possible of these unique documents. At present Hoover has more than 160 different serial titles, amounting to nearly a thousand individual issues.

In addition to these serial publications, Hoover's East European Collection has amassed hundreds of pieces of organizational materials generated by Solidarity and other groups. These items include statutes and bylaws, minutes of meetings, communiqués, letters of protest to government officials, and political posters and cartoons.

THE CZECHOSLOVAK COLLECTION

The Hoover Institution Library's collection on Czechoslovakia consists of over 26,000 volumes of monographs and pamphlets, runs of over 300 periodicals, and files of some 150 newspapers. It is one of the more important resources in the West on twen-

tieth-century Czech and Slovak history and politics. Although the collection officially begins with the independence of the Czechoslovak state in 1918, it includes
valuable background materials concerning the development of the Czech and Slovak
national movements, especially for the period of World War I. Other important
sources for Czechoslovak history can be found in other collections, particularly
those of Austria and Hungary.

One of the strongest points of the Czechoslovak Collection is the impressive holdings of periodicals and newspapers. These serials cover the entire period from the
late 1800s to the present. Particularly well documented are World War I, the 1930s,
World War II, and the period from the late 1960s to date.

The Czechoslovak Collection has several other areas of strength. For the World
War I period, there are significant holdings on early Czech and Slovak political parties, the so-called "Czech mafia," the Hapsburg political reprisals and trials, and the
Czechoslovak legions on the western and Russian fronts, as well as major holdings
dealing with the Czech and Slovak delegations to the Paris Peace Conference in 1919.

For the interwar period of 1919–1939, the collection is especially strong in government documents and materials on contemporary political parties. Another area
in which the Hoover Institution excels is the short-lived Slovak Soviet Republic of
1919. This small but significant collection includes runs of the communist newspaper
Červené noviny (Budapest, 1919) and *Armáda proletáru* (Bratislava, 1919), as well
as a number of pamphlets, bulletins, leaflets, and other propaganda of the Slovak
revolutionaries.

World War II and the German occupation of Czechoslovakia are well documented
with materials pertaining to the German "protectorate" of Bohemia and Moravia,
the Slovak Autonomous State, the Czechoslovak government-in-exile in London, and
the activities of Czech and Slovak Communists in the USSR, 1939–1945.

The immediate postwar period of 1945–1948 is covered reasonably well with documentary and secondary works. The history of the communist-dominated Czechoslovak state after 1948 and especially the history of the Czechoslovak Communist Party
is superbly well documented in the Hoover Library. Included are original and re-
printed minutes and protocols of all Communist Party congresses from 1923 to the
present (original editions from 1949 on), as well as records of the plenums of the
Central Committee from 1958 to 1960 and from 1962 to the present. Other important sources are numerous memoirs and writings of leading members of the party.
The library holds a valuable body of material concerning the political trials and
purges held in Czechoslovakia from the early 1950s until 1962. Among these holdings is a complete copy of the manuscript of the Kaplan Report, a candid and critical
study of the purge trials of the 1950s by a special committee of the Czechoslovak
Communist Party under Dubček in 1968.

With regard to the events of 1968 and the Soviet invasion, the Hoover Institution
has collected many official and clandestine ephemeral underground newspapers,
brochures, and leaflets. In addition to the published sources, the Institution has acquired some unpublished materials (letters, lists of persons involved, etc.) and has
put together a collection of clippings from the U.S. and European press regarding the
events leading to and following the Warsaw Pact invasion.

Since the 1968 invasion, many cases involving human rights violations have occurred in Czechoslovakia. A most important event was the founding in 1977 of a
major dissident group known as Charter '77 after its founding declaration. The library has sizable holdings of the group's clandestine publications, *Dokumenty Charty
77* and *Informace o Chartě 77*, as well as the reports (*Sdělení*) of a related organization, the Committee for the Defense of the Unjustly Prosecuted (Výbor na Obranu

Nespravedlivě Stíhaných). Recently the archives has begun to receive a major collection of unpublished dissident material (correspondence, reports, protests) smuggled out of Czechoslovakia and gathered by Czech exile groups in Western Europe.

The Hoover Institution Archives contains some forty manuscript collections dealing specifically with Czechoslovakia. Among the most important are the papers of Ladislav K. Feierabend (Czechoslovak minister of agriculture, 1938–1940; and minister of finance of the Czechoslovak government-in-exile, 1941–1945), Joseph Lettrich (president of the National Slovak Council and the Slovak Democratic Party, 1945–1948; an organizer of the Slovak national resistance movement, 1944–1945; and founder of the Council of Free Czechoslovakia), Štefan Osuský (Czechoslovak ambassador to Great Britain, 1918–1920; and to France, 1920–1940), Juraj Slavik (Czechoslovak envoy to Poland, 1936–1939; minister of the interior, 1940–1945; minister of foreign affairs, 1945–1946; and ambassador to the United States, 1946–1948), the diary of Štefan Tiso (brother of the leader of the Slovak Autonomous State, Jozef Tiso), and the records of the Československý Armadní Sbor v SSSR (the Czechoslovak army in the Soviet Union during World War II under Gen. Ludvik Svoboda).

THE YUGOSLAV COLLECTION

The Yugoslav Collection of the Hoover Institution, with more than 20,000 volumes of books, 350 runs of periodicals, and 180 files of newspapers, originated with material gathered early in 1921 by Professor Golder in the newly formed Kingdom of Serbs, Croats, and Slovenes. Golder was charged with collecting materials throughout Europe concerning the origins and results of World War I. He did not, therefore, attempt to acquire great amounts of materials on the historical development of Yugoslavia or other countries involved.

Later, in the 1930s and 1940s, it was decided to expand the scope of the collection to include all social, economic, political, and historical movements of the twentieth century. This brought about the broadening of the Yugoslav Collection as well as others to the point where it is today. Over the years, as scholars have been drawn to the collection, both the primary archival materials and the library's secondary, documentary materials have grown to support their research needs. A significant portion of the growth resulted from gifts of materials that the scholars themselves had collected. The holdings have reached the point of being quite adequate for advanced study.

The points of concentration of the materials are in such areas as the late nineteenth-century national and social movements among the South Slavs, including the rise of the idea of a confederation of the Southern Slavs, or the feelings for a "Yugoslavia." The origins of socialism in the area are also well covered. Documentation for the period of World War I, the causes of the war, as well as its sociopolitical consequences, is strong. The formation of the Kingdom of Serbs, Croats, and Slovenes is documented in detail. As is the case for most European areas, the Hoover collection on the delegations of the various South Slavic groups to the Paris Peace Conference is outstanding.

For the interwar period source materials on the development of Yugoslav political parties, including the Communist Party of Yugoslavia, are especially abundant. A major part of the collection deals with the World War II occupation and resistance, the Independent State of Croatia, Gen. Draža Mihailović and his Chetniks, and Josip Broz Tito and his Partisans.

Presently the largest segment of the collection is concerned with the development of a socialist society in Yugoslavia after 1945. Particularly well covered are the development and the role of the communist party (League of Communists of Yugoslavia), including its conflict with Moscow and the Cominform in 1948 and its decision to follow its own economic path of "socialist self-management."

The Hoover Institution Archives holds many valuable unpublished documents relating to Yugoslavia, such as the papers of Dragiša Cvetković (prime minister of Yugoslavia, 1939–1941), Konstantin Fotić (Yugoslav ambassador to the United States, 1935–1944), Milan Gavrilović (Yugoslav ambassador to the Soviet Union, 1940–1941; member of the Yugoslav government-in-exile in London, 1941–1943), Dragoljub Jovanović (Yugoslav politician), Vladimir Milanović (Yugoslav ambassador to Bulgaria, 1940–1941; assistant to the foreign minister, Yugoslav government-in-exile, 1941–1944), Dušan Petković (Yugoslav diplomat in Turkey during World War II), Žarko Popović (Yugoslav military attaché to the Soviet Union, 1939–1941), Božidar Purić (premier of the Yugoslav government-in-exile, 1944), and Mladen Žujović (a chief adviser to Gen. Draža Mihailović during World War II).

THE HUNGARIAN COLLECTION

The Hungarian Collection consists of some 14,000 volumes of monographs and pamphlets, runs of approximately 200 periodical titles, files of 42 newspaper titles, and a unique assemblage of archival collections. Exchange programs established with the library of the Institute of Party History and the Széchényi National Library in Budapest have strengthened the acquisitions program considerably.

Officially the Hungarian Collection begins with the period of World War I, and the strength of the collection is greatest for the period 1914 to the present, but holdings on pre–World War I history are substantial. Some of this early material is cataloged under the Austro-Hungarian Empire. Other works dealing with minorities within the former empire are cataloged under the various nations that gained independence after 1918 (for example, Czechoslovakia).

The collection for the period from 1914 to the present comprises primary and secondary sources; official documents; memoirs; biographies and autobiographies; and studies relating to wars and revolutions, political, social, and economic problems, and antigovernment and left-wing labor movements. The strongest areas of coverage are the Hungarian Soviet Republic established by Béla Kun in 1919, the Paris Peace Treaty, the Trianon Treaty establishing Hungary's boundaries, World War II, the 1956 Hungarian Revolution, the history of the communist party (Hungarian Socialist Workers' Party), and the Social Democratic Party. The congresses, plenums, conferences, sessions, and activities of the Central Committee of the Hungarian Socialist Workers' Party are all documented in the collection.

There is also a considerable amount of material, chiefly secondary sources, on questions and problems of nationalities in Hungary; Hungarian minorities in territories lost to other nations, especially for Transylvania; anti-Semitism in Hungary; the history of the Hungarian labor movement; Imre Nagy; and Cardinal Mindszenty. Generally, the history, politics, and economy of Hungary since 1960 are very well covered.

In addition to the library's published materials, the Institution's archives has impressive unpublished, documentary collections. Among the more important of those dealing with Hungary are the papers of Tibor Eckhardt (Hungarian politician, delegate to the League of Nations, 1934–1935), a handwritten autobiography of Miklós Horthy (regent of Hungary, 1920–1944), two collections dealing with the Hungarian Soviet Republic of 1919, the records of three Hungarian embassies (in Moscow, 1934–1941; in Madrid, 1937–1944; in Switzerland, 1920–1945), the papers of Ferenc Marosy (Hungarian diplomat, minister to Croatia, 1941–1943; minister to

Dr. Ralph H. Lutz managed to get a valuable batch of materials from the short-lived communist Béla Kun government of Hungary in 1919. But by the time the documents were ready for shipment to the United States, the Communists had been ousted from power. Officials of the new government had orders to seize and burn all communist files. The Bolshevik records were about to go up in smoke when an American official was able to convince the Hungarians that the interests of history would best be served if the documents were safely deposited in an American research center. Unfortunately the documents were lost en route to Stanford.

Finland, 1944), the papers of Elemér Radisics (Hungarian statesman; member of the Ministry of Foreign Affairs; editor of *Budapesti Hirlap*; member of the Secretariat of the League of Nations, 1931–1940), the papers of János Radványi (a diplomat at the Hungarian embassy in the United States, 1962–1967), and the papers of Rusztem Vámbéry (Hungarian lawyer and politician, Hungarian ambassador to the United States, 1946–1948).

THE ROMANIAN COLLECTION

The Romanian Collection contains some 13,000 volumes of monographs and pamphlets, runs of over 60 periodicals, and about 50 files of newspapers. Although not extremely large, it is capable of supporting advanced research in a number of areas.

The strongest points include Romania's participation in World War I and the peace treaty, the conflicts with the Soviet Union over Bessarabia and with Hungary over Transylvania, interwar political parties (significant documentation for the Partidul Naţional-Liberal, Partidul Naţional-Ţărănesc, Partidul Conservativ, Partidul Poporului, and Partidul Naţional-Democrat), and interwar problems with the monarchy. The foreign policy of Romania for the interwar years is also covered as are internal developments. Materials on the Romanian Communist Party (Partidul Communist Român) form an important part of the collection. The coverage of publications of and about the communist party is especially good for the years 1945–1960 and 1965 to the present. Reports, speeches, and writings by the two general secretaries of the party, Gheorghe Gheorghiu-Dej, who died in 1965, and his successor, Nicolae Ceauşescu, are virtually complete. Speeches and reports of the general secretary are the most important primary sources for the study of Romanian foreign policy, planned economy, education, internal affairs, and policy in general since only a limited number of monographs on these subjects are published.

The archives of the Hoover Institution possesses significant manuscript material for the study of twentieth-century Romanian history, politics, and society. Among these materials are the letters of Ferdinand I, king of Romania, to Aristie Dissescu (1916–1927); and the papers of George Caranfil (Romanian ambassador to Bulgaria, 1941–1943; ambassador to Finland, 1943–1945), Grigore Constantinescu (Romanian diplomat; minister-counselor to Great Britain, 1946–1947), Alexandre Cretzianu (Romanian minister to Turkey, 1943–1946), George I. Duca (Romanian diplomat; chief of mission to Sweden, 1944–1947), Ion George Duca (Romanian minister of education, 1914–1918; minister of agriculture, 1919–1920; minister of foreign affairs, 1922–1926; minister of interior, 1927–1928; and prime minister, 1933), Radu Irimescu (Romanian minister of air and navy, 1932–1938; ambassador to the United States, 1938–1940), Sabin Manuila (Romanian politician), Nicolas Michael Petresco-Comnene (Romanian delegate to the League of Nations, 1923–1928 and 1938; ambassador to Germany, 1927–1929 and 1932; minister of foreign affairs, 1938), Dimitri G. Popescu (private secretary to the undersecretary of state for foreign affairs, 1940–1946), Nicolas Titulescu (Romanian minister of finance, 1920–1922; ambassador to Great Britain, 1922–1927; minister of foreign affairs, 1927–1928 and 1932–1936), and Constantin Visoianu (Romanian minister of foreign affairs, 1945–1946); and the records of the Romanian National Committee, Washington, D.C. (1946–1975).

THE BULGARIAN COLLECTION

The library of the Hoover Institution has one of the major Bulgarian collections in the United States. It consists of somewhat over 10,000 volumes of monographs, runs of approximately 100 periodicals titles, and files of 41 newspapers. As a whole, the collection constitutes an excellent reference source.

The subject areas in which the collection is strongest are Bulgaria's participation in the Balkan Wars of 1912–1913 and Bulgaria's involvement in World War I on the side of the Central Powers. For the interwar period, Hoover has significant holdings on Bulgarian political parties and a complete run of the country's official gazette, *Dŭrzhaven vestnik*. There are also considerable materials on Bulgaria's part in World War II. Among the best-covered areas are the history of the Bulgarian Communist Party (Bŭlgarska Komunisticheska Partiia) and its publications. The decisions and policy statements of the communist party between 1891 and 1955 are reproduced in the work Bŭlgarskata Rabotnicheska Partiia (kommunisti) v rezoliutsii, konferent-siite i plenumite na Tsk (Sofia, 1947–1955). The collection also contains the minutes of all postwar party congresses and individual reports given to the congresses by Georgi Dimitrov, Vŭlko Chervenko, and Todor Zhivkov, as well as various directives, resolutions, and a large number of reports issued by plenums of the Central Committee of the Bulgarian Communist Party. The extensive documentary holdings are supported by quite comprehensive holdings of published collected works, speeches, and writings of the leading postwar party members.

The archives holds a number of interesting unpublished collections dealing with Bulgaria. Among these are some of the writings of Georgi M. Dimitrov (Bulgarian émigré politician; leader of the International Peasant Union), the papers of Racho Petrov (Bulgarian politician and general), Atanas Slavov (Bulgarian émigré author), and Dimitri Stanchov (Bulgarian diplomat; minister of foreign affairs, 1906–1908; minister to France, 1908–1915; minister to Great Britain, 1920–1924). Other collections relating to Bulgaria are the papers of George Caranfil (Romanian ambassador to Bulgaria, 1941–1943) and Vladimir Milanović (Yugoslav ambassador to Bulgaria, 1940–1941); and certain records of the Polish legation in Bulgaria, 1919–1931.

THE GREEK AND ALBANIAN COLLECTIONS

The Hoover Institution's collections on Greece and Albania are relatively small, but do offer research possibilities in certain areas. The Albanian Collection consists of approximately 1,500 volumes of monographs, runs of 21 periodicals, and files of 15 newspapers. Considering the amount that the Albanians have published, and what others have published about Albania, dealing with twentieth-century history, politics, and various social science issues, Hoover's collection is fairly complete. It contains virtually all pertinent works dealing with the independence of Albania in 1912, Albania during World War I, the interwar period and King Zog, World War II, and Enver Hoxha's partisans. For the postwar communist era in Albania, all works by and about the Albanian Communist Party (Partia së Punës të Shqipërisë) are held, as are the writings of Enver Hoxha; the leader in disgrace, Mehmet Shehu; the up-and-coming leader, Ramiz Alia; and most other prominent party leaders. The writings of these individuals are especially important for the study of Albania due to the extreme concentration of power in the hands of a few persons.

The Greek Collection is larger and somewhat more diverse than the Albanian. It consists of some 3,500 volumes of monographs, runs of 115 periodicals titles, and files of 45 newspapers. It also includes a number of archival collections.

Coverage of the era of Eleutherios Venizelos's leadership between 1910 and 1920, including the Balkan Wars and World War I, is fair. The Paris Peace Conference is well covered, and there is good documentation for the period of the Greek military regime, 1967–1974. By far the strongest part of the collection, however, are the years from 1936 to 1949. This encompasses the time of the Metaxas dictatorship (1936–1941), the invasion and occupation by the Axis powers, national resistance and guerrilla warfare, and the Greek Civil War (1946–1949). Holdings of materials on resistance movements, especially the leftist EAM group, are particularly strong. All the various groups are well documented from their inception during the world war through the Civil War. The collection also has materials on the Greco-Turkish disputes over Cyprus.

Archival collections include the papers of Costa G. Couvaras (reports and transcriptions of radio messages relating to the activists of the Greek resistance organization EAM-ELAS during World War II), the George Grivas Collection (materials relating to the revolutionary activities on Cyprus of the Greek underground organization, EOKA, led by G. Grivas, 1955–1959), and the Leften S. Stavrianos Collection (material relating to political and military developments in Greece and Cyprus, especially during the Civil War period, 1946–1949).

5 | THE CENTRAL AND WESTERN EUROPEAN COLLECTIONS

Agnes F. Peterson
Curator

Agnes F. Peterson, Curator,
West European Collection

At the suggestion of Angelica Bala-
banoff, Lutz paid a visit arranged
with conspiratorial care to Rosa
Luxemburg's secretary, who handed
over to him for preservation Lux-
emburg's 1918 prison diary, a set
of her original letters, and corre-
spondence from her family.

The plight of noncombatant Belgium in World War I first raised Herbert Hoover's interest in documenting the causes, the conduct, and the results of this vast struggle. He himself undertook the first collecting effort. As an American delegate to the Paris Peace negotiations, he was inundated by the publications of the various interest and pressure groups. This material was collected into the Official Paris Peace Delegation Propaganda Collection, the beginning of the library of the Hoover Institution.

In the aftermath of World War I, the obvious approach to collecting contemporary historical sources was to concentrate on Europe. At the insistence of Herbert Hoover, Ralph H. Lutz, a young Stanford historian, was released from service in Army Intelligence and went to work to lay the foundations for what eventually became the Central and Western European collections. Lutz had studied in Heidelberg, knew prewar Europe well, and was eager to document the far-reaching social, political, and economic changes taking place. He was particularly interested in German affairs and had an uncanny ability to predict developments.

In the 1920s and early 1930s, the collection was as yet undifferentiated by areas. Efforts were made to collect parliamentary debates, reports of ministries, documents on foreign affairs, and the monographic literature in the various European languages in the fields of history, politics and government, economics, and international relations. The collectors emphasized newspapers and periodicals and publications of various interest and pressure groups. A strong commitment to document the various mass movements—communism, fascism, and national socialism—increased the library's holdings on these subjects tremendously. Library personnel recruited bookdealers and purchasing agents in the various countries to obtain specialized studies, checked dealers' catalogs and national bibliographies, drew up want lists, and organized search trips. The publications of the League of Nations, which came on deposit, formed a basic collection of important international documents. Trading on Herbert Hoover's name and reputation, the library's "historical sleuths" also received gifts of documents, files of newspapers, and records of parties or interest groups. Among them, for instance, were the diaries and the 2,500-volume book collection of noted Austrian lawyer and pacifist Alfred Fried, who was a friend of Bertha von Suttner of "Lay Down Your Arms" fame and a winner of the Nobel Peace Prize in 1911.

Growth was steady during the 1920s and 1930s but slowed abruptly after World War II broke out. Lutz arranged with the library's old and trusted bookdealers in Austria, France, Italy, and Germany to set aside items for the Hoover collections, confident that after the hostilities ended, Hoover personnel would be able to pick up the material. In a number of cases this foresight paid off, and valuable materials carefully packed and stored were waiting at war's end.

During the war, the library's mission grew from a Europe-directed undertaking to one encompassing much of the world. Increasing interest in the non-Western world resulted in a division of the collection into various geographic areas. The Central and Western European collections formed a massive cornerstone of this new structure.

The Central and Western European collections cover the following countries (listed in order of size and importance of the holdings): the two Germanys, France, Great Britain, Italy, Spain and Portugal, Belgium and the Netherlands, Ireland, Austria, Finland, Norway, Sweden and Denmark, Switzerland, and Luxembourg. Coverage in most of the collections begins in 1914 with the outbreak of World War I and concentrates on the fields of government and politics with special attention to labor movements, the rise of social democracy, the two world wars, and the subjects of peace and neutrality. Of particular importance are the materials of regional organizations, such as the European Economic Community (for which the Hoover Institution has functioned as a depository library since 1963), NATO, and the Nordic Council.

In his 1939 trip report, Lutz noted "this unusual opportunity to arrange for the establishment of collecting agencies for current historical materials in accessible belligerent and neutral countries, with the understanding that the material is to be held until peace is declared."

THE TWO GERMANYS

Coverage in the German collections begins with the founding of the First Reich and the Reichstag debates of 1871. Documentation on the German participation in European politics and in World War I is extensive, ranging from trench papers like *Die Bugzeitung* (1915–1918) to the standard works *Die grosse Politik der europäischen Kabinette, 1871–1914* and *Amtliche Urkunden zur Vorgeschichte des Waffenstillstands*, to personal accounts of participants (listed in the catalog under "European war, 1914–1918. Personal narratives—German"). Two useful tools for the study of conditions in wartime Germany are *Daily Review of the Foreign Press* (1915–1919), issued by the British General Staff, and *Bulletin périodique de la presse allemande* (1916–1940) of the French Ministry of Foreign Affairs. Manuscript materials, prisoner-of-war letters and sketchbooks, and posters are available in the archives. A number of important newspaper files for the wartime period, such as *Frankfurter Zeitung, Leipziger Volkszeitung*, and *Münchener Neueste Nachrichten*, can be consulted on microfilm. The period of the November 1918 Revolution and its aftermath, the founding of the Kommunistische Partei Deutschlands, and its journal, *Die Rote Fahne*, are amply covered in documentary studies, journals, and revolutionary tracts, as are other parties, such as the Sozialdemokratische Partei, the Unabhängige Sozialdemokratische Partei Deutschlands (USPD), the Deutsche Zentrumspartei, and the Deutsche Volkspartei.

The history of the Weimar Republic is documented in an extensive collection of secondary literature, in official files such as the *Verhandlungen des Reichstags* and the *Reichsgesetzblatt*, and in periodical literature such as *Alldeutsche Blätter* (1914–1928), *Archiv für Politik und Geschichte* (1924–1929), *Kulturwille* (1924–1932), and *Weltwirtschaft* (1915–1928). A useful, little-known, and little-used source is the weekly cable letters of the Berliner Handelsgesellschaft for 1925–1928.

The Mensing family papers held in the archives include diaries and logbooks of Adm. Franz Mensing (1843–1911) and papers and correspondence of his sons Carl Friedrich (1888–1975) and Franz (1890–1918). Interesting for social studies and the position of women are the diaries of the family's housekeeper for the period 1899–1906.

Origin of the Gestapo state—the
early diaries (1914–1922) of
Heinrich Himmler, the chief of
the nazi secret police. The
diaries formed the basis of a
Himmler biography by
Bradley F. Smith, published by
the Hoover Institution.

The increasing economic difficulties, the weakness of the multiparty system, the radicalization of public opinion, the failure of constitutional emergency powers, the rise of the Nazi Party, and the collapse of parliamentary government are extensively documented.

The National Socialist period from 1933 to 1945 is represented by abundant holdings of the writings of the chief actors of the time, such as Adolf Hitler, Joseph Goebbels, Heinrich Himmler, Alfred Rosenberg, by a nearly complete edition of the *Völkischer Beobachter*, and by representative files of periodicals such as *National-sozialistische Monatshefte* (1930–1943), *Militärwissenschaftliche Rundschau* (1935–1944), and *Zeitschrift für Geopolitik* (1924–1944).

In the 1920s and 1930s, the Institution collected contemporary publications issued by the Nazi Party and the various government offices. It is now endeavoring to collect historical assessments of the Third Reich as they are published. One valuable historical source is the 150 microfilm reels of the records of the NSDAP (National-sozialistische Deutsche Arbeiterpartei) Hauptarchiv, which the Hoover Institution filmed at the Berlin Document Center in 1959–1960 with approval of the Department of State.

Library holdings covering World War II from the German perspective include the official, multivolume history *Kriegstagebuch des Oberkommandos der Wehrmacht, 1940–1945*, a vast array of regimental histories and personal memoirs, individual studies, and microfilms available from the National Archives in Washington of "Captured German Documents," for which 86 guides covering documentation of the Nazi Party and military, political, and economic affairs are now available. A fascinating and nearly complete file of *Zeitschriftendienst* (1939–1944), issued by the Propaganda Ministry, mirrors wartime conditions inside Germany in its pointed press and censorship directives.

The collection includes extensive literature on concentration camps and the Holocaust. The records of the German Foreign Office from 1920 to 1945 were among the "Captured German Documents" microfilmed at Whaddon Hall in England prior to being used for the still incomplete series *Documents on German Foreign Policy, 1918–1945*. The photo blowups made for the use of the American editors were given to the Hoover Institution by the Department of State and form a small Politisches Archiv des Auswärtigen Amts here. To make the microfilms more useful to scholars, the Hoover Institution published the four-volume *Catalog of Files and Microfilms of the German Foreign Ministry Archives, 1920–1945*, edited by George O. Kent (1962–1972).

Holdings for the immediate postwar period include publications of the various zonal governments. A major project of the Bundesarchiv in Koblenz and the Institut für Zeitgeschichte in Munich has been the microfilming of the records of the occupation in the American zone. The Hoover Institution holds a set of OMGUS (Office of Military Government, US) data sheets for this filming project, which can be used as a reference guide to the American occupation material stored by the National Archives and the microfilms available at the Bundesarchiv.

Records from the Soviet Zone are sketchy, but the Briegleb and the William Sander collections in the archives contain reports on political, economic, and social conditions for the years 1945–1959.

The records of the International Military Tribunals at Nuremberg made a vast body of historical materials public. Originally the Hoover Institution was one of the depository libraries for these records. Because of the poor quality of the paper, however, the photocopies tended to self-destruct. In the early 1980s, the National Ar-

As a matter of course, because it seemed interesting, Ralph Lutz bought the first edition of the first volume of an unknown political writer in 1925. The volume was Mein Kampf.

Professor Theodore Abel of Columbia University organized a prize competition in 1934 asking a self-selected group of party members why they had joined the Nazi Party. About 500 of these autobiographical sketches are held in the archives and give some clues as to the appeal of the party.

A view of the Document Room at the International Military Tribunal, Nuremberg, during the 1946–1948 period

chives microfilmed a complete set, and a copy of the microfilm is available at the Institution. The minutes of the 121 sessions of the 1961 Eichmann trial in Jerusalem are also available.

Since the founding of the Federal Republic and the Democratic Republic in 1949, the library has attempted to document events in both parts of Germany, their relations to each other and to the rest of the world, and their self-image and self-doubts. Documentation on the student revolt in the late 1960s and its forerunner, the youth movement of the 1920s, consists of leaflets and periodicals issued by the various groups and of later academic studies. The library has systematically collected the publications of the different parties in the West, such as the Christliche Demokratische Union (CDU), Sozialdemokratische Partei Deutschlands (SPD), Freie Demokratische Partei (FDP), and Deutsche Kommunistische Partei (DKP), and of the ruling party in the East, the Sozialistische Einheitspartei Deutschlands (SED). Records of congresses and *Parteitage* are available, as are materials on the various general elections. The special problem of Berlin is covered in academic publications: in the stenographic reports of the Stadtverordneten Versammlung von Gross-Berlin (1946–1949); in books, pamphlets, and pictures on the airlift of 1948–1949 and on the raising of the wall in 1963; and finally in the proceedings of the Quadripartite Treaty settling the position of the city in 1972. Materials that deserve special mention because of their uniqueness or importance are the six reels of microfilm of listeners' mail to RIAS (Radio in the American Sector) (1961–1963), a substantial collection of CDU pamphlets from 1953 to the present, and a set of some fifty reports by onetime political prisoners in East German jails (1950–1975), brought together by a high school teacher from Hannover.

Ongoing collecting strategies aim at documenting the efforts of the peace movement in both parts of Germany and the current unease in transatlantic relations and at keeping up with the never-ending flow of books, pamphlets, periodicals, and newspapers describing and analyzing current political, economic, and social conditions.

The coverage of the French collections essentially starts with the outbreak of World War I and carries through to the present, but the holdings are uneven since collecting intensity varied. Among the more substantial areas of coverage are the two world wars, foreign relations in the interwar period, decolonization, the war in Algeria, the establishment and growth of the Fifth Republic, the May 1968 student uprising, the change in 1981 from a conservative to a socialist government, and all general elections from 1958 to 1981.

FRANCE

For the history of World War I, important holdings include the 92-volume *Les Armées françaises dans la grande guerre*, issued by the Imprimerie Nationale, and the 100-volume *Collections de mémoires, études et documents pour servir à l'histoire de la guerre mondiale*, issued in Paris between 1920 and 1936, which covers both official and unofficial propaganda and information efforts.

Of particular interest is the set of foreign press surveys issued by the French Foreign Ministry entitled *Bulletin périodique de la presse étrangère* (1916–1940). This survey was resumed after 1945 in a new series entitled *Bulletin quotidien de la presse étrangère* (1946–1953) and continued in abbreviated fashion by *Chroniques étrangères* (1946–1967), which covered events only in Germany, Spain, the United States, Great Britain, Italy, and the USSR.

A bibliographic treasure is the fifteen volume set of Marshal Pétain's report as commander in chief for the French Army of the North and Northeast in 1918. The volumes had originally belonged to Marshal Foch, but were then given, suitably inscribed by Pétain, to John D. Rockefeller III, who in turn presented them to the Hoover Library.

Holdings for the post-WWI reconstruction period include the papers of Louis Loucheur (1872–1931), who as minister of reconstruction was intent on accommodation with Germany. A few files for the period 1916–1955 of the important industrialist and engineer Ernest Mercier can also be consulted.

For the interwar period, the eighteen scrapbooks of Stéphane Lauzanne, who as editor of the influential newspaper *Le Matin* from 1920 to 1940 was in an excellent position to watch French policy, are available. The same period is covered by the sometimes muckraking periodical *Documents politiques, diplomatiques et financiers* (1920–1940), published by Roger Mennevée.

A file of records of the congresses of the Parti communiste français is available for 1922–1981; holdings of the PCF newspaper *L'Humanité* (1914–1981) and journal *Cahiers du communisme* (1924–1939, 1945–1983) are good. Substantial files of records of the congresses of the Parti socialiste (1905–1965) and its journal *Le Populaire de Paris* (1916–1969; partly on microfilm) also exist. Documentation on the Parti républicain radical et radical socialiste includes microfilm records of its party congresses for 1933–1938 and 1944–1962.

Of particular interest for students of events of the 1930s leading up to World War II are the records of the postwar government investigation entitled *Commission chargée d'enquêter sur les événements survenus en France de 1933–1945* (11 vols., 1949–1950) and the *Documents diplomatiques français, 1932–1939*, which are at long last being issued by the French Ministry of Foreign Affairs.

In 1958 the Institution received a request from the French government to microfilm the entire collection. The reason given was that the original documents existed but were scattered through many archival sections. The collection at the Hoover Institution was efficiently organized and easy to use.

World War II is amply covered both from the Vichy and the Free French side. Some aspects of the "phony war" can be traced in a collection of about fifty trench papers issued in 1939–1940.

Of special interest is a collection of material on Vichy France, including depositions on Pierre Laval, by his collaborators, brought together by his son-in-law René de Chambrun. For industrial and trade union activities, the Victor-Louis Chaigneau collection on the Charte de Travail and the Georges Lefranc collection of writings and reports relating to social conditions and trade union movements during and after the war should be consulted.

Files of periodicals for this period include *L'Atelier* (1940–1944), *Le Cri du peuple* (1940–1944), *Idées* (1941–1944), *La Voix ouvrière* (1942–1944), and newspapers such as *Les Nouveaux temps* (1940–1944), and *La France socialiste* (1941–1944).

Files of the Free French *Journal officiel*, issued in London and in Algiers, are available, as are *Les Cahiers français* (1941–1944), *La France libre* (1940–1947), and *Tricolore* (1941–1945), all issued in London. Free French files issued in the United States include, among others, *France-Amérique* (1943–1948), *La République française* (1943–1949), and *La Victoire* (1942–1946).

A fine collection of primary sources on the French resistance includes, among other materials, a substantial set of minutes of COMAC (Comité d'action militaire du Conseil national de la résistance). Members of a special committee set up in Paris under the leadership of Louis Chevrillon in 1946 typed copies of all of these documents, and the Hoover staff has made detailed inventories and registers of these materials.

By their very nature, underground newspapers and periodicals are difficult to collect in large runs. A special index, available in the public catalog room, has been compiled for the great number of titles represented by only a few issues. Among the better-known Resistance papers in the collection are *Action, Aurore, Défense de la France, Les Forces unies de la jeunesse, Franc-tireur, Libération,* and *La Voix du nord*. An underground journal surfacing later was *Le Maquis*, held by Hoover for 1944–1957.

The papers of Gaston Bergery (1892–1974), the wartime French ambassador to the Soviet Union and to Turkey, are also open for research. A number of biographies are available on French leaders, the greatest number, of course, being on Charles de Gaulle. The general's published writings are held in both French and English.

In general the postwar reconstruction and the Fourth Republic are covered somewhat scantily, with the exception of Pierre Poujade's movement and his journal, *Fraternité française*, for which the library holds a run from 1956 to 1973.

The library made an intense effort to collect materials on the establishment and consolidation of the French Fifth Republic under Charles de Gaulle. Ephemeral material, such as leaflets, pamphlets, and posters can be found in the archives' French Fifth Republic Collection, which is part of the French Subject Collection. The *professions de foi*, issued for the general elections from 1958 to 1981 by the various prefectures for the candidates of all parties, are also located in this collection. Monographs, biographies, memoirs, and studies in a variety of languages can be found in the catalog under the subject heading "France—Politics and government, 1958– ."

The journal of the Union de la nouvelle république, *Courrier de la nouvelle république* (1960–1962), is available, as are the official newspaper of the party, *La Nation* (1962–1974), and a confidential newsletter with much inside information, the *Bulletin d'André Noël* (1958–1967). The war in Algeria and its settlement were the central concern at the beginning of the Fifth Republic. The war was indeed responsible for the advent of de Gaulle to power, and the library collected extensive materials on the war. The names of three important files, *Le Bled: Hebdomadaire militaire d'information* (1958–1962), *L'Echo d'Alger* (1957–1961), and *Le Pied noir* (1963–1966), stand for many other titles. The library holds the major clandestine journal of the Algerian Front of National Liberation, *El Moudjahid* (Freedom fighter) from 1957 to 1962 in the edition issued in Tunis, as well as a later reprint issued in Yugoslavia. Some materials on the Organisation de l'armée secrète (the French secret army), which opposed de Gaulle's policies, can be found in the materials on the generals' revolt in Algiers in April 1961 in the John K. Cooley Collection and in the Yves Godard papers. Concerns with defense policy can be traced from 1945 to 1981 in the collection of speeches and writings of Gen. Pierre Gallois.

The other event of inordinate concern and far-reaching consequence was the French student revolt in May 1968. Short runs of periodicals, sets of leaflets, some posters, appeals and flyers, newspaper issues, and cartoons can be found in the French Student Revolt Collection, which also forms part of the French Subject Collection in the archives. Monographs, reminiscences, studies, and accounts are cataloged under the headings "Students–France–Revolts of May 1968" and "Students–Paris–Political Activities."

The presidencies of Georges Pompidou and Valéry Giscard d'Estaing are covered, and special efforts were made to collect documentation on the presidential elections of 1969, 1974, and 1981. Ongoing efforts aim at documenting the government of François Mitterrand.

"Perhaps the best collection that I have," wrote Donald Baker, a Stanford graduate who happened to be in Paris and started collecting for the Hoover Institution before even being asked, "is that from the Beaux Arts, where student artists have been turning out memoranda by the yard. Posters are hard to get, as artists (the printing shops were closed) took an oath not to give or sell them to anyone but revolutionaries who would be sure that they got glued to walls, but I have a handful anyway."

GREAT BRITAIN

The British Collection is one of the oldest and most established at the Hoover. Because no foreign language was involved in its acquisition, materials were easier to obtain, handle, and organize. The main interest centers on acquiring materials on the two world wars, British foreign relations between the wars, decolonization and the changing of the Empire into the Commonwealth, and, most important, the rise and possible demise of the Labour Party.

Student protest posters, May–June 1968, Paris

Since the Wellington House material had to be moved quickly, a Hoover Library staff member armed with rolls of packing paper and twine, tied up everything on the assigned shelves in small bundles, and to the amazement of passersby hired a fleet of taxis to convey those bundles from Downing Street to the Institution's book-dealer, Stevens and Brown in Trafalgar Square, which shipped them to Stanford.

One of the first major acquisitions in 1919 was the Wellington House library of British wartime propaganda pamphlets. These samples of propaganda had been stored on the top floor of the Foreign Office in Downing Street and were in imminent danger of being scrapped. The official history of World War I can be consulted here under the title *First World War, 1914–1918*, and events from the British point of view can be followed in *Documents on British Foreign Policy, 1919–1939*, in *Survey of International Affairs* (1920–1962), and in *Documents on International Affairs* (1928–1963). The French series *Bulletin périodique de la presses anglaise* (1916–1940), the *Bulletin quotidien de la presse étrangère* (1946–1953), and the *Chroniques étrangères: Grande Bretagne* (1952–1967), give a capsule view of fifty years of British history.

The tension-ridden period between the wars is highlighted by special materials on the General Strike of May 1926 (a collection of London newspapers), by the publications of the International Brigade Association, such as *Volunteer for Liberty* (1940–1945), for the Spanish Civil War, and by the newspaper *New Times and Ethiopian News* (1936–1956), which was founded to cover the Abyssinian war.

Documentation on the official history of World War II is shared with Green Library. The Hoover Institution holds the United Kingdom Civil and Military Series; Green Library is responsible for the Medical Series. Over the years the Jonsson Library of Government Documents at Green Library has built an excellent collection of *Hansard* (1803 to the present) and has extensive holdings on microfilm of Cabinet Office and Foreign Office materials, including Cabinet Office minutes for 1916–1939 and War Cabinet minutes for 1939–1945, as well as papers from the Prime Minister's Office for 1938–1946.

Holdings of the general correspondence of the Foreign Office files on microfilm go back to 1805 and include sets of Confidential Prints for Africa, Russia, Japan, and China and the correspondence of the British embassy in the United States (1903–1948), among others. These materials, usually acquired after joint consultation and sometimes with joint funds, are all housed at the Jonsson Library of Government Documents in Green Library.

An excellent source on internal politics and social policy is Tom Harrison's Mass Observation Archive, which is now available on microfilm for 1937–1941. The filming of this archive will be continued. This set is held at the Hoover Institution.

Another collection highlight is the microfiche package brought together by Harvester Press entitled *Britain and Europe Since 1945*, in which all the ephemeral literature for and against the British entry into the European Communities is contained, as is documentation on Britain's uneasy and tempestuous membership.

The heart of the British Collection consists of a rich selection of material published by the various political parties. Among these, the most important and substantive is the documentation on the Labour Party and its various predecessors and allies, such as the Independent Labour Party and the Fabians. The pamphlets and leaflets of the Independent Labour Party are available on microfiche from 1893 to 1975, as are the "Minutes and Related Records" from 1894 to 1956 and the pamphlets and leaflets of the Social Democratic Federation from 1893 to 1931.

The Labour Party Collection was begun by Professor Carl F. Brand (1892–1981), and its growth can be attributed to his unceasing efforts to gather documentation.

Holdings of the reports of the annual conferences of the Labour Party from 1901 to 1982 are nearly complete: the minutes of the National Executive Committee on microfiche cover the period from 1900 to 1966. A set of pamphlets and leaflets covering 1900 to 1969 from the Archives of the Labour Party also exists on microfiche.

The books and pamphlets of Clement Atlee, Ernest Bevin, Sir Stafford Cripps, Hugh Dalton, Arthur Greenwood, Arthur Henderson, George Lansbury, Harold Laski, J. Ramsay MacDonald, Herbert Morrison, Noel Baker, Philip Snowden, Harold Wilson, James Callaghan, Tony Benn, and Neil Kinnock can also be consulted.

Substantial periodical files include *Fact* (1941–1956), *Notes for Speakers* (1929–1947), *This Week* (1962–1971), *Commonwealth* (1959–1966), *Left* (1936–1950), *Labour Research* (1919–1982), and *Labour Weekly* (1972–1982). Notable newspapers available are *Bradford Pioneer* (1913–1936), *Lansbury's Labour Weekly* (1925–1927), and *Workers' Dreadnought* (1914–1924).

Complementing these holdings on the Labour Party are the general minute books of the Trades Union Congress available on microfilm for 1921–1946, and its pamphlet and leaflet series from 1887 to 1966.

Substantial runs of trade union periodicals include *Scottish Miner* (1962–1982), *Man and Metal* (1962–1980), and *Data Journal* (1965–1971).

The collection also includes the pamphlets and leaflets of the British Conservative and Unionist Party from 1868 to 1956, the Executive Committee minutes of the National Union of Conservative Associations from 1897 to 1956, all on microfiche, a set of pamphlets on microfilm of the Communist Party of Great Britain for 1947–1982, and files of *The Daily Worker* (1943–1966), and *Morning Star* (1966–).

For the contemporary political scene, the library is actively collecting the publications of the Social Democratic Party under Shirley Williams and Roy Jenkins and materials of the Campaign for Nuclear Disarmament. Extensive secondary documentation exists on the war in the Falklands, and a concerted effort has been made to gather the position papers, leaflets, and posters from the June 1983 general election.

IRELAND

The Irish Collections were begun by James A. Healy (1891–1975) of New York, a longtime friend of Herbert Hoover and a passionate collector of materials on Irish history. Healy's interest also extended to art and literature, and he gave a very fine collection of writings by authors of the Irish Literary Movement to the Green Library.

The printed and published volumes of the Healy Collection are housed as a special collection in the Tower; the manuscript and clipping sections are in the archives. The latter contain Healy's correspondence with Herbert Hoover and Sean T. O'Kelley, president of Ireland from 1949 to 1959. Also included are newspaper clippings, pamphlets, and special newspaper issues for the period 1896–1966, all relating to political and economic conditions in twentieth-century Ireland. The collection emphasizes 1916 and the Easter Uprising, Sir Roger Casement, the establishment of the Republic of Ireland in 1921–1922, Irish involvement in World War II, and the civil war in Northern Ireland since 1969. The debates of Parliament in Dublin are available from 1922 to 1980.

The A. J. and Ann Monday Collection on contemporary Irish history and politics, established in 1976, contains a selection of pamphlets, leaflets, posters, and phonograph records relating to the Ulster conflict and is being kept up to date.

Some of the records of the Parliament of Northern Ireland are shared between the Hoover Institution and the Jonsson Library of Government Documents at Green Library. The Hoover Institution holds the records (journals, documents, notices, and debates in hard copy) of the House of Commons and the Senate of the Parliament (Stormont) of Northern Ireland in Belfast from 1921 to 1925. The Jonsson Library holds the same materials on 95 reels of microfilm from 1921 to 1972.

Of special interest is a collection on microfilm, entitled *Northern Ireland Political Literature, 1968–1975*, brought together by the Linenhall Library in Belfast. The extensive set *Irish Political and Radical Newspapers of the 20th Century, 1895–1941*, also on microfilm, is shared between the Hoover Institution and Green Library.

Current acquisition interest centers on the initiatives developed by the New Ireland Forum.

BELGIUM   The collection's great interest in Belgium originated in Herbert Hoover's leadership of the Commission for Relief of Belgium during and after World War I. The files of the commission are kept in the archives.

The collection stresses Belgian foreign relations, underground and resistance activities during the two wars, Belgium's colonial empire in Africa and the subsequent decolonization, its membership and integration in the European Communities, its cooperation in NATO, activities of political parties, and the French-Flemish problem.

Materials of special nature that deserve mention are *An Annotated Listing of Clandestine Publications Issued in Belgium During the German Occupation, 1914–1918*, by Ruth Perry (Berkeley, 1939), and a file of *La Libre belgique* (1915–1918, 1940–1944 [underground], 1944–1977).

For World War II, the bibliography of George Tanham's thesis, "Belgian Underground Movement, 1940–1944" (Stanford, 1951), provides a detailed evaluation of Belgian underground materials available at the Institution.

For the official government record, a file of the *Moniteur belge* (1914–1924, 1935–1940, 1940–1944 [London], 1944–1975) can be consulted. The deliberations of parliament can be traced in the *Annales parlementaires* (1918–1926, 1934–1939, 1944–1977/78). Materials of the WWI German occupation administration can be found in *Militärverordnungsblatt des Generalgouvernements in Belgien* (1915–1918) and in the *Gesetz und Verordnungsblatt für die okkupierten Gebiete Belgiens* (1914–1917).

For World War II, an extensive collection of German propaganda can be found under the heading "Nationalsozialistische Deutsche Arbeiterpartei, Propaganda Abteilung Belgien, Gruppe Presse," as well as in the *Verordnungsblatt des Militärbefehlshabers in Belgien und Nordfrankreich . . .* (1940–1944).

A discussion of the royal question and documentation pertaining to Leopold III can be found in the various materials issued by the Secrétariat du roi.

Miscellaneous papers of Henri de Man (minister of public works, 1935–1936, and minister of finance, 1936–1938), who was active in Belgian politics and convicted for collaborating with the Nazis, are available.

For materials specifically on Flemish interests, files of the daily *De nieuwe Gids* (1951–1954) and the monthly *De nieuwe Maand* (1965–1982) should be consulted.

The Comité belge pour la Communauté Atlantique furnished an extensive clipping collection on NATO taken from the Belgian press from February to August 1959. More recent NATO materials include annual conference reports from 1975 on and the records of the deliberations in various committees of the North Atlantic Assembly from 1971 on, as well as a stream of publications issued by the Information Office of NATO headquarters in Brussels.

From the headquarters of the European Communities in Brussels, the Hoover Institution has acquired extensive materials of the old Coal and Steel Community from 1952 on, as well as for three emerging communities (Coal and Steel, Common Market, and Euratom [nontechnical materials]) from 1957. In 1963, the Institution became a depository library for all publications of the European Communities in its fields of interest of politics and government. A special collection includes propaganda materials issued by various groups and parties for the first European parliamentary election in June 1979 and the second one in June 1984.

The outstanding aspect of the holdings on the Netherlands is their coverage of World War II and the Dutch underground. A key to the Dutch underground material in the collection can be found in the bibliography of the thesis by Werner Warmbrunn, "The Netherlands Under German Occupation, 1940–1945" (Stanford University, 1955). In this connection should be mentioned the holdings in the Nijhoff Collection of Books Published by Underground Presses, which contains books and pamphlets of exceptional design, printing, and binding published clandestinely during the German occupation.

The collection includes the publications of the Royal Netherlands Institute for War Documentation, of which *Nederland in oorlogstijd* (1946–1951) is of special interest, and the official Dutch government inquiry: *Enquête commissie Regeringsbeleid, 1940–45* (8 vols., 1949–1956).

The record of the trial of Anton Mussert (1894–1946), leader of the Dutch Nazis, is available, together with some of Mussert's writings. A substantial collection of underground pamphlets issued by various opposition groups, as well as leaflet and manuscript material covering especially the medical doctors' opposition, rounds out the Institution's holdings.

The collection has large runs of the following clandestine periodicals: *Christofoor*, *Het parool*, *Je maintiendrai* (various editions), *Marx-Lenin-Luxembourg front*, *Bulletin*, *Trouw*, and *Vrij Nederland*. There is also a substantial file of *De Vliegende Hollander* (1943–1945), a weekly newspaper produced jointly by the U.S. Office of War Information and the political intelligence division of the British Foreign Office, dropped by the Allied Air Force, and distributed by the Dutch underground.

Policies of the German occupying powers are documented in a large run of *Verordnungsblatt für die besetzten niederländischen Gebiete, 1940–1945*.

General laws and statutes are covered in the Hague edition of the *Nederlandsche Staatscourant* (May 24, 1940–March 19, 1945). The German Army in the Netherlands issued a monthly periodical entitled *Vuur: Officieel orgaan voor de Weermacht* (1942–1943). Holdings of publications issued by collaborating organizations include *Deutsche Zeitung in den Niederlanden* (1940–1945; broken file), *Dinaso Orde: Weekblad van het Verdinaso-Nederland* (1939–1940; issued by the Verbond van Dietsche Nationaalsolidaristen), and *Storm: Weekblad der Germaansche in Nederland* (1941–1945).

The roots of the present-day Dutch peace movement date back a long time; included in the collection are considerable materials on the Nederlandsche anti-oorlograad, such as *Holland News*, *Nouvelles de Hollande*, *Holländische Nachrichten* (1914–1919), as well as files of *Vrede door Recht* (1913–1916), *De Toekomstige Vrede* (1915–1919), and *Na-Oorlogse Rechtspraak Zwolle* (1946–1951). Another file covering literature on war and peace is entitled *Nieuwe literatuur over oorlog en vrede* (1964–1967).

Among archived materials, the Louis Raemaekers (1869–1956) Collection of correspondence and particularly of about 600 original political cartoons deserves special mention. Raemaekers's biting anti-German World War I caricatures were distributed by the British Ministry of Information in more than twelve languages; the political cartoons of the 1920s and 1930s were published by the *Amsterdam Telegraaf*.

THE NETHERLANDS

Original drawing of Dutch cartoonist Louis Raemaekers, famous for his pro-American and anti-German cartoons during World War I, symbolizes the landing of American forces in Europe with President Woodrow Wilson as a conquering American eagle and Kaiser Wilhelm II in caricature.

A selection of Raemaeker's original sketches was exhibited in 1982 at the Hoover Institution to celebrate 200 years of friendly relations between the United States and the Netherlands.

LUXEMBOURG   Holdings on the Grand Duchy of Luxembourg are very small and deal with questions of attempted neutrality in both world wars.

Of importance is a complete file of the German occupation laws for World War II, *Verordnungsblatt für Luxemburg, 1940–1944*.

Luxembourg has a small, but vocal communist party, and its point of view is represented in *Zeitung vum Letzeburger Vollek*, which the library holds for 1979 to the present.

The headquarters for both the European Court of Justice and the European Parliament (which, however, holds its meetings in Strasbourg) are in Luxembourg. Shipping operations for all publications issued by the European Communities, for which the Hoover Institution is a depository library, have recently been transferred to Luxembourg.

ITALY   The Italian section is one of the larger constituents of the Western European Collection and spans the period from 1914 to the present. There are several areas of special interest and emphasis, including the fascist era, World War II, the Italian underground movement, and political developments from the late 1950s on.

For the first part of the century, a good set of parliamentary debates and documents exists from 1909 to 1938 for the proceedings of the Chamber of Deputies and from 1909 to 1944 for those of the Senate. The Commissione per la pubblicazione dei documenti diplomatici is slowly issuing volumes of diplomatic documents for the years 1914–1943, and the Hoover is acquiring these as they appear.

Italian participation in World War I is covered by holdings of various official publications issued by the Corpo di stato maggiore, Officio storico, such as *L'esercito italiano nella grande guerra, 1915–1918* and *Collana di monografie storiche sulla guerra del 1915–1918*.

Personal accounts and narratives can be located in the 24-volume *Collezione italiana di diari, memorie, studi e documenti per servire alla storia della guerra del mondo*, edited by Angelo Gatti. Also available are the Rome dailies *Corriere d'Italia* (1915–1918) and *Idea nazionale* (1914–1919), as well as the Milan quarterly *La Guerra* (1916–1921).

The fascist period from 1922 to 1943 is documented by *La legislazione fascista* (1922–1943, with a few gaps); *News Notes on Fascist Corporations* (1932–1936), issued by the Ministero della corporazione; the periodical *Gerarchia: Rassegna mensile della rivoluzione fascista* (1922–1942); the daily *Popolo d'Italia* (1915–1922, 1931–1933, 1940–1943); and the *Atti* of the Partito nazionale fascista (1932/33–1939/40). The microfilms of the *Corriere Padano* (1925–1945) mirror the regional impact of fascist policies in Ferrara.

The collection includes Benito Mussolini's *Opera omnia*, edited by Eduardo and Dulio Susmel, as well as studies and biographies by de Felice, Delzell, Hilbert, Kirkpatrick, Mack Smith, Salvemini, Sarfatti, and Seldes, among others. Of particular interest is a 47-page account on microfilm by Franco Maugeri, *Mussolini m'a detto*. Maugeri was the naval officer responsible for Mussolini's custody after his fall from power.

There is ample League of Nations documentation on the Italian-Ethiopian war. A number of secondary works deal with Italian military involvement in the Spanish Civil War.

The library holds a number of exile publications issued in France, Great Britain, and the United States during the entire fascist period, including a series of irregular periodicals published by Giustizia e libertà, under that name from 1934 to 1947 and the monthly *Contro corrente: Organo d'agitazione e di battagli contro il fascismo*, which appeared in Boston from 1938 to 1951.

For World War II, the official histories of both the army and navy are available, and various problems are illuminated by fragments of historical materials brought together in special collections such as the collection of propaganda leaflets issued by the German High Command in Italy, 1944–1945, directed to the Italian population under German occupation. The resistance movement is represented by original documents of the Comitato di liberazione nazionale and the Partito d'azione and by files of their publications.

For the postwar period the Institution's holdings of the proceedings and the documents of the Constituent Assembly are invaluable for studying the reorganization of the government apparatus.

A great effort has been made in the Italian section to bring together significant political party materials. A set of 25 microfilm reels of correspondence and reports relating to communist and anarchist movements from 1902 to 1934 assembled by the Public Security Office of the Ministry of the Interior merits special attention.

For the communist party, important files like *L'ordine nuovo* (1919–1925) and *Rinascita* (1944–) can be consulted, supplemented by a somewhat broken file of *L'unità*, the communist daily (1924– , partly on microfilm), by *Critica marxista* (1966–), and lately by a good file of *Il Manifesto* (1977–).

The Partito socialista italiano is represented by an incomplete file of *Avanti* (1896–1960; a large part on microfilm), *Il Soviet* (1918–1922), *Critica sociale* (1891–1926, 1945–1975), and *Mondo operaio* (1966–1981).

The voice of the Partito della democrazia cristiana can be checked in *Il Popolo* (1966–) and in *Discussione* (1962–), as well as in a large collection of memoirs, studies, accounts, and earlier periodical files.

The Partito liberale italiano is represented with a file of *Nuovi argomenti* (1953–) and the neo-fascist Movimento sociale italiano by *Il secolo d'Italia* (1972–).

Major current newspaper files consist of *Giornale nuovo* (1977–), *La Nazione* (1966–), *Repubblica* (1980–), and *La Stampa* (1962–1977, 1981–). Older files include *Corriere della sera* (1906–1926, 1940–1943, 1945–1953) and *Osservatore Romano* (1914–1918, 1949–1953, 1966–1970).

Collecting emphasis centers on the seesaw between the political parties, the redevelopment of the Mezzogiorno, the history of the fascist era, the Red Brigades, and Italian integration into the European Communities.

It proved difficult to subscribe to Il Manifesto. By chance a young Italian-language professor at the University of California at Santa Cruz was looking for a library to house her backfiles of the newspaper. The Institution acquired her file and took over her subscription.

SPAIN

The heart of the Spanish collections is the substantial holdings of books, newspapers, periodicals, ephemeral materials, and archival documents covering the Civil War (1936–1939). These materials were gathered by three American correspondents assigned to cover the Spanish Civil War, Burnett Bolloten, Jay Allen, and Milly Bennett.

Under the heading "Spain–History–Civil War," holdings on the following subtopics are especially rich: foreign participation, personal narrative, pictorial works (including most of the graphic propaganda emanating from all sides), and regimental histories. Under the latter may be found rewarding materials on the International Brigades.

Since 1941, Burnett Bolloten has donated more than 2,000 books and pamphlets, some of them exceedingly rare. In addition, about 12,000 newspaper titles from the

Civil War period have been integrated into the library's general holdings; the library also holds a set of microfiches covering the 680 pamphlets of the Blodgett Collection collected by Harvard. Of greatest importance, however, is the large collection of primary documents (in 54 manuscript boxes, ten large scrapbooks, and on 60,000 frames of newspaper microfilm) brought together by Bolloten and used by him to write the *Grand Camouflage* (1961) and *The Spanish Revolution* (1979).

Archival materials on the Spanish Civil War can also be found in the papers of Bertram Wolfe and in the archive of Joaquín Maurín, the founder of the Partido Obrero de Unificación Marxista (POUM), whose papers yielded a file of the newspaper *La Batalla* (1923–1937). More documentation can be found in the papers of H. H. Fisher, the Müller and Gräff miniature poster collection, and on reel 19 of the microfilm of the André Marty archive.

During the Franco period (1939–1975), appropriate monographs in the Hoover Institution's field of interest were acquired as well as newspapers such as the falangist *Arriba* (1939–1974) and periodicals like *Revista de Estudios Internacionales* (1950–). The Institution also collected opposition, separatist, and exile publications, such as *El Socialista: Organo del Partido socialista obrero español* (1948–1957), Toulouse; *Nouvelles d'Espagne* (1962–1969), Toulouse; *Alderdi: Euzko alderdi jeltzaliu ren deya* (1951–1974); and the *Spanish Labor Bulletin* (1938–1939), New York.

In the post-Franco period, the library has paid great attention to the establishment of the new democracy under Juan Carlos and also to the attempted coup against this democracy in 1980. The *Boletin oficial de las Cortes españoles* (now *Cortes generales*) has been received since 1971, but it has assumed greater constitutional importance since 1977, as has the *Gaceta de Madrid: Boletin oficial del Estado*, which has been received in various series (1936–1961, 1961–1975, 1977–). The proceedings of both the Chamber of Deputies and of the Senate are available since 1979.

The files of the daily *El País* are available since 1976 as are the weekly *Cambio 16* since 1975 and the monthly *Historia 16* since 1976. The Spanish Communist Party is represented by its weekly paper, *Mundo Obrero* (1976–), and some earlier underground files. The conservative *Vanguardia Española* has been acquired on microfilm since 1975.

The bimonthly *El Socialista*, published in France from 1973 to 1976 and now representing the viewpoint of Felipe Gonzáles and the Socialist Party, is available from 1973 on.

PORTUGAL   For many years, the Portuguese Collection grew very slowly and formed only a background and framework to the burgeoning collections on the wars and events in Portuguese Africa (see Chapter 7). Since the Salazar and Caetano regimes discouraged political publications, the main collecting effort was devoted to government documents, official publications, and periodicals.

After the 1974 revolution, a great publishing renaissance took place on all points of the political compass. The Hoover Institution has attempted to collect as much material in its traditional fields of interest as possible in the face of unsettled conditions, small press runs, confiscations, and skyrocketing prices.

For the pre–World War I period, Richard Hammond's *Portugal and Africa, 1815–1910: A Study in Uneconomic Imperialism* is especially helpful to users of the Hoover Institution's collections. Professor Hammond turned over to the Institution much of the source material he used in writing the book.

The Institution holds many substantial files on several ministries and agencies responsible for colonial affairs since World War I (see Chapter 7).

Archival materials are thin for this period. The most substantial collection, 29 manuscript boxes of correspondence, memorandums, reports, and government documents covering 1919–1950, came by an accident of location from the files of the Polish legation in Lisbon. Also useful are the British Foreign Office and Colonial Office Confidential Prints (Africa Series) that dealt with Portuguese-British relations in Africa.

Official documentation can be found in *Diario do governo*, Series I, II, and III (1914–1975). This file continues in the post-1974 period as *Diario da Assembleia da Republica* (1976–). For the Assembleio nacional, the *Diaro das sessoes* (1935–1952, 1962–April 1974) is available. The Camara corporativa is represented by *Actas da Camara corporativa* (1964–1968, 1970–1973). Holdings on the earlier Congresso consist of *Diario do congreso* (1913–1920) and *Summario das sessoes do congreso* (1913–1917) as well as the *Anais da assemblea nacional e da camara corporativa* (1935–1943). A long run of the official collection of laws and statutes can be found in *Colecção oficial de legislação portuguesa* (1922–1958; 1950–1954 missing).

A series of pamphlets dealing with overseas policy, corporative organizations, labor policy, youth training, church-state relations, and economic development was issued for the period 1940–1945 by the Secretariado nacional da informação, cultura popular e turismo. This same government office also issued *Portugal: Bulletin of Political, Economic and Cultural Information* (1937–1956), which was superseded by *Portugal: An Information Review*, for the years 1956–1964 and 1970–1973.

Listings of the published works of Antonio Salazar and Marcello Caetano can be found in the main catalog. Also available are the published proceedings of the trial of Henrique Galvao in 1952 and the memoirs of Humberto Delgado.

The Revolution of the Flowers of April 1974 brought about far-reaching changes in Portugal, divested it of its overseas empire, and established a democratic government in the homeland, which found itself threatened successively by the army, the Left, and the Right.

Noteworthy materials for this period of change include the second edition of Antonio Spinola's influential *Portugal e o futuro*; the published works of Mario Soares, the head of the Socialist Party; the memoirs of Marcello Caetano, *Depoimento*, published in Brazil, and their refutation by Col. Antonio Cruz; as well as the publications of Alvaro Cunhal, the leader of the communist party.

The *Diario* of the Assembleia Constituente is available for 1975; it continued as *Diario da Assembleia* (1976–). Of particular interest is the rare file of *Boletim informativo* (1–25, no. 8 missing; September 1974–August 1975), issued by the Movimento das forcas armadas. A collection of posters and ephemera relating to the revolution brought together by Cornelius Drijver documents the more colorful aspects of the changes.

A visiting Canadian scholar who had spent the summer of 1975 at Hoover was instrumental in acquiring a nearly complete file of the Boletim informativo *of the Armed Forces when he found various numbers in Lisbon during his stay there.*

Phonotapes of interviews with British, Portuguese, and South African diplomats, politicians, economic advisers, businessmen and journalists relating to the April 1974 events can be consulted in the Robert Keith Middlemas Collection.

Publications by members of the government and leaders of political parties can be found under the subject heading "Portugal–History–Revolution 1974." The Institution continues to collect descriptive and analytical accounts of political events and developments and maintains substantial files of periodicals such as *Baluarte*, *Economia*, *Estudos sobre o comunismo*, *Portugal socialista*, *Portuguese Studies Newsletter*, and *Povo livre* and of newspapers such as *Avante*, *Diario de noticias*, *Expresso*, and *O Jornal*.

FINLAND   The Finnish Collection proper begins in 1918–1919 with the establishment of an independent state, but earlier materials go back to 1907 and stress Finnish efforts to separate from Russia.

In some form, the Institution has been receiving the debates and documents of the Finnish parliament (Valtiopaivat) in Finnish and in Swedish since 1907. A good file of *Virallinen lehti* (official journal) is available from 1941 to the present, as is a file of *Finlands Forfattningssamlings* (laws and statutes) from 1914 to 1927 and 1942 to the present and the treaty series of this set (*Finlands Forfattningssamling-Fordrags-serie*) from 1935 to 1950 and 1951 to the present.

The library made a special effort to collect materials on the Winter War (1939–1940), in particular narratives and accounts by German armed forces personnel in Finland during World War II. Extensive documentation for this period can be found in the records of the Finnish war guilt trials (*Sotasyvllisprocessi*) held in 1945–1946, housed in the archives. The official history of World War II, *Suomen Sota, 1941–1945* (10 vols., 1951–1965), is also available. A few archival materials center around the memoirs of Rudolf Holsti (1881–1945) and Hjalmar Procopé (1889–1954).

For the postwar period, the library has tried to follow Finland's uneasy position as a neutral, a member of the Nordic Council, and a neighbor of the Soviet Union and has collected the writing of its presidents, Karl Gustaf Mannerheim, Juho K. Paasikivi, Urho Kekkonen, and Mauno Kovisto.

The library has maintained a subscription to the Finnish Communist Party newspaper *Tyokansan Sanomat* (1947–1956) and its successor, *Kansan Uutiset* (1956–), as well as to the recently established Marxist-Leninist version, *Tiedonantaja*.

DENMARK   The Danish Collection is small and covers only a few subjects in depth. The current acquisitions program is purely a holding operation. Since Denmark is a member both of NATO and the European Communities, its participation in both organizations is covered, as are its activities in the Nordic Council.

Denmark was neutral during World War I, but found itself under German occupation in World War II and was made to serve as a showcase for occupation policies. The collection contains some resistance materials both in pamphlet and in periodical form, as well as documentation issued by the Danish government under German pressure. The official parliamentary inquiry on the period of German occupation can be found in *Folketinget: Kommission af 15. Juni 1945 i henhold tie Grundlovens #45* (15 vols. and supplements, 1945–1968). Among the larger runs of underground or exile journals are *Dansk presse* (1943–1945), *De frie Dansk* (1943–1945), and *Frit Danmark*, London (1941–1945). The German journal for the period is the semi-monthly *Skaggerak: Zeitschrift der Deutschen in Dänemark*, published in Copenhagen from 1942 to 1945.

The collection holds a few party publications and journals. Only the Danish Communist Party is represented with a longer file (*Land og folk*, 1943–1945, 1950–1952, 1967–).

A great deal of documentation on the Scandinavian countries in wartime can be found in the Harvester Press microfilm publication filmed from British Foreign Office records entitled *Conditions and Politics in Occupied Western Europe, 1940–1945*; Parts 2–6 contain materials on Denmark.

NORWAY   Since Norway is a member of the Nordic Council and of NATO, certain present-day aspects of Norwegian policy are covered by holdings of the publications of these two organizations. In general the collection is small, and its holdings concentrate on social and economic questions during World War I and the 1920s and on the German occupation and Norwegian resistance in World War II.

The campaign in 1940 against the invading German army is recounted officially in eleven volumes published by the Norwegian Defense Department (Norway. *Forsvarsdepartment Krigshistorisk Avdeling*) between 1952 and 1963.

German materials for the occupation can be found in *Verordnungsblatt für die besetzten norwegischen Gebiete* (1940–1945) and in *Deutsche Monatshefte in Norwegen* (1940–1945).

The collection contains much of the writings of Vidkun Quisling (1887–1945), as well as pamphlets put out by Quisling's party, Nasjonal Samling, and two monthlies: *Heim of Aett* (for women, 1942–1945) and *Gjallarhorn* (1942–1945). Available as well is a transcript on microfilm of Quisling's trial for treason.

Substantial files of the following anti-nazi underground movement publications are available: *Alt for Norge* (1941–1945), *Nordisk front* (1943–1945), and *Jossingposten* (1941–1942). Also available are several publications of the Norwegian government-in-exile in London: *Det Frie Norge* (1941–1945), *Fram* (1942–1945), *Norsk Tidend* (1941–1945), *Norwegian Monthly Review* (1942–1945), and *Weekly News Summary* (1942–1947).

Hoover has a substantial number of wartime Norwegian anti-nazi books, which could not be published in occupied Norway and were printed and distributed in Sweden.

SWEDEN

For the period of the two world wars, collecting efforts stressed foreign policy materials as Sweden struggled to maintain its neutrality. At present only Swedish involvement in the European Free Trade Association (EFTA) and the Nordic Council and the active peace movement are covered.

Since Sweden was officially neutral during 1914–1918 and 1939–1945, both sides used Stockholm as a convenient information center. Newspapers and periodicals published in wartime Sweden were extremely important for their news and often for their intelligence value. Sweden's exposed position in World War II vis-à-vis Germany and its sympathies both with Finland, involved in an anti-Russian war, and with Norway, involved in an anti-Hitler struggle, made the realistic pursuit of a neutralist foreign policy extremely difficult. After an extensive inquiry in 1946 into the motives and handling of Sweden's foreign policy, the Swedish Foreign Office published *Svensk utrikespolitik unter andra varldskriget: Statsradstal, riksdagsdebatter och kommunikeer* and *Aktstyken: Handlingar rorande Sveriges politik under andra varldskriget*. Both are available.

The files of *Svenska Dagbladet*, the Stockholm conservative daily, for 1914–1918 and 1939–1946 chronicled world events as seen from Sweden, as did the liberal *Dagens Nyheter*, again for the wartime years. The quarterlies *Nordisk Tidskrift* and *Svensk Tidskrift* dealt with science, art, and industry in wartime. The *Goteborgs Handels-och Sjofarts Tidning* (1939–1946) furnished an account of trade and shipping in the Baltic at critical times.

Special materials in the library are the protocols and documents of the espionage trial of Col. Stig Wennerstrom in 1964, the files of the social-democratic newspaper *Social demokraten* (1914–1918, 1933–1938, 1939–1946 [on microfilm]), and the extensive files of *Ny Dag*, the communist party newspaper (1939–1946, 1969–). The publications of the Stockholm International Peace Research Institute (SIPRI) are also collected.

Present interests center on international relations and the very active peace research effort. Periodical files are maintained for *Cooperation and Conflict* (1965–) and *Internasjonal Politik* (1977–). Three weekly newspapers, the conservative *Farmand* (1976–), the communist *Friheten* (1966–), and the Marxist-Leninist *Klassenkampen* (1970–), arrive on subscription.

AUSTRIA   The Austrian Collection tends to mirror the many facets of a large, multilingual empire at the beginning of the century and its subsequent shrinking in size and importance after World War I. The collection also documents Austria's struggle to maintain its independence against its powerful German neighbor during the 1930s, its wartime involvement on the side of the Axis, its occupation by the Allied victors from 1945 to 1955, and its emergence as a truly independent, neutral state after 1955.

Among the archival and special collection materials that deserve mention are the Alfred H. Fried Collection of about 2,500 items, which belonged to the famous Austrian writer, pacifist, and Nobel Peace Prize winner of 1911; the papers of Heinrich Kanner (1864–1930), an editor of the Viennese newspaper *Die Zeit*; and the Gilchrist Baker Stockton papers, which contain material on the American Relief Administration in Austria for 1919–1920; as well as documents on Austrian–United States relations for 1930–1933.

Archival material for the period immediately before the outbreak of World War I is furnished by eight reels of microfilm made by the Haus-Hof und Staatsarchiv, which include documents on the Austrian policy in Herzegovina; the wartime occupation of Serbia and Poland, 1914–1917; and the antimonarchical movements of South Slav immigrants to the United States, Chile, and New Zealand.

Of an entirely different provenance but dealing with similar materials are the 28 rolls of microfilm of U.S. State Department records (decimal file) relating to the internal affairs of Austria-Hungary and Austria from 1910 to 1929.

For the upheaval and the civil war in 1934, there are various small collections listed under the names of the warring factions, groups and parties, such as Republikanischer Schutzbund Österreich, Revolutionäre Sozialisten Österreichs, Rote Hilfe Österreichs, and Sozialdemokratische Arbeiterpartei Deutsch-Österreichs.

Also of an archival nature are 23 reels of microfilm detailing the proceedings of the Allied Commission for Austria, 1945–1955, covering the Four Power administration of the country in the early post–World War II period.

The parliamentary debates for the imperial period can be found in the *Stenographische Protokolle* of both the Abgeordneten Haus and the Herrenhaus from 1866 to 1900 at the Jonsson Library of Government Documents at Green Library and from 1891 to 1918 at the Hoover Institution.

Among the Institution's holdings documenting the history of the reduced Austrian state after the Treaty of St. Germain are the debates of the Provisorische Nationalversammlung (1918–1919), of the Konstituierende Nationalversammlung (1919–1920), and of the Nationalrat and the Bundesrat (1920–1934) and finally the protocols of the Bundestag (1934–1938).

A useful documentary source for the period of the Anschluss is *Der Hochverratsprozess gegen Dr. Guido Schmidt vor dem Wiener Volksgericht* (1946).

For the post–World War II period, the protocols of the Bundesrat and the Nationalrat are available from 1945 to the present.

Of particular importance are major newspaper and periodical runs, such as the extensive files of *Die Arbeiterzeitung* (1914–1955), the voice of socialism; a long run of *Die Fackel* (1899–1936), edited by Karl Kraus; important holdings of *Neue Freie Presse* (1864–1938), a good news source; and the conservative *Reichspost* (1914–1925). Of great importance for the study of economic conditions is the file of the *Österreichische Volkswirt* (1908–1962), which spans the empire, World War I, the interwar years, and the post-WWII period (publication was suspended while Austria was part of the Third Reich).

For the period before the Anschluss in 1938, files like *Der Anschluss* (1927–1933), *Deutsche Einheit* (1926–1935), and *Österreich-Deutschland* (1924–1933) are available. The wartime years are covered in a series of small exile publications, such as *Free Austria* (London), but also of course by publications issued in Austria itself. The Hoover Institution holds a partial file of the Vienna edition of the *Völkischer Beobachter* (1939–1945).

In cooperation with Green Library, the Hoover Institution currently collects materials on internal politics and government, neutrality, and foreign relations. Current subscriptions include periodicals, such as *Arbeit und Wirtschaft* (1966–), expressing the point of view of the Austrian trade unions; *Der Donauraum* (1956–); *Österreichische Zeitschrift für Aussenpolitik* (1960–); *Wiener Tagebuch* (1971–); *Weg und Ziel* (1946–), the journal of the Austrian Communist Party; *Die Zukunft* (1946–), the voice of the Socialist Party; and the daily *Presse* (1969–), which furnishes general information.

SWITZERLAND

Emphasis in the Swiss Collection is on the documentation of Switzerland's efforts to remain neutral in the last two wars, as shown in the recently published series *Documents diplomatiques suisses*, particularly from volume 6 (1914–1918) on. The library has taken special care to acquire studies on neutrality, such as the magisterial multivolume work of Edgar Bonjour, and the report of Gen. Henri Guisan on how this neutrality was safeguarded in World War II.

Since Switzerland was at the crossroads of all European information and intelligence activities, newspapers covering the war periods are of particular importance. Substantial runs are available, such as *Basler Nachrichten* (1914–1919, 1935–1942, 1944–1948), *Berner Tagwacht* (1914–1954), *Journal de Genève* (1914–1923), *National Zeitung* (1939–1945), and *Neue Zürcher Zeitung* (1914–1945, 1947–1952, 1976–).

Switzerland was and is the home of a great many international organizations, and it was relatively easy to collect the publications of a number of these organizations. Special mention should be made of holdings of the documentation issued by the League of Nations, the International Red Cross, and the International Commission of Jurists.

The archival collections contain the papers of William Martin, the Paris correspondent of the *Journal de Genève* for 1915–1933, and a small anti-Hitler opposition collection brought together by Alhard Gelpke, which contains some items issued by the Bewegung Freies Deutschland in der Schweiz. Of political interest are the writings of Fritz Platten, Robert Grimm, and Jules Humbert Drosz.

An interesting collection of pacifist materials was brought together by the Bund für Menschheitsinteressen und Organisierung Menschlichen Fortschritts, which had offices in Bern and Stuttgart. The following files are available: *Dokumente des Fortschritts: Internationale Revue* (1907–1914, Berlin; 1915–1918, Bern), *Lettres politiques* (1923–1925), *Politische Briefe* (1923–1925), *Die Versöhnung* (1917–1919), and *La Voix de la humanité* (1916–1921).

One Swiss periodical deserves special mention. The file of the Friedenswarte *founded by Alfred Fried extends from 1899 to 1966. It was edited with skill and knowledge from 1924 to 1962 by Hans Wehberg. Fittingly the journal published its last volume in 1966 as a memorial issue to Wehberg.*

The holdings cover internal Swiss politics only sketchily, but the library made a special effort to document the youth riots in Zurich in 1980 and to obtain the official Swiss government report issued by the Eidgenossische Kommission für Jugendfragen. One longtime general periodical is available in the files of the *Schweizer Rundschau* (1939–1978), and opposition on the part of young people, antimilitarists, and the communist party can be found in periodical files such as *Tell* (1979–), *Virus* (1978–), and *L'Etincelle* (1964–1969). Files of *Vorwärts* (1947–1955, 1968–) and *La Voix ouvrière* (1945–) document the Socialist Party.

6 | THE EAST ASIAN COLLECTION

Ramon H. Myers
Curator

Yuji Muramatsu, the distinguished Japanese scholar, has written of the East Asian Collection: "I think this collection is simply unique not only in this country but in every other country except China. At least present-day Japan has nothing to compare with this." Many others have concurred with his views.

Two factors were crucial in the origination of this collection: an imaginative and forward-looking program befitting an institution dedicated to the study of war, revolution, and peace and a group of outstanding individuals able to carry out this program.

THE EARLY YEARS

In January 1945, Harold H. Fisher, then-director of the Hoover Institution, launched a long-delayed program to collect materials on contemporary China and Japan. In keeping with the Institution's aims, he established three guidelines for the collecting program:

> Under "war," the collection would concentrate on "the causes and results of war rather than military operations";
>
> Under "revolution," the collection would deal with "all types of revolutionary movements";
>
> Under "peace," the collection would encompass "the whole field of international relations—political, economic, and cultural, [and] the organization of peace."

Dr. Fisher's first step was to consult with officials in the Department of State and others in Washington, D.C., on how to approach this task. He also received help from former President Herbert Hoover and various friends of the Hoover Institution. By 1946, he had at his disposal an entire network of dedicated people in China and Japan, most of whom were Stanford alumni or former Stanford professors.

In Japan, the collecting program was entrusted to a special organization set up in

Ramon H. Myers, Curator, East Asian Collection

November 1945 by permission of Gen. Douglas MacArthur and was supervised by Lt. Col. Hubert G. Schenck, a Stanford professor of geology. The Tokyo Office, as it became known, was quartered in the Nihon Zasshi Kinen Kaikan building in Kanda, the center of the book trade in Tokyo. Under the management of Yoshio Higashiuchi, a member of the Stanford class of 1937, the staff searched the book stalls and shops in Kanda for rare items and other materials requested by the Hoover Library. Over a two-year period, they amassed some 5,000 books and as many magazines, together with newspapers, official documents, and other items by the ton. Between November 1945 and December 1947, the Tokyo Office shipped almost 300 boxes of Japanese materials to Stanford.

In China, collecting presented more problems. Raging inflation made collection and shipment difficult; civil war made them hazardous. Nevertheless, ways were found. On several occasions when American channels could not be used, Canadian friends forwarded materials to Stanford through Ottawa.

From 1946 until the spring of 1947, the Hoover Library's principal representatives in China were historians Mary and Arthur Wright. Peking was their home base, but this did not limit their activities. Thanks to the U.S. Air Force, Mary Wright flew to Yenan, capital of the Chinese Communists, before it fell to Nationalist troops. The newspapers, pamphlets, and books that she shipped back to Peking are a priceless and irreplaceable record of those troubled times.

After the Wrights left China, Ann N. Bottorff assumed responsibility for collecting materials in the Peking region. By November 1948 the Hoover Library had representatives in many Chinese cities. In Shanghai there was John Berentz; in the communist areas, William C. Berges; in Chungking, H. H. Hopkins, as well as Shu-pan Wu of the Education Ministry; in Tihua, Sinkiang, J. Hall Paxton; in Nanking, Pardee Lowe; in Canton, Ding U. Doo and the Reverend Harry Hainz; in Hong Kong, the Hsin-min ch'u-pan-she; and in Taipei, Richard P. Conlon. By late 1949, when communist forces overran the mainland, large quantities of Chinese materials had already found their way to Stanford. The Tokyo Office alone had shipped 450 boxes containing some 5,000 volumes, many of them rare.

Mary Wright, former curator of the Chinese Collection, and her husband, Arthur, rode in everything from military aircraft to vegetable carts in their quest for materials in China in 1945. At one point in Peking they found certain valuable records being used as wrapping paper for fruits and vegetables. Their trip eventually brought 9,000 pounds of documents on China to the library.

THE SCOPE OF THE COLLECTION

The opening of diplomatic and commercial relations between East Asia and the West represented a turning point in world history. Since World War I, the balance of global power has gradually shifted eastward. In today's multipolar system, the roles of China and Japan are pivotal.

The rich holdings of the East Asian Collection challenge traditional historiography. Since they leave few aspects of human activity undocumented, they provide the basis for a new history of modern China and Japan—a history grounded in the methodology of the social and behavioral sciences. In East Asia as elsewhere, war, revolution, and peace are important parameters of human experience.

The collections include approximately 153,800 titles in 286,100 volumes. About 40 percent of these deal with politics, law, economics, public finance, sociology, statistics, education, and defense; 25 percent with history and geography; 17 percent with language and literature; 10 percent with science and technology—a category that includes agriculture as well as industry; and 8 percent with other areas. Chinese-language materials account for about 60 percent of the collection; Japanese-language materials for some 40 percent.

Serial holdings are unusually comprehensive. Outstanding among the 6,000 titles in the Chinese Collection are those dating from before 1949. They include government documents, statistical reports on commerce, and numerous periodicals. The Japanese Collection has 1,800 serial titles. Of special interest here are many left-wing journals of the 1920s and their right-wing counterparts of the 1930s and 1940s.

China

In the Chinese Revolution of 1911, army officers, intellectuals, and students educated abroad combined to overthrow the Ch'ing government. The ensuing political anarchy was accompanied by widespread institutional change. Winston Hsieh's *Chinese Historiography on the Revolution of 1911* (Hoover Institution Press, 1975) is based entirely on materials in the East Asian Collection. In addition to monographs, collected works, pamphlets, and periodicals, it lists 340 Chinese bibliographies. All are fuel for the continuing debate over the revolution's nature and influence, particularly with regard to the erratic course of modernization in China.

The collection also has rich resources for studying the tumultuous history of the Chinese Communist Party. Formed in 1921 by a small group of Shanghai intellectuals, the party was all but destroyed in 1927 by the Kuomintang. Mao Tse-tung and others revived it in Kiangsi, where it consolidated a base during the 1931–1934 period. It was greatly expanded after the Long March to the northwest in 1934 and 1935. Much of the collection's coverage of these events is cited in Chün-tu Hsüeh's two bibliographies: *The Chinese Communist Movement, 1921–1937* (1960) and *The Chinese Communist Movement, 1937–1949* (1962). Others are cataloged in *Hoover Institution Microfilms* (1976) and its *Asian Supplement* (1977), which lists 128 microfilm reels describing communist base areas during the civil war of 1945 to 1949. (All of these works were published by the Hoover Institution Press.)

Like other countries that have modernized hastily by borrowing from abroad, China acquired a whole range of new institutions without foreseeing the consequences. This was especially true of the new schools and universities launched by the

In 1952, the library of Gen. Huang Ch'iang, best known as chief of staff of the Chinese 19th Route Army during its legendary stand against the Japanese in 1932 at Shanghai, came up for sale in Hong Kong.

The Hoover Institution cabled an offer, admittedly far below the average market price. General Huang, an acute student of politics as well as an accomplished military leader, immediately accepted the offer.

"These books should go to the Hoover Library," the Chinese general commented. "I will consider the difference between the library's offer and the current market price as my donation to its work."

Rare photo taken in 1937 in Yenan of Mao Tse-tung, the political leader, and Chu Teh, the military commander of the Chinese Communist Party. The Institution has extensive holdings of original materials on Chinese communism.

Mao Tse-tung and other leaders of the Chinese Communist Party in their mountaintop fortress in Yenan, 1937, taken by Edgar Snow and his first wife, Helen Foster Snow. (From Nym Wales Collection)

Mao-Tse-tung in Yenan, 1943

Ch'ing regime and continued by subsequent administrations. The result was a dissatisfied young intelligentsia, critical of its parents and hostile to established authority. Students often resorted to street demonstrations, sometimes inspiring segments of the populace to support them in boycotts of foreign goods or demands for political and legal reforms. Materials in the collection that refer to these events are cited in John Israel's *Chinese Student Movement, 1927–37* (1959).

Among the other aspects of modernization on which the collection can support research are organized labor (especially strikes), rural markets, railroads, urban banks, and rural land tenure (see G. William Skinner and Winston Hsieh, eds., *Modern Chinese Society: An Analytical Bibliography*, Vol. 2, *Publications in Chinese, 1644–1969*, Stanford University Press, 1973).

In 1949, the Kuomintang moved from the mainland to Taiwan. The evolving Chinese community on this island underwent massive change. Taiwan's social evolution, less rapid but just as remarkable as its economic growth, has been in the direction of a free and open society with a diversity of public opinion. Many overseas Chinese draw inspiration from a lifestyle that has yet to be studied in depth. Taiwan's recent progress is well represented by materials in the collection.

Japan

Japan's attack on China, and the Pacific war, was preceded by attempts to compete with the Western powers in China by acquiring territory there. This course of action can be examined not only through the East Asian Collection's studies of Sino-Japanese diplomatic relations but also through its records of Japan's policy toward

Generalissimo and Madame Chiang Kai-shek at the Cairo Conference in 1943

China, Japanese treatises on colonial theory and management, and a vast store of administrative records and field studies relating to the empire's daily affairs. An important bibliographical guide to the collection's holdings in this area is another volume in the series published by the Stanford University Press, G. William Skinner and Shigeaki Tomita, eds., *Modern Chinese Society: An Analytical Bibliography*, Vol. 3, *Publications in Japanese, 1644–1971* (1973).

The collection has many documents relating to the Japanese occupation of Manchuria in the early 1930s. In addition to contemporary newspapers and pamphlets, researchers may consult publications of the famous South Manchurian Railway Company and of the puppet Manchukuo government. Another puppet regime, maintained in north China by the Japanese after 1937, is also well covered (see Frederick W. Mote, *Japanese-Sponsored Governments in China, 1937–1945* [1954]).

Between 1895 and 1945, Japan's leaders created an empire of remarkable size, extending from Sakhalin Island in the north to Korea, the Liaotung peninsula, Taiwan, and the South Sea Mandate islands acquired from Imperial Germany in 1918. Japanese officials controlled this sprawling empire closely but modernized agriculture and opened these territories to world trade. Michiko Kiyohara's *Checklist of Monographs and Periodicals on the Japanese Colonial Empire* (1981) provides an impressive listing of the East Asian Collection's holdings pertaining to this colonial empire.

Researchers interested in Japan's domestic history will find extensive documentation of the social and economic turmoil that followed that nation's plunge into modernization after 1868. Japanese peasants migrated in increasing numbers to cities ill-prepared to receive them. Strikes, food riots, and bitter disputes between landlords and tenants were numerous during this turbulent period. During the 1910s and 1920s, the government reacted with stronger police measures to suppress laborers and tenant farmers, by then better educated and informed, who had become increasingly active in their demands for a fair share of the social product. Through government reports and other materials in the East Asian Collection, these events can be followed in detail.

Such conditions made it possible for extremist groups of varying ideologies to emerge and flourish. The obscure origins of these groups, their political platforms, and their organizing activities are recorded in party newspapers, pamphlets, and other documents in the collection (see Nobutaka Ike, *The Hoover Institution Collection on Japan* [1958]).

During the 1930s, the Japanese government moved to stamp out leftist organizations. Many leaders of the Left were arrested by the police and tried. Notes of their interrogations and secret records kept by defense attorneys can be found in the Japanese Collection.

As Japan's military leaders silenced opponents at home and expanded their military activities in China, they found it necessary to mobilize the entire society. This huge effort required the creation of new associations, patriotic societies, and new organizations to control business—in other words all the structures of a totalitarian state. Many of the collection's holdings describe these new state activities in vivid detail and show how the regime mobilized manpower, financed the war effort, educated the young to obey unquestioningly, and recruited the old to support the nation's efforts. Pamphlets and magazines depict the activities of the newly founded patriotic societies. Numerous biographies of important people provide personal accounts of life in that remarkable period.

After Japan's defeat in 1945, the Allied occupation authorities introduced a series of institutional reforms. The constitution was rewritten; large business corporations

In Seoul, Korea, in 1945, the Japanese, about to surrender to the Americans, indulged in an orgy of record destruction. But they reckoned without Mr. Shinn, a Korean who had worked as a clerk in army headquarters. For years Mr. Shinn had been secretly photographing documents and burying the plates. The Japanese burned their documents and evacuated. A year or so later, Miss Rae Gilman, an American Red Cross worker attached to the United States Army of Occupation, met the Korean and learned about the buried plates. Shinn declined to send them to Mr. Hoover but offered, if Miss Gilman could get enough photographic paper and chemicals, to make two sets of prints, one for himself and one for Mr. Hoover. Miss Gilman radioed the Institution, papers and chemicals were flown out by military transport, and in due course the prints documenting the Japanese occupation of Korea reached the Hoover Institution.

were broken up; virtually every sphere of activity, from education to agriculture, underwent significant change. Thanks in no small part to these measures, Japan once again became a world power. This time, however, the power was almost exclusively economic.

The emerging picture is a complex one. The ruling Liberal Democratic Party, for long an important conservative force, is internally divided and will be seriously challenged by other parties. This realignment of political power will sorely test Japan's democratic institutions and its leaders.

The East Asian Collection's large holdings on postwar Japan include government white papers, journals, newspapers, business histories, and personal diaries. These materials represent a fascinating resource for anyone prepared to cope with their complexity.

ACTIVITIES SINCE 1949

Although collecting in China ceased after 1949, purchasing continued in Hong Kong. Since the Tokyo Office closed in 1952, materials from Japan have been acquired through dealers. The collecting program has assumed new forms, including gifts and special acquisitions.

Rich materials have arrived in both ways. In 1959, Nym Wales (Mrs. Edgar Snow) presented to the Hoover Institution her Yenan notebook, together with Chinese documents on left-wing artists, Chinese women, student movements, and the Sian Incident of 1936 in which Generalissimo Chiang Kai-shek was kidnapped by a Chinese warlord.

Of the special acquisitions projects, two in particular are noteworthy. In 1958 Tamotsu Takase, curator of the Japanese Collection, obtained microfilm copies of documents of Prince Fumimaro Konoye, a major figure in the interwar and wartime regimes. Three years later, Eugene Wu, who succeeded Mary Wright as curator of the Chinese Collection and became the first person to act as curator for both collections, gained permission from the National Defense Ministry of the Republic of China to microfilm all of its materials on the 1931–1934 Chinese Soviet Republic.

Since 1967, when the East Asian Collection moved from the Tower to the Lou Henry Hoover Building, its holdings have steadily expanded. Curators and their assistants have paid special attention to adhering to the tradition of acquiring unique historical materials at the cutting edge of contemporary research interests.

CHINESE
HISTORICAL MATERIALS

Ten compendiums (each consisting of twelve volumes) containing household customary law contracts have been received from Taiwan. The Library of Congress, Harvard's Yenching Library, and the Academia Sinica in Taiwan are the only other repositories of these materials. These documents offer a rich assortment of private contracts, many dating from the eighteenth century, between both households and individuals covering land exchanges, credit procedures, inheritance, and land tenure relationships. This collection alone contains more examples of customary law contracts than exist for all of mainland China now held in libraries outside of China.

In the 1970s and 1980s many young Taiwanese became involved in attempts to build a political coalition outside the Nationalist Party (Kuomintang). The government banned many of their publications because of their inflammatory rhetoric. A great number of these materials found their way outside of the country; the East Asian Collection has probably the largest collection of these political tracts, including many election pamphlets and rare journals.

One example of the wealth of documentation on Chinese history: a mural poster issued by the Chinese Ministry of Education showing Mao celebrating the unification of Chinese minorities. Other posters in this series of ten describe the rights and duties of citizens, the importance of local governments, the redistribution of taxes for the community benefit, and the respect due to minorities.

In the late 1970s, the collection became the repository for eleven cassette tapes and numerous questionnaire forms from the China Research Institute of Land Economics of Taipei. These materials represent a multiyear oral history project initiated at the request of Dr. Ramon H. Myers, who became curator of the collection in 1975. They cover interviews with ten officials in high government offices who were deeply involved in the important financial and trade reforms of the 1950s and 1960s that played such an important role in transforming that island-state into an export-oriented, modernizing country. Many of these documents focus on the perceptions and views of these officials about the efficacy of the reforms and their likely impact on the economy. A second collection of oral interview tapes and documents was obtained from another dozen officials who participated in the monumental land reform between 1950 and 1953 that made it possible for hundreds of thousands of tenants to buy and acquire land. Their comments provide an insider's view of the evolution of the reform and the obstacles that were overcome. These materials are located in the archives of the Hoover Institution.

Because access to historical materials in Communist China has been extremely difficult, the documents arriving from that closed society to the outside world have typically been newspapers, journals, and standard monograph publications that the regime allows to be exported. Aside from these items, the East Asian Collection has been fortunate to receive from private parties a variety of rare and unusual historiographical materials that Peking did not license for export.

Two local newspapers covering the years 1957–1960 and 1972–1975 for Shun-te county in the southeastern province of Kwangtung reveal much about local conditions in one small part of this complex country. For the same area, the collection also possesses various government directives, textbooks, and an assortment of folio-size materials dealing with agricultural affairs in the organizations created by the communist party to control and manage rural activities.

A flood of underground magazines and publications appeared in China in 1979 and early 1980 before the regime clamped down and arrested their authors and printers. The collection has received some one hundred of these items from a variety of sources and visiting scholars who gathered these documents during brief sojourns in China. The library also holds several tapes and documents describing a student hunger strike at Hunan Normal College from Liang Heng, a student leader of that movement who later married an American scholar and migrated to the United States. His tapes recorded the passionate speeches made during the demonstrations protesting the communist party's interference in the election of local representatives.

From Hong Kong, the collection has received over the years an assortment of land deeds, merchant account books, lineage records, and private Chinese association handbooks from a collector in the colony, a British civil servant named James Hayes. Hayes visited bookstores every week and purchased these items whenever they came on the market. Through his efforts, the collection has a file of rare late nineteenth- and early twentieth-century local Chinese materials on the management of economic and social affairs by associations and households.

In 1983, the East Asian Collection entered into an agreement with the Library of the Bureau of Investigation in Taipei of the Republic of China to exchange rare materials on the origin and rise of the Chinese Communist Party. The bureau had collected, prior to 1949, numerous party documents showing internal organization and tactics to establish communist control in rural areas. While a few scholars in Taiwan have used these materials, these documents have yet to be really examined by American scholars. Under the agreement, Hoover will not sell any of the bureau's materials to other libraries, the East Asian curator alone can grant permission for their use, and users can reproduce only a very limited part of any document.

JAPANESE HISTORICAL MATERIALS

Since the mid-1970s, the Japanese collection has almost doubled in size, and several thousand reels of microfilm have been acquired. A small portion of the materials flowing into the collection covers the pre-1850 period in order to support faculty and graduate student research, but the primary emphasis of acquisitions has been the building of modern Japan in the late nineteenth and the twentieth centuries. In particular, acquisitions have stressed primary materials published in large sets and careful selection of the best scholarly materials published in Japan.

For the phase of state building known as the Meiji period (1868–1911), basic historical materials include the records of the Japanese cabinet (*Nihon Naikaku Shiroku*) and the proceedings of the Imperial Diet (*Teikoku Gikai Gijiroku*) from 1890 until 1946. Noteworthy for its coverage of political party affairs is the ten-volume set of reports of the Liberal Party (*Jiyūtō Tōhō*) for the years 1891–1898. Economic development during this period can be examined from the perspective of the annual reports of major business companies contained in such collections as the *Eigyō Hōkokusho Shūsei* and the *Hompō Shōkō Kaigisho Shiryō*, which documents the activities of Japanese chambers of commerce. The histories of the Yokohama Specie Bank (8 vols.) and Mitsui Bank (6 vols.), as well as of the Bank of Japan depicted in *Nihon Ginkō Enkakushi* (47 vols.) and *Nihon Ginkō Hyakunenshi* (7 vols.), shed light on Japan's finance, both public and private.

The critical educational reforms undertaken during this period are presented in

60 microfilm reels entitled *Meiji Zenki Kyōikushi Shūsei*, along with assorted volumes describing education in major universities and colleges. Nor have intellectual currents of this period been neglected; special efforts have been made to acquire a variety of important journals such as *Meiroku Zasshi* (1874–1901), *Kokuryū* (1901–1908), and early issues of *Chūō Kōron*, which began publication in 1887.

The period of modernization and crisis between 1912 and 1945 is complex and tragic, for it involved overseas expansion of an unprecedented nature for the Japanese, defeat in war, the loss of colonial territories, and a ravaged homeland. In that period unique individuals shaped historical events, and primary materials relating to their activities have been collected whenever possible. The personal papers of Viscount Okuma Shigenobu, 1838–1922, are reproduced in 170 microfilm reels, and the papers of Count Gotō Shimpei, 1857–1929, in 88 microfilm reels.

Cumulative statistical surveys of the Taishō (1912–1926) and early Shōwa (1925–) periods can be found in prefectural reports, of which 1,456 reels have been acquired for all of these years, as well as for Meiji period. Important documents on the land system between 1890 and 1927 are contained in *Tochi Keizai Shiryō* (110 microfilm reels). A systematic effort has been made to expand the collection's holdings relating to Japan's overseas empire by acquiring 31 microfilm reels called *Kyū Gaichi Kankei Shiryō*, which contains 103 titles and lists very rare and valuable research studies on villages, crops, land tenancy, land taxation, and general economic conditions in Manchuria and north China by Japanese researchers. In particular, the hard-to-find research documents and reports issued by the South Manchurian Railway Company have been purchased from bookdealers whenever they became available in Japan, Korea, or Taiwan.

The Japanese carried out remarkable surveys in their colonies and in the wartime occupation areas. The light these surveys shed on the lives and condition of local inhabitants is often not matched by the historical records produced by those same societies, and a vigorous effort has been made to develop this area of the collection to make it superior to all other library holdings outside of Japan. The East Asian Collection has acquired the surveys of traditional land systems in the cities of north and central China produced by the South Manchurian Railway Company between 1941 and 1942 (*Shina Toshi Fudōsan Kankō Chōsa Shiryō*); the annual statistical reports of the Kwantung Leased Territory between 1906 and 1942 (*Kantōkyoku Tōkeisho*); the monthly research reports of the South Manchurian Railway Company between 1919 and 1944 (*Mantetsu Chōsa Geppō*); the Manchurian review, published between 1931 and 1945 (*Manshū Hyōron*); the Supreme Court monthly review published in Taiwan between 1905 and 1942 (*Hōin Geppō*); the annual report of basic agricultural data published by the government-general of Taiwan between 1920 and 1944 (*Nōgyō Kihon Chōsasho*); and the Taiwan Daily News (*Taiwan Nichinichi Shimpō*), the officially recognized newspaper of that colony, issued between 1898 and 1944 under the colonial authority.

Japan's rise to world power status since 1945 can be documented in many of the materials acquired by the East Asian Collection. The collection holds complete runs of such important newspapers as the *Japan Times* and the *Asahi Shimbun*. A valuable eight-volume collection describing the post–World War II land reform is *Nōchi Kaikaku Shiryō Shūsei*. More volumes recording the history of major industrial companies and financial agencies have been acquired through gifts and the assistance of the Japan-U.S. Economic Council and the Japan Business Administration Research Institute. Works on labor unions and studies of minority groups such as the Koreans, the Burakumin, and women have been acquired as they appeared in Japan. Works on

Mimeographed police record of 12,000-page autobiography of Japanese Marxist writer and onetime Tokyo University professor Omori Yoshitarō (1898–1940). This oral statement was taken down by the Japanese special political police in 1938, soon after Omori's arrest, and depicts in detail Japanese Marxists' activities during the 1920s and 1930s.

From left: Deputy Curator Emiko Moffitt, Research Fellow Fu-mei C. Chen, Deputy Curator Mark Tam. Seated at computer terminal: Curator Ramon H. Myers

radical student movements of the 1960s and early 1970s number approximately 500 volumes; 250 of these volumes were donated by an American activist who gathered them in Japan at the peak of these movements.

OTHER RELATED
ACTIVITIES

In recent years two important developments have enhanced the use of the collection and expanded the services it offers. The first was cooperation between the East Asian Collection and the East Asiatic Library and Center for Chinese Studies Library of the University of California at Berkeley. Commencing in 1977 through the efforts of Dr. Robert Ward and Dr. Ramon H. Myers at Stanford and various faculty at Berkeley, a series of arrangements allowed students, faculty, and visiting researchers at one institution to acquire borrowing privileges at the other institution.

At the same time, new procedures were developed to initiate closer contact and coordination between the collections to avoid duplication of expensive materials. The three libraries also reached an agreement to allocate the purchase of recently published mainland Chinese publications in microfilm and printed forms, which now extends to items published by the China National Microforms Import and Export Corporation, New China Microfilm Company, and the reprint series of the China National Publishing Industry Trading Corporation. Another agreement divided local and regional histories geographically, allocating certain prefectures in Japan and certain provinces in China to each collection for acquisition in future years. Finally, a rapid delivery service of materials between the two campuses was established.

Another area of cooperation involves publication of checklists of materials contained in both libraries. The two libraries have already produced lists of Chinese and Japanese local histories, Japanese company histories, and Japanese newspapers. Other checklists of Japanese government materials and Chinese newspapers are also being prepared and will be published in the near future.

In 1983, the East Asian Collection became a pilot library, along with several other libraries in the United States, for the developmental usage of computer terminals. These machines have the capability to store and retrieve Japanese-, Chinese-, and Korean-language records and allow the collection to computerize its catalog. All records of the materials cataloged since October 1984 are on-line and retrievable, and the conventional card catalog system will eventually be terminated. This system also has the capability to machine-record all acquisitions made by the East Asian Collection.

7 | THE AFRICAN COLLECTION

Karen Fung
Deputy Curator

The African collections at Stanford University are housed mainly in the University (Green) Library and the Hoover Institution Library. Other Africana may be found in the Food Research Institute, Art Library, Earth Science Library, Education Library, and the Business, Medical, and Law School libraries. The curator of Hoover's Africa Collection is also curator for the Green Library's Africa Collection and assists the branch and other coordinate libraries by referring titles to them so that Africana materials are acquired in all fields.

HISTORY

Karen Fung, Deputy Curator, African Collection

The Africa Collection in the Hoover Institution began in 1919 when the Belgian government presented Herbert Hoover with a collection of official Belgian documents and reports, including many pertaining to the Belgian Congo and Ruanda-Urundi. In the fall of 1919, an agent of the provisional German government contributed a large number of maps and documents on Africa. After the establishment of the Hoover War Library in 1922, Nina Almond, the first librarian, expanded the collection by securing the reports of the League of Nations Mandates Commission and many official gazettes and annual reports of colonial governments. The library now has reports from all the former League mandates in Africa and from the United Nations trust territories. Files of older official gazettes from the various African countries include those for Tanganyika (1920–1937, 1957–1964), South-West Africa (1916–1963), the Gold Coast (1917–1957), Nigeria (1914–1937, 1952–1962), Gambia (1914–1961), the former French Cameroun (1919–1956), French Equatorial Africa (1939–1949), French West Africa (1905–1959), and Senegal (1856–1891, 1901–1961).

The Africa Collection is unusually strong in that it covers all the former colonial territories in a manner rarely paralleled elsewhere. Students of comparative colonialism further benefit from the wealth of material on the metropolitan powers contained in the Western European collection. The Africa Collection covers a broad range of subjects—political, administrative, military, economic, and social. (Material concerned with anthropological research may be found in the Green Library.) Printed material has been supplemented by research notes supplied by some of the foremost scholars in their respective fields. The library does not acquire current gazettes (with the exception of selected titles such as the Owambo [Namibia] Official Gazette). Stanford readers can obtain fairly up-to-date gazettes on microfilm through interlibrary loan from the Cooperative Africana Microform Project (CAMP), the New York Public Library, and the Library of Congress.

With the appointment of Ruth Perry as part-time curator of the Africa Collection in 1956, acquisitions were extended and expanded. Ms. Perry's trips to Africa greatly strengthened the holdings on Ghana and Nigeria. Following the appointment of Dr. Peter Duignan as full-time curator in 1959, the holdings increased significantly. Dr. Lewis Gann, a historian, and Karen Fung, a librarian, joined the staff in 1964 and 1966 respectively.

SCOPE

The Africa Collection is integrated into the general collections and holdings of Hoover Institution, which uses the Library of Congress classification system. Approximately 80 percent of the Africa Collection's holdings are cataloged. The remaining 20 percent are listed under country or organizational headings. The collection concentrates on the period from 1870 to the present in Africa south of the Sahara and on the fields of history, politics, government, and economics. In 1976, with the establishment of the Hanna Collection on the role of education in twentieth-century society, acquisitions of publications on education as it relates to political and social developments in African countries increased.

There are no specific limitations on language coverage, but the vast majority of the material is in English, French, German, Italian, and Portuguese with important holdings in Swahili, Afrikaans, and Russian.

SIZE AND STRENGTHS

The Africa Collection contains approximately 60,000 volumes of monographs, government publications, and pamphlets. Many older serials are held—both those produced in the metropole, for example *Revue française d'histoire outre-mer* (Paris, 1913–1938, 1945–1979) and the *Revue indigène* (Paris, 1906–1914, 1916–1932), as well as in Africa itself, such as *Uganda Journal* (Kampala, 1934–) and *Tanganyika Notes and Records* (Dar Es Salaam, 1936–).

The library attempts to acquire legislative proceedings from all of Sub-Saharan Africa. Hoover has, for example, older debates for Chad (1952–1958), the Gold Coast (1928–1957), French Equatorial Africa (1947–1956), French West Africa (1947–1959), Kenya (1907–1966), and Zimbabwe (1899–). Along with having one of the most extensive current African newspaper collections in the United States, the Hoover Library holds valuable runs in print and on microfilm of older titles, including *African Times* (London, 1862–1902), *Ashanti Pioneer* (1939–1962), and *Gold Coast Leader* (Accra, 1901–1929). The serial holdings of the University Library and Hoover Library were partially inventoried by Peter Duignan and Kenneth Glazier in *A Checklist of Serials for African Studies* (1963). The library has holdings of such rare journals as the *Zambesi Mission Record* (1898–1934), in effect a history of the Catholic church in Zimbabwe; *Nouvelles du Zambèze* (1898–1934); *Revue d'histoire des missions* (Paris, 1924, 1926–1937); and *Tropiques: Revue des troupes coloniales* (Paris, 1902–1953). Other major scholarly journals held by the Hoover include *Sudan Notes and Records* (1918–1974) and the *Zambia [Northern Rhodesia] Journal* (1951–1965).

Political ephemera such as election material, party pamphlets, and trade union

Police in Nairobi,
Kenya, ca. 1900

literature constitute an important element in the collection. For example, the library has the Immanuel Wallerstein Collection of political ephemera and journals from liberation movements of Angola, Mozambique, Guinea-Bissau, Namibia, South Africa, and Zimbabwe as well as its own extensive collection of such materials. The library houses runs of South African Communist Party (SACP) newspapers and numerous pamphlets issued by the SACP.

Trade union material includes the William H. Friedland Collection on Tanzanian trade unions (1929–1967); the Martin Lowenkopf Collection on Liberian economic conditions and labor relations; the Jay Lovestone Collection (partially restricted), which includes letters regarding the African-American Labor Center (1969–1974); the African Labor College in Kampala (1959, 1963–1965); letters from Tom Mboya (late 1950s–1960s); letters from John K. Tettegah, a Ghanaian labor leader (early 1960s); letters from G. Mennen Williams (early 1960s, and letters and reports on trade union activities during the late 1950s–1960s in Nigeria, Kenya, Congo-Leopoldville, Congo-Brazzaville, Cameroun, Tanganyika, Rhodesia, Uganda, Ghana, Ethiopia, Mauritius, Gabon, and the Sudan); and the Paul Lubeck Collection on the trade union movement in Africa, primarily during the 1960s.

The library attempts to obtain the newsletters and newspapers of important trade unions. Holdings include *Advance* (Nigerian Trade Union Congress, 1966–1976), *Eveil du travailleur togolais* (Confederation nationale des travailleurs du Togo, 1982–), *FOSATU Worker News* (Federation of South African Trade Unions, 1980–), *Labour Mirror* (Trade Union Council of South Africa, 1976–), *Mfanya-kazi* (National Union of Tanganyika Workers, 1968, 1972–), and *Walike* (Confederation nationale des travailleurs de Guinée, 1975–).

Coverage for all African states for the period since independence is very extensive and includes official publications, newspapers and journals, scholarly series and proceedings of institutes, party and trade union publications, and locally produced books and ephemeral materials. Military and police journals, if available, are acquired for all countries.

As a member of the Cooperative Africana Microform Project (CAMP) of the Center for Research Libraries, Chicago, the Hoover Institution has available on interlibrary loan the over 3,000 entries in this collection of rare journals, newspapers, books, pamphlets, government documents, and archival collections on microform. (Many of these are rare and expensive to obtain, such as the Archives of the Council for World Mission and the Church Missionary Society.) A published catalog listing materials in the CAMP collection is available.

ANGLOPHONE AFRICA

During the colonial era, the British created an infrastructure of colonial archives, research institutes, and similar bodies as well as numerous missionary and exploration societies. The work of these government and private organizations was documented in a vast body of publications ranging from legislative proceedings, departmental annual reports, and investigatory commissions to mission society correspondence and reports—both on the metropolitan and local levels. Anglophone Africa is one of the best documented of colonial ventures in world history. The holdings of the Hoover Institution and the University Library are exceptionally rich in these areas, and this chapter can make only brief and selective references to the material in the Institution's possession.

Government publications fall into two major categories, material produced in Great Britain and local publications centering on specific territories, designed as reference tools, as records of past achievement, or as instruments of reform. On the metropolitan level, for example, a major series is the Confidential Prints relating to colonial Africa, produced for internal use by the Colonial Office and the Foreign Office in London. (The Hoover has microfilmed a large proportion of these.) Equally valuable are the "command papers" produced for the British Parliament on a great variety of topics under debate. Other categories include the *Annual Lists* of the Colonial and Foreign offices (with information on personnel) and a variety of reports, all of them well represented at Stanford. Of equal value are the reports of investigatory commissions. Some of these are major works of scholarship in their own right. (For instance, the *Report of the Commission Appointed into the Financial and Economic Position of Northern Rhodesia* [London, 1938] still stands as a basic economic and administrative history for the period.)

Regent's Palace, Zanzibar, symbol of British colonial power

Corresponding material was issued on the local level in the shape of the legislative council debates of individual territories and reports issued by territorial census, archives, agricultural, mining, and other departments. Equally informative were the reports of local commissions of inquiry. (For example, the *Evidence Taken by the Commission Appointed to Enquire into the Disturbances of the Copper Belt, Northern Rhodesia* [Lusaka, 1938] remains one of the most valuable sources for this particular aspect of labor history in Zambia.)

Government publications are supplemented by a broad range of serials put out by private and semiprivate bodies both in Britain itself and in the various African countries. The Hoover is rich in such holdings. These include, among many others, *NADA* (the journal of the Southern Rhodesia Native Affairs Department, 1923–1963); *Rhodes-Livingston Journal* (1944–1967), produced by a sociological research institute set up in 1937 in what is now Zambia; and the various publications (held in the Stanford University Library) of the National Museum of Southern Rhodesia, set up in 1901. Journals produced in Great Britain are even more varied in their provenance and coverage; they range all the way from those published by geographical societies, anthropological societies, and research institutes to private publications issued by specialized societies. There are likewise journals of opinion such as *Round Table* (in the Stanford University Library) begun in 1910 as a journal specializing in Commonwealth affairs and the multifarious publications of lobbies or of societies such as the Royal Commonwealth Society (originally set up in the 1860s as the Royal Colonial Institute).

FRANCOPHONE AFRICA

Holdings from Francophone Africa include the *Annuaire du gouvernement général de l'Afrique Occidentale Française* (1867, 1872–1915/16, 1922); the *Bulletin administratif du Sénégal* (1819–1908); and the *Journal officiel* for Dahomey (1908, 1918–1959, 1963–1968), for Guinea (1901–1959), and for Senegal (1856–1891, 1901–1961). This material provides a detailed conspectus of what might be called the French colonizers' "official mind" and of Africa as seen through the rulers' eyes. Material from Senegal is strong, with publications coming from the Institution's long-standing exchange arrangement with the Senegal National Archives.

The library has the *Bulletin officiel* of the French Ministère des Colonies (later Ministère de la France d'Outre-mer and Ministère de la Cooperation) for 1914–1948 with scattered earlier volumes.

The publications of the Institut Fondamental de l'Afrique Noire (formerly Institut Français d'Afrique Noire) are divided between the Hoover Library and the University Library, with Hoover holding the series *Etudes sénégalaises* (1949–1966) and *Etudes eburnéennes* (1951–1960).

Other valuable serials in the collection include *Réveil Dakar* (1944–1950), the organ of the Federation d'A.O.F.; *Guinée française* (Conakry, 1947–1952); *L'Afrique française* (Paris, 1891–1940, 1952–1960); *La Quinzaine coloniale* (Paris, (1897–1914), organ of the Union Coloniale Française; and *La Revue indigène* (Paris, 1906–1914, 1916–1932), organ of Intérêts des Indigènes aux Colonies et Pays de Protectorat.

Covering former Belgian Africa are the *Bulletin de l'Office Colonial* (1910–1940), the *Bulletin de colonisation comparée* (1908–1914), and the *Bulletin de l'Agence Générale des Colonies* (1911–1929). Also held are the *Bulletin officiel* of the former Belgian Congo (1910–1959); the Académie Royale des Sciences d'Outre-mer, *Bulletin des seances* (Brussels, 1930–); *Congo Mission News* (Leopoldville, 1912–

1946); and *Congo: Revue générale de la colonie belge* (1920–1940), which was superseded by *Zaïre* (Brussels, 1947–1961).

Holdings on independent Zaïre include *Cahiers du CEDAF* (Brussels, 1971–), *Cahiers économiques et sociaux* (Kinshasa, 1962–), *Mwana Shaba* (Lubumbashi, 1964–), and *Problèmes sociaux zaïrois* (Lubumbashi, 1946–).

LUSOPHONE AFRICA

The Lusophone Africa collection was strengthened by Curator Duignan's 1971 and 1974 trips to Portugal and then–Portuguese Africa. It is now one of the strongest colonial history collections in the United States. For the pre-independence period, the library holdings include the *Studia* issued by the Centro de Estudos Historicos Ultramarinos (Lisbon, 1958–1980), *Colecção Oficial de Legislação Portuguesa* (1922–1958), *Moçambique* (Lourenco Marques, 1935–1957, 1959–1961), *Defesa Nacional* of the Ministerios da . . . Guerra (Lisbon, 1934–1975), and *Revista Militar* (Lisbon, 1849–).

The Hoover and Green (University) libraries hold most of the publications of the Agência Geral do Ultramar and the Junta de Investigações do Ultramar and its various series: *Estudos, Ensaios e Documentos*, and *Estudos de Ciências Políticas e Sociais*, the *Anais* (1946–1957), and *Garcia de Orta* (1959–1971). Also held are *Ultramar: Revista da Communidade Portuguêsa e da Actualidade Ultramarina Internacional* (1961–1970); the *Boletim Geral do Ultramar* (1925–); the *Anuário do Ultramar Portugues* (1935–1946); *Portugal em Africa* (1894–1910, 1944–1973), a Catholic monthly; and the *Revista Portuguêsa Colonial e Marítima* (1897–1910). Other retrospective journals published in Africa include the *Boletim Cultural de Guiné Portuguêsa* (1948–1973) and the *Boletim of the Instituto de Angola* (1953–).

The late professor Richard Hammond of the Food Research Institute at Stanford

Left: FRELIMO poster. "The liberation of the Mozambican woman is necessary to the revolution. It is the guarantee of its continuity. It is a condition for its success. April 7, Day of the Mozambican Woman." Right: Election poster, Zimbabwe, 1980

acquired an extensive collection of books and pamphlets on nineteenth- and twentieth-century Lusophone Africa in the course of a research project. This material has been integrated into the Stanford Library collections.

The Hoover Library's holdings of publications of the various liberation groups in exile from Angola, Mozambique, and Guinea-Bissau include *Angola Operaria* (Kinshasa, 1971–1973), which was superseded by *Ondinga Upange* (Kinshasa, 1974–1975); *Mozambique Revolution* (Dar es Salaam, 1964–1975); and *PAIGC Actualités* (Conakry, 1969–1973/74).

For independent Lusophone Africa, holdings are extensive and include *Jornal de Angola* (Luanda, 1976–); *Voz di Povo* (Praia, Cape Verde, 1975–); and its predecessor, *Novo Jornal de Cabo Verde* (1974–75); *No Pintcha* (Bissau, 1975–1978); *Diario de Moçambique* (Beira, 1968–1971, 1981–); and *Combate* (Forcas Armadas, Maputo, 1983–).

Special collections include files on each liberation movement, such as the MPLA, FRELIMO, and PAIGC, in the African Revolutionary Movements Collection in the archives. Other special collections include Ronald Chilcote's fifteen-reel collection, *Emerging Nationalism in Portuguese Africa*, which contains publications (political ephemera, journals) of all the Lusophone African nationalist groups as well as relevant U.N. documents; the Immanuel Wallerstein Collection of political ephemera of the liberation movements of Lusophone Africa and Anglophone Southern Africa, 1958–1975; and the Robert Keith Middlemas Collection on Portugal and South Africa, 1966–1976, which contains notes and tapes of interviews with British, Portuguese, and South African diplomats, politicians, economic advisers, journalists, and businessmen as well as correspondence and writings.

FORMER GERMAN AFRICA

Rebel leader and master guerrilla Witboi in German Southwest Africa, ca. 1906

The Hoover Institution has approximately 1,200 volumes dealing with the history and administration of the German colonies and with German attitudes toward colonial questions. Hoover's German colonial collection is one of the strongest outside of Germany. The 40 volumes of *Die grosse Politik der europäischen Kabinette* (1871–1914) are basic sources. Every aspect of German colonization is widely covered in the publications of the Kolonialamt. These include source books and interpretations of laws on subjects such as commerce and banking, agriculture, education, labor, insurance, taxes, income, inheritance, prices, the military, and maritime, constitutional, and electoral law. Holdings of important official publications include *Deutsches Kolonialblatt* (1890–1921), edited by the Colonial Office, and the *Verhandlungen des Reichstags: Stenographische Berichte* (1871–1938). These and the accompanying *Anlagebande* plus the *Beilage* to the *Deutsches Kolonialblatt* contain not only all the debates on colonial questions but also numerous documents, committee reports, correspondence, and the official reports of the Colonial Office. Of an unofficial or quasi-public nature are reports of colonial societies like the Deutsche Kolonialgesellschaft, whose official organ, *Deutsche Kolonialzeitung*, is available for the years 1884–1922, 1929–1932, and 1935–1942. Other important titles for German colonial affairs in the early part of the twentieth century are the *Zeitschrift für Kolonial-Politik, Kolonialrecht und Kolonialwirtschaft* (1899–1911) and the *Koloniale Rundschau* (1909–1927, 1929, 1932, 1937–1943), a paper critical of German overseas policy.

Since special attention was given to collecting colonial publications for the war years, the library has holdings of the Kolonialinstitut of Hamburg's *Abhandlungen* (1910–1921), *Mitteilungen* (1914–1917), and *Bericht über das Studienjahr* (1910–1921). National Socialist publications treating the history of the German colonies are also numerous. The Stanford University Library holds journals such as *Afrika und Übersee* (1910–) and *Zeitschrift für Volkskunde* (1891–1940).

Important archival materials on former German Africa filmed from the Deutsches Zentralarchiv in Potsdam include the minutes and correspondence of the Deutsche-Ostafrikanische Gesellschaft (Berlin) board of directors (1885–1898); official documents of German Southwest Africa (1914–1915); selected files of the Reichs-kolonialamt (1884–1894); and minutes, protocols, and reports of the Kolonialrat (1890–1906).

Other noteworthy holdings include Charles Cecil Ferquharson Dundas's report on German administration in East Africa (1919); the diary of Franz Koehl (1913–1914), which describes the situation in German East Africa and the Belgian Congo; the Karl Peters papers, 1881–1903; and *Die Deutschen Kolonien* (1938), a collection of photographs and maps of former German African colonies from the Reich-kolonialbund. Contemporary journals dealing with Africa include *Afrika* (Bonn, 1963–), *Afrika Heute* (Bonn, 1961–1975), and *Afrika Spectrum* (Hamburg, 1967–).

HORN OF AFRICA

For former Italian Africa the library holds the *Revista Coloniale* (Rome, 1906–1927), *Revista delle Colonie: Rassegna dei Possedimenti Italiani* (Rome, 1927–1943), *Rassegna Economica dell'Africa Italiana* (1913–1943), *Africa* (Naples, 1882–1921, plus scattered issues from the 1930s), and the *Annuario dell'Africa Italiana . . .* (Rome, 1926–1940).

After the demise of the Italian empire, research into the history of the former empire reverted to the Minestero degli Affari Esteri, which sponsored the series *L'Italia in Africa*, held by the library.

Special collections include the diary (1927) of Luigi Federzoni, Italy's minister of colonies, and the papers of Ruth Ricci Eltse, a nurse in the Ethiopian-Italian War (1935–36) and a photographer-journalist in North Africa (1936–1939).

Current Italian journals on Africa include *Africa* (Rome, 1947, 1950, 1978–) and *Nigrizia* (Verona, 1963–).

The library holds publications from opposition groups in Ethiopia, such as the Eritrean Liberation Front, the Eritrean People's Liberation Front, and the Tigray People's Liberation Front.

SOUTHERN AFRICA

The library collections are particularly strong for this region. Special collections providing regional coverage include the Immanuel Wallerstein Collection, cited above in the Lusophone Africa section, which also contains publications of liberation groups in Zimbabwe (Rhodesia), Namibia (South West Africa), and South Africa.

The African Revolutionary Movements Collection contains files on such liberation movements as MPLA, FNLA, UNITA, UPA, GRAE, FRELIMO, COREMO, ANC, PAC, SASO, SWAPO, SWANU, ZANU, ZAPU, and FROLIZI.

The Southern Africa Collection (1969–) contains political ephemera, pamphlets, and photographs of political action groups and other organizations (Gulf Boycott Coalition, SWA 1975–76 Constitutional Conference, South African Congress of Trade Unions, Urban Foundation, American Committee on Africa, Episcopal Churchmen for South Africa, Washington Office on Africa, African National Council [Zimbabwe], Friends of Rhodesia, and Zimbabwe Rhodesia Elections [1979–1980]).

The S. Herbert Frankel Papers (1925–1975) contain his writings, correspondence, reports, and proceedings of commissions he served on, relating to economic conditions, finance, agriculture, mining, and transportation in South Africa, Zimbabwe, and East Africa.

NAMIBIA

For Namibia, the library holds the legislative proceedings for the following: South West Africa Legislative Assembly/National Assembly/Legislative Assembly for the Whites, *Debates* (1965–1980, 1979–1980), *Votes and Proceedings* (1926–1962, 1967–), *Eastern Caprivi* (1973–), *Kavango* (1972–), *Owambo* (1968–1970, 1972–1979, 1981–), *Rehoboth* (1979–), and *Nama* (1981–).

Holdings of journals published by the South West Africa People's Organization (SWAPO) include *Current Events in Namibia* (Dar es Salaam, 1975–1976), *Namibia News* (London, 1968, 1970–1978), *Namibia Today* (Lusaka, Dar es Salaam, Luanda, 1965–1969, 1971–), *Namibia Youth* (Stockholm, 1982–), *Solidarity* (Cairo, 1962–1967, 1974–1975), and *SWAPO Information Bulletin* (Luanda, 1980–).

SOUTH AFRICA

The library tries to elucidate South Africa's complex problem by drawing on every possible source—official publications, materials produced by political parties and by the legal and the underground opposition, and private sources of every description. The library attempts to obtain every important South African government publication, including commission reports, such as the seventeen-volume Tomlinson Report (Commission for the Socio-Economic Development of the Bantu Areas, 1955), the Odendaal Report (Commission of Inquiry into South West Africa Affairs, 1964), and the Cillie Report (Commission of Inquiry into the Riots at Soweto . . . 1976 . . . 1977, 1980). There are significant holdings on nationalist and other opposition groups. Included are the following journal and newspaper titles: *A.P.O.* (Cape Town, 1909–1915, 1922); *The International* (Johannesburg, 1915–1924); *Umsebenzi* (Johannesburg, 1926–1938); *The Spark* (Cape Town, 1935–1939); *Guardian* (Cape Town, 1937–1952); *Inkundla Ya Bantu* (Verulam, 1944–1951); *Challenge* (Johannesburg, 1951–1953); *New Age*, also called *Clarion, People's World*, and *Advance* (Cape Town, 1952–1962); *African Communist* (London, 1959, 1961–); *Counter Attack* (Johannesburg, 1961–1962); and *Fighting Talk* (Johannesburg, 1954–1958, 1960–1963).

The library holds various journals issued by present-day nationalist groups, such as the African National Congress's *Sechaba* (London, 1967–) and *ANC Weekly News Briefing* (London, (1981–) and the Pan Africanist Congress's *Azania News* (Dar es Salaam, 1968–).

Special holdings on South Africa include four microfilm reels on the black consciousness movement of South Africa (material from the collection of Gail Gerhart); the 71-reel Carter-Karis Collection, which includes documents on South African politics from 1882 to 1964 collected by Gwendolyn Carter and Thomas Karis; 3 reels of papers (1933–1948) of the South African Communist Party and related organizations, held by the South African Public Library, Cape Town; *South Africa: A Collection of Miscellaneous Documents, 1902–1963*, in 15 microfilm reels, which includes publications of the South African Congress of Trade Unions, South African Indian Congress, Pan Africanist Congress, African National Congress, Congress of Democrats, Liberal Party, African Political Organization, and African People's Organization; 15 reels on the treason trial in South Africa (1956–1960), for which the Hoover Institution Press published a guide prepared by Dr. Thomas Karis; 10 microfilm reels, covering the years 1921–1949, of papers of Dr. Alfred B. Xuma, president of the African National Congress in the 1940s, including correspondence, political pamphlets, party policy statements; and three boxes of records of Dom Polskich Dzieci in Oudtshoorn, covering the years 1942–1947, containing correspondence and reports on the establishment and operation of this home for Polish war orphans from Russia.

ZIMBABWE

The library has attempted to obtain the publications of the various African nationalist groups, such as *Zimbabwe Review* (1968–1979) and *Zimbabwe News* (1964–1979), as well as current titles, such as *Social Change and Development* and *Moto*. The Zimbabwe collection includes many records and files from the pre-independence period. Holdings of government commission reports include *Report of the Land Commission of 1894, Papers Relating to the Southern Rhodesia Native Reserves Commission of 1917*, and the *Native Labour Committee of Enquiry Report* (1921). The library also holds a 1971 guide, on microfilm, "The Historical Manuscripts of the National Archives of Rhodesia and Nyasaland," as well as runs of important serials.

SPECIAL COLLECTIONS

The library has a substantial collection of materials, many of which are not to be found anywhere else. These special collections, derived from the private holdings of officials and scholars, include the following:

David B. Abernethy Collection, 2 ms. boxes. Notes, pamphlets, etc., 1949–1964, relating to political, educational, economic, and social affairs in Nigeria.

Henry Bienen Papers, 1961–1967, 1 ms. box. Reports, pamphlets, clippings, etc., on political developments in Tanzania.

L. Gray Cowan Papers, 1952–1970, 11 ms. boxes. Reports, articles, speeches, etc., on political, economic, educational and social conditions in various African countries.

Joseph Boakye Danquah studies, 1961–1963, 1 ms. box. His typescripts of "Revelation of Culture in Ghana" (1961) and "Sacred Days in Ghana" (1963).

Lewis Henry Gann Papers, 1950–1976, 30 ms. boxes. Correspondence, interviews, research notes, drafts of books/papers relating to Gann's research on German colonialism in Africa and on pre-independence Malawi, Zambia, and Zimbabwe.

Harvey Glickman Papers, 1955–1969, 2 1/2 ms. boxes. Notes, speeches, pamphlets, reports, etc., relating to the Tanganyika African National Union and to political developments in Tanzania.

Great Britain. Colonial Office. East African Pamphlets, 14 reels.

Great Britain. Colonial Office. Pamphlets about Africa, 1870–1940s, 24 reels covering West and Central Africa plus Mauritius.

Samuel I. Hayakawa Papers. Hayakawa was U.S. senator for California; the collection is closed until May 1985. File and reports on his 1978 and 1982 Africa trips (Liberia, Kenya, Zimbabwe, South Africa, Botswana); printed material from SWAPO, National Unifying Force, Rhodesian government, FLEC Cabinda Enclave Liberation Front; Hayakawa's press conferences in Zambia, Botswana, and South Africa (1978); letters on Zimbabwe and other Africa-related matters from N. Sithole, George McGovern, William Tolbert, Abel Muzorewa, etc.; videotapes of press conference with Ian Smith; photographs of Bishop Abel Muzorewa and aides, Ian Smith, Rev. N. Sithole.

George D. Jenkins Papers, 1903–1969, 24 ms. boxes. Writings, notes, correspondence, pamphlets, etc., relating to politics in Nigeria, especially to the government of Ibadan.

Kenya National Archives, Annual Reports, 1904–1963, 63 reels. Handing Over Reports, 1910–1963, 14 reels. Intelligence Reports, 1921–1951, 12 reels. Miscellaneous Correspondence, 1894–1961, 11 reels. Provincial and District Record Books, 1902–1958, 18 reels.

Ernest W. Lefever Papers, 1956–1969, 3 ms. boxes. Writings, correspondence, reports, interviews, pamphlets, etc., on political developments in Zaïre, Ethiopia, and other African countries.

René Lemarchand Papers, 1920–1972, 3 ms. boxes. Government reports, political ephemera, interviews, correspondence, printed matter, etc., on political developments in Zaïre, Burundi, and Rwanda.

Intelligence Reports on Southern Nigeria, 16 reels. Unpublished reports by British colonial officials, 1932–1942.

Frederick Quinn Papers, 1822–1974, 16 ms. boxes, 4 tapes. Research notes, writings, interviews, copies of government documents, tapes, photographs on Beti society in Cameroun.

American Committee to Keep Biafra Alive, St. Louis Chapter, 1967–1970, 4 ms. boxes, 2 motion picture reels, 2 phonorecords. The committee's files contain publications of private and government organizations such as the U.S. Agency for International Development, the governments of Biafra and Nigeria, press releases, periodical literature, etc., relating to the Nigerian Civil War.

Documents on the Southern Sudan, 1962–1968, 2 ms. boxes. Letters and pamphlets from individuals and groups opposed to the central government, including missionary letters and reports.

Tanganyika Provincial and District Books, 1900–1950, 27 reels.

Herbert J. Weiss Collections on the Belgian Congo, 1947–1963, 10 reels. Political ephemera, police reports, correspondence, legislative debates, government documents, government and party newspapers, journals, etc. Also from Professor Weiss: the Conseil National de Liberation, Commandement des Forces Armées Populaires. Etat-Major Général. Records, 1964, 5 ms. boxes. Correspondence, reports, battle plans relating to military and political aspects of a rebellion in Kwilu, Zaïre.

PHOTOS AND SLIDES

The archives also houses a large photo and slide collection. Many African governments and colonial governments have provided pictures, for example, 220 photos of Angola and Mozambique and 50 from the Ministry of Information of the Sudan. Several individuals have donated their private collections, and Curator Duignan took hundreds of pictures of South Africa in 1979, especially of Durban, Port Elizabeth, Soweto, Cape Town, and Windhoek (Namibia) and the war zone in the north of Namibia.

AMERICANS IN AFRICA

The United States' links with Africa have been close, not only because of the slave trade, but also because Americans (as whalers and shippers, traders and merchants, explorers and missionaries, frontiersmen and soldiers, tobacco experts and mining engineers, government officials and Peace Corps volunteers) played a significant role

Booker T. Washington, president of Tuskegee Institute, and his secretary Emmett Scott, who sent a team of black scientists to Togo to teach Africans to grow cotton

in the history of the continent. Because of the extent of American commercial, missionary, philanthropic, scientific, and governmental contacts with Africa since the seventeenth century, resources are numerous and the Africa curator has tried to cover all aspects of this involvement. Holdings of papers and records of Americans serving and working in Africa include the following:

Thomas Jefferson Bowen Papers, 1 reel. Reverend Bowen served in Nigeria from 1849 to 1856 as missionary, explorer, linguist.

R. Dorsey Mohun Papers, 1892–1913, 3 reels. Mohun was U.S. commercial agent, Boma, Congo Free State, 1892–1895; U.S. consul, Zanzibar, 1895–1897; and agent of the Rubber Exploration Company of New York in South Africa, 1910–1911.

Henry Shelton Sanford Papers, 9 reels. Sanford was representative of the United States at the Berlin Conference, 1884, and at the Anti-Slavery Conference in Brussels, 1890. He served on the executive committee of the International Association, which sent Henry Morton Stanley to the Congo.

International Association of the Congo. Letters and documents . . . as collected by Lievin Van de Velde, Vivi Station, Congo, 1882–1883, 1 reel. Lt. Van de Velde accompanied Stanley to the Congo [Zaïre]. Included are letters of Henry Morton Stanley.

Presbyterian Church in the U.S., Board of Foreign Missions. Correspondence and report files, 1837–1903, 31 reels. Covers Liberia (including many letters of E. W. Blyden), Equatorial Guinea, Cameroun, and Gabon (in the Stanford University Library).

United States. Department of State. Dispatches from U.S. consuls/ministers to/in Liberia, 1863–1906 (14 reels); Lourenco Marques, 1854–1906 (6 reels); Tamatave, Madagascar, 1853–1906 (11 reels); and Zanzibar, 1836–1906 (11 reels). Records of the Department of State relating to internal affairs of British Africa, 1910–1929 (33 reels); Liberia, 1910–1929 (34 reels).

United States. Navy Department. Letters received by the secretary of the Navy from commanding officers of the squadrons, U.S. Navy, Africa Squadron, 1843–1861 (11 reels).

Marshall Bond Diary, 1927, 2 vols. Description of Bond's trip from Cairo to Cape Town; addendum on "African women" by Margaret Davidson.

Frederick R. Burnham Papers, 1876–1964, 7 ms. boxes. Burnham was an explorer and a major in the British Army during the Boer War. Correspondence, writings, photographs, etc., relating to the Southern Rhodesia Matabele wars of 1893 and 1896, the Boer War, and exploration in Africa.

Robert F. Corrigan Papers, 1958–1975, 1 folder. Corrigan was ambassador to Rwanda, 1972–1973. Includes reports, clippings on the visit of President Sekou Toure to the United States in 1959, and U.S. investment in Africa.

David W. King Papers, 1/2 ms. box. King was a consular official in Ethiopia in 1926 and served in the Office of Strategic Services during World War II, covering North Africa.

William D. Moreland, Jr., Papers, 1949–1965, 6 ms. boxes. Moreland was U.S. consul, Dakar, 1949–1951; includes correspondence, reports, photographs on political, economic, and social conditions in West Africa.

Eddie Smith Diary. Manuscript of Mr. Smith's diary while serving in the Peace Corps in Ghana, 1963–1964.

8 | THE MIDDLE EAST AND NORTH AFRICAN COLLECTIONS

Edward Jajko

Bibliographer

Edward Jajko, Bibliographer,
Middle East Collection

The Middle East Collection was formally established in 1948, nearly thirty years after the founding of the Hoover Institution. Having been founded on collections of materials from World War I, the Institution already had valuable holdings for research on the region since the Ottoman Empire had been a belligerent. Among them were documents on the role of the Ottoman Empire in the Great War, such as original sketches of the Gallipoli campaign by Lt. Col. M. J. W. Pike of the Royal Irish Fusiliers. Other holdings were included in the records of the American Relief Administration (ARA), which had maintained an office in Constantinople; the American National Red Cross; and the Near East Relief, which had cooperated with the ARA and the Red Cross in Turkey, Iran, and Syria. From an earlier period, the Institution had the papers of M. D. Skobelev, commander of the Russian forces in the Russo-Turkish War of 1877–1878.

The Institution's voluminous documentation on the Paris Peace Conference contained much material on the Middle East, which was one of the principal regions for the application of the new mandate system devised by the peacemakers. The papers of the House Inquiry, the research arm of the U.S. delegation to the conference, included data on the Middle East, as did the papers of George D. Herron, unofficial adviser to President Wilson. The Institution also possessed at this early stage the following special collections relating to the Middle East: E. J. Fisher, T. E. Lawrence, Eliot G. Mears, Mary M. Patrick, Ernest W. Riggs, and Arnold Toynbee.

Other pre-1948 holdings included materials produced by British organizations such as the British Palestine Committee, the English Zionist Federation, the Zionist Organization, and Friends of Armenia, as well as those produced by corresponding American groups—the American Jewish Committee, the Federation of American Zionists, the Zionist Organization of America, and the New Syria National League. Professor Graham Stuart and Dr. Luella Hall contributed books, manuscripts, pamphlets, and clippings on Morocco, Tangier, and other parts of North Africa. Materials such as these served as a basis for a distinguished collection on the Middle East.

Upon establishment of the Middle East Collection of the Hoover Institution in

1948, Dr. Christina Phelps Harris was named its first curator. During the first years of the collection, a concerted effort was made to define its scope and nature, to acquire materials, and to establish programs of study and research on the Middle East at Stanford University and the Hoover Institution.

The staff of the new collection established contacts with agents who served Hoover well, securing important materials on the history and dynamic social change of the modern Middle East. Among those agents were Jibran Bikhazi of the American University of Beirut, Professor Pertev Naili Boratav, and Dr. Andreas Tietze. Gifts came from Jamal-el-Din al-Muzaffar and his two brothers in the eastern Arab countries and from Hafez Farman-Farmaian in Iran.

In this initial stage in the history of the Middle East Collection, elaborate plans for programs of study on the Middle East were drawn up. Proposals for funding went out to foundations, to industries with Middle Eastern connections, and to individuals experienced in the area and with contacts in positions of influence. Efforts were made to establish programs in Middle East studies and to acquire funds to support those programs and library resources to give them substance. During Dr. Harris's curatorship, the Middle East Collection acquired two rich libraries, the Heyworth-Dunne and the Dağdeviren. These, with later significant additions of other materials, formed the backbone of Hoover's Arabic and Turkish holdings.

In these years, large basic sets were acquired, like the encyclopedia *Dā'irat al-Ma'ārif* of Butrus al-Bustani and serial sets like *al-Manār*. Along with these large sets, the collection secured significant histories of the revolutions in Egypt and Iraq in 1881, 1919, and 1952; books and pamphlets on the Muslim Brotherhood; and materials on the Baghdad Pact and the Suez War of 1956. A special effort was made to complete the sets of the writings, autobiographies, and biographies of prominent public figures and authors in the Middle East. Gifts included a collection of British propaganda leaflets dropped on Egypt during the Anglo-French invasion in November 1956 and files of *al-Istiqlāl* and other newspapers from French North Africa, some of which had been banned by the French government.

Dr. Harris served as curator until September 1957. She continued to teach in the Department of Political Science at Stanford until 1967, giving the collection the benefit of her knowledge, experience, and counsel. During her tenure as curator, she received valuable help from a staff that included graduate students who became eminent scholars, such as Sherif Mardin, later professor at the University of Ankara and author of *The Genesis of Young Ottoman Thought*; Amin Banani, later professor at the University of California, Los Angeles, and author of *The Modernization of Iran, 1921–1941*; and Nasuh Adib, later an official of the United Nations.

Another assistant, Dr. Eleanor Bisbee, rendered yeoman service in building up the Turkish side of the collection. Author of *The New Turks: Pioneers of the Republic, 1920–1950*, Dr. Bisbee had been a professor of philosophy at Robert College and the American College for Girls in Istanbul for six years, and she had excellent connections in Turkey. Thanks to a grant from the Ford Foundation, Dr. Mohamed Kafafi and Dr. Sami N. Özerdim, both accomplished professional librarians, came on leaves of absence from Cairo University and the National Library of Turkey respectively to help catalog the collection's holdings. Mrs. Samahat Turan, a librarian from Istanbul, also worked for two years cataloging Turkish materials.

Dr. Harris was succeeded as curator in 1957 by Dr. John Derek Latham, on leave from his position in charge of Middle East collections at the University of Manchester in England. In late 1958, Dr. Nicholas L. Heer, who had lived in the Middle East for some years, took the place of Dr. Latham and served as curator until June

1962. He was also assistant professor of Arabic in the Department of Asian Languages at Stanford. The collection then came under the wing of the curator of the Africa Collection, Dr. Peter Duignan.

Largely because of the absence of a program of Middle East studies in the Stanford University curriculum—a condition that still exists as of this writing—the collection for a while fell on hard times. In 1962, there was talk of putting it in mothballs, and other universities made approaches to the Hoover Institution for the possible purchase of the collection. Subscriptions to a number of publications on the Middle East were canceled. At the urging of Dr. Duignan, Director W. Glenn Campbell made several new appointments—in August 1962, Michel Nabti became assistant curator of the collection; and in September 1963, Dr. George Rentz became curator. Dr. Rentz had spent 24 years in the Middle East as a teacher, an official of the U.S. government, and director of research in Arab affairs for the Arabian American Oil Company (ARAMCO).

During the Rentz-Nabti period, the collection profited greatly from the Hoover's participation in the Library of Congress Public Law 480 Program for the Middle East. PL-480 provided for the use of a portion of "excess" counterpart funds in blocked currencies held by U.S. embassies in various countries, one of which was Egypt, for the acquisition of books and serials for the Library of Congress and selected American research libraries. Under the program, on-site acquisitions offices, run by the Library of Congress, acquired tens of thousands of books and hundreds of thousands of individual serial pieces for participating libraries. In return for a token membership fee, the Hoover Institution received several thousand volumes a year in Arabic and other languages along with thousands of issues of several hundred newspapers and periodicals. Most were Egyptian imprints. But many materials from Lebanon, Syria, North Africa, and the eastern Arab countries were also included (based on availability on the Egyptian market). Hoover participated in the PL-480 program for Egypt from 1963 until the late 1970s. In 1983, the Institution joined the program again, in its reincarnation as the dollar-funded Middle East Cooperative Acquisitions Program.

Dr. Rentz retired in 1976. A year later, Mr. Nabti left the Hoover. The Middle East Collection once again fell on hard times, as the Institution tried to determine the role of a distinguished Middle East Collection in the midst of a university that has never developed programs in Middle East studies and in the face of tightening budgets. The collection itself was absorbed into the Africa Collection. Dr. Peter Duignan, already curator-scholar of the Africa Collection, was named curator-scholar of the combined Africa and Middle East Collection in 1976. For the next six years, acquisitions of Middle East materials were largely confined to those in Western languages. The scope of collecting was reduced by subject as well as by language. Ms. Karen Fung, deputy curator for Africa, did yeoman service in maintaining Western-language acquisitions and in the continuing acquisition of a reduced list of vernacular newspapers and serials.

Despite the curtailment of activity in the Middle East Collection, the Hoover Institution increased its research program on the Middle East. Twice as many books were produced under Dr. Duignan's direction as in all previous periods put together. The importance of the collection, its continuing use by a steady stream of researchers, and the significance of the Middle East in world affairs were all convincing arguments favoring restoration of the collection to full activity. This was effected in January 1983 with the hiring of Edward Jajko as Middle East bibliographer, charged with the duties of selection, acquisition, cataloging, and reference work for Middle East materials in Arabic, Persian, Turkish, Hebrew, and other languages, under the general direction of the curator-scholar, Dr. Duignan. Active once again, the collection has an ongoing program for acquisitions from the Arab countries and Turkey, is building an acquisitions program for Iran, and has rejoined the Library of Congress Middle East Acquisitions Program.

The Hoover Institution's Middle East Collection is a study in paradoxes: it is one of the newest of Hoover's collections, but it is based on some of the oldest holdings of the Hoover Library and Archives; it is one of the older Middle East collections in the country, but one that is experiencing a rebirth after a long dormancy.

SCOPE OF THE MIDDLE EAST COLLECTION

The scope of the Middle East Collection has changed over the years. The present collecting policy, which is expected to remain in effect permanently, brings the collection in line with the rest of the Hoover Library (with the exception of the East Asian Collection). The Middle East Collection now collects books, serials, and other materials on the history, politics, and economics of the twentieth century. Attention is also paid to twentieth-century military affairs and to education as a factor in political and social change. Materials are acquired in support of a new area of concern, U.S. national security interests. Responsibility for collecting materials in subjects outside the Hoover's areas of specialization lies with the appropriate Stanford University library.

This represents a historic change in the mission of the collection. Until 1977, the Middle East Collection held responsibilities paralleling those of the East Asian Collection. As the only repository on the Stanford campus of books from the Middle

Sample of Islamic calligraphy in the Middle East Collection

East, it collected materials in a number of fields, ranging from philosophy and religion to classical Islamic texts to modern Arabic and Turkish literature. Acquisition of the James Heyworth-Dunne Collection both reflected and helped shape this policy since that collection was extremely strong in classical Islamic texts. The Middle East Collection still has good, basic holdings on the history, literature, and religion of classical or medieval Islam and on modern literature.

The near-closing of the collection in 1977 provided the opportunity to focus the collection on the Hoover's areas of interest—as well as the impetus to do so. Middle East Collection policy statements produced at that time stated that the Hoover would collect Western-language materials only, strictly in the Institution's areas of concentration: twentieth-century history, politics, and economics. With the reopening of the collection in 1983, that collecting policy was expanded by type of material. The collection now acquires materials from and on the Middle East in Western languages, which are added to the Western-language collections in the Tower stacks. In addition, the collection now once again acquires Arabic, Persian, and Turkish materials, which are added to the Middle East Collection proper. Concentrating on development of holdings of materials on the history, politics, economics, and military and educational affairs of the twentieth century enables the Hoover to build library resources of extraordinary depth and richness.

Since its beginnings, the Middle East Collection has concentrated on the development of holdings in Arabic, Turkish, and Persian to the exclusion of Hebrew, Coptic, Kurdish, Pushto, or other Middle Eastern languages. There were numerous reasons for this policy, among them the proximity of good holdings, particularly in Hebrew, at the University of California at Berkeley, and insufficient human and financial resources. This policy will, most probably, continue. The Hoover will most likely not develop large holdings in Hebrew, but will collect selectively. (The Hoover will continue to acquire materials in other languages from and about Israel/Palestine.) As for the minor languages, Coptic is now out of scope; other languages, such as Kurdish and Pushto, will not be developed systematically, but only if an abundance of resources allows.

As for other "minority" languages, Hoover does have small but valuable holdings of materials in the Turkic and Iranian languages of Central Asia. These include several years' worth of the Uighur newspaper from Urumchi, Sinkiang, *Sin Can Gazeti*, and numerous issues of Uighur serials and pamphlets. In addition, the Russian/ Soviet and East European Collection administers small holdings of valuable and rare books and pamphlets in Uzbek, Azeri, Kazakh, Chuvash, Bashkir, Kirghiz, Yakut, Balkar, and other languages of Soviet Central Asia, as well as several hundred volumes in Crimean and Volga Tatar. Notable among these Tatar books are two works by Gaziz Gubaydullin, *Tatarlarda sinflar* (Kazan, 1925) and *Tatar tarihi* (Kazan, 1924).

STANFORD UNIVERSITY LIBRARIES

The Middle East Collection is complemented and enriched by the holdings of the Stanford University libraries. Certain materials are to be found in campus libraries other than the Hoover because of the historical division of collecting responsibilities and because of unique strengths in other libraries. As of mid-1984, Green Library does not have significant holdings in Arabic or other Middle East vernaculars, but it does have important and growing Western-language holdings on the Middle East before 1900 and on philosophy, religion, and literature, as well as on contemporary Middle East history and politics. The Middle East Collection generally does not acquire American university press publications, which are to be found rather in Green

Library. Additionally, the Jonsson Library of Government Documents in Green Library has taken over the major role in acquisition of foreign government documents and is developing an excellent and constantly growing collection. The Hoover's specialty is older documents. The Green Library also holds the Israeli bibliographic journal *Kiryat Sefer*, and its excellent reference collection includes many titles of prime importance to researchers on the Middle East, including the printed catalogs of the University of California at Berkeley, the School of Oriental and African Studies, and the British Library.

A collection like the Middle East Collection is notoriously hard to quantify. No accurate count has ever been made, only general estimates that have not specified whether titles, bibliographic volumes, or physical volumes have been counted. A further complication is that, in addition to books, the Hoover's shelves hold serials, bound and unbound; newspapers, loose, bundled, and bound; pamphlets; photographs; films; maps; manuscripts; and other types of documents. Another factor is the holding of several thousand titles in unclassified "miscellaneous" collections and in uncataloged backlogs. At this point, short of actual physical counting of each piece in the collection, the only way to measure it is by estimating, based on shelf-list measurements and averaging of per-shelf holdings. Positing an arbitrary unit, equaling one title (monographic or pamphlet) or one bibliographic volume (serial or newspaper), but not including manuscripts, photographs, maps, etc., the Middle East Collection consists of the following units (approximately):

SIZE OF THE COLLECTIONS

Arabic	20,000	titles (monographs and pamphlets)
	10,000	volumes (serials and newspapers)
Turkish	5,000	titles (monographs and pamphlets)
	20,000	volumes (serials and newspapers)
Persian	500	titles (monographs and pamphlets)
	500	volumes (serials and newspapers)
Western Languages	40,000+	monographs, pamphlets, serials, and newspapers

The Arabic Collection is the largest and most varied vernacular component of the Middle East Collection. Its size arises from Arabic's position as the major language of the Middle East; its variety developed in part from the history of the mission of the collection. Because the Middle East Collection previously took within its purview most areas of scholarly interest, including philosophy, religion, the arts, and literature, and because a scholar's library particularly strong in classical and premodern Islamic and Middle East studies was the foundation of the collection, the Arabic Collection has excellent holdings on Arabic philology, Islamic and Middle East history from the rise of Islam to early modern times, and on the beginning of modernization in Egypt and elsewhere in the Middle East. Further, holdings in modern social sciences and literature are excellent, thanks to Hoover's participation in the Library of Congress PL-480 program for the Middle East and also to perspicacious purchases. Thus, although the Middle East Collection now primarily develops its holdings in the history, politics, and economics of the twentieth century, it remains a library rich in Islamica and Arabica on a broad range of subjects. These materials are supplemented by excellent holdings of translations and studies in the Western-language collections and by uncataloged materials in the Heyworth-Dunne Collection. For the

ARABIC COLLECTION

modern period, Hoover has good holdings in Arabic literature, with the works of authors like Tharwat Abazah, Najib Mahfuz, Tawfiq al-Hakim, Yusuf al-Siba'i, and Taha Husayn well represented.

This part of the collection, now out-of-scope, continues to be heavily used and of major interest to Stanford faculty and students.

Still, despite the excellence of these holdings and their evident popularity and usefulness, they are not in the Hoover's areas of specialization and are no longer developed. Of greatest significance to this survey are the considerable holdings in modern social sciences. Particularly strong are the holdings on the history of Saudi Arabia, Egypt, and Palestine; Arab-Israeli relations, and the wars of 1948, 1956, 1967, and 1973; the Muslim Brothers; the origins and systematization of socialism in Egypt; communism and communist parties in the Arab world; oil, economic development, and the new wealth in the Middle East; and Lebanese party politics, civil wars, and foreign occupation.

The Middle East Collection contains a wide range of official publications from Arab countries, including Egypt, Lebanon, Syria, Saudi Arabia, Kuwait, and the United Arab Emirates. Palestine under the British Mandate and Israel (Arabic being an official language) are well represented, as are provisional governments, such as Algeria before independence, and governments-in-exile, such as the Imamate of Oman. These publications include parliamentary debates, official gazettes, and reports of ministries, development boards, banks, chambers of commerce, and state railways.

The Middle East Collection is especially strong in materials on Islam and Arab nationalism in the modern period. For years, the collection developed holdings on industrialization, agriculture, land tenure and agrarian reform, irrigation, education, communications, public health, and law. Special attention is given to the oil industry. Activities of the Arab League, the Organization of Arab Petroleum Exporting Countries, and other regional bodies are well documented.

The section of the Heyworth-Dunne Collection on the modern Middle East covers the period from the 1860s to the early 1940s. Along with publications by prominent figures of the time, there are many reports, pamphlets, offprints, and other opuscula, including a considerable body of clandestine materials on revolutionary movements. Heyworth-Dunne's working notes on a variety of subjects are to be found in the Hoover Archives.

An extremely important recent addition to Hoover's collections is that of materials acquired from Richard P. Mitchell, professor of history at the University of Michigan. The late Dr. Mitchell was the leading authority on the Society of the Muslim Brothers and on Islamic fundamentalism in general. The first part of his collection is located in the Hoover Archives. In mid-1984, the Institution received the second part, consisting of more than 400 books and hundreds of newspaper and magazine articles. Dr. Mitchell collected them from Morocco to India for a new edition of his seminal work on the Muslim Brothers, which he had been working on at the time of his death. The world of learning was robbed of a revision of this major work at a time when Islamic resurgence makes such materials especially valuable. But generations of scholars will find in the Hoover Institution an important center for the study of the Muslim Brothers and of Islamic fundamentalism, thanks to the efforts of this collector and the Hoover Institution's support of his research.

Finally, the Middle East Collection makes available to researchers a broad range of ancillary materials, such as the latest edition of the Wehr-Cowan dictionary; dictionaries and encyclopedias such as Lane and Dozy, as well as specialized dictionaries for business, diplomacy, petroleum sciences, and other métiers; indexes and collections of abstracts such as *Index Islamicus* and *Middle East: Abstracts and Index*; the Harvard, Utah, and British Museum catalogs (other printed catalogs are available in Green Library); the periodical index *al-Fihrist*; and a growing number of bibliographic tools, like *al-Bibliyūghrāfiyā al-Waṭanīyah al-Urdunīyah* and *al-Kitāb al-Maghribī*. *Mideast File* is currently available to Hoover readers in the Dialog databank and in hard copy. Lastly, because of the peculiarities of the collection's history, readers can still get a good idea of Hoover's holdings from *The Library Catalogs of the Hoover Institution on War, Revolution and Peace, Stanford University: Catalog of the Arabic Collection* (Boston: G. K. Hall, 1969).

TURKISH COLLECTION

The Turkish Collection is perhaps the most distinguished component of the Middle East Collection. The Turkish Collection was considerably strengthened early in the history of the Middle East Collection, in 1952, with the purchase from Mrs. Saadet Dağdeviren of the library of her late husband, Hidayet Dağdeviren, a businessman, scholar, and former member of the Turkish parliament, who had begun assembling his collection before the Young Turk Revolution of 1908. The library consisted of books, pamphlets, and a profusion of manuscript documents, clippings, and other unique or rare items. The importance of the Hoover Turkish Collection was recognized soon afterward. In 1954, Celal Bayar, president of Turkey, visited the Hoover Institution. As noted in a report written later that year,

> President Bayar of Turkey was sufficiently impressed by our display, chosen from our collection on the National Struggle (*Milli Mücadele*) and economic and government materials, to devote treble the time allotted in his program to seeing the display (a

Poster depicting victorious cavalry, headed by Mustafa Kemal Ataturk, founder of the Turkish Republic, entering Izmir on September 9, 1922, on a road strewn with flowers (Hoover Institution Archives)

compliment to our collection, which, however, gravely disrupted
the rest of the program!). He commented, as other eminent
Turkish visitors have, on various items and files which he was
sure were not as complete, or even available, in Turkey today;
and he asked for photostats of certain items.

In 1957, a grant from the Rockefeller Foundation enabled the Hoover Institution
to bring together a panel of twelve of the foremost Turcologists in the United States
and Canada for a thorough examination of the Turkish section. The panel con-
cluded: "Taking into consideration the length of the period covered and the topical
range, this collection may be considered to be unique in the United States and Canada, and possibly outside Turkey."

In 1968–1969, the Institution made another major acquisition from Turkey—the
private library of M. Hüseyin Tutya of Istanbul. This collection of 10,122 volumes,
mostly in Ottoman, built up by three generations of the Tutya family in Istanbul and
Izmir, was particularly well stocked with works in history, geography, politics, military affairs, law, and Islam.

The catalogs of the Hoover Turkish Collection list some 266 newspaper titles, all
but a few of them in Ottoman Turkish. This represents the richest single collection of
Turkish newspapers outside Istanbul. Newspapers from 1870 to the late 1970s are
held, for Istanbul, Ankara, and numerous provincial cities and towns, and areas outside Turkey, such as Saloniki, Crete, Aleppo, London, Mosul, Batum, and Beirut.
The great majority of the files date from the 1880s to the 1920s. Many files contain
only a single year or a portion of a year; many have spotty holdings—some consist of
only one issue. In the aggregate, however, the Hoover's holdings of Turkish newspapers are a uniquely rich resource, which attracts scholars and inquiries from
around the world, for unparalleled access to documentation of the commercial and
political life of late imperial and early republican Turkey.

The Hoover's holdings of Turkish serials are also extremely rich; the catalogs list
over a thousand titles, in Ottoman, Modern Turkish, and other languages. Turkish
newspaper, serial, and monograph holdings are listed in detail in *The Library Catalogs of the Hoover Institution on War, Revolution and Peace, Stanford University:
Catalog of the Turkish Collection* (Boston: G. K. Hall, 1969).

The Dağdeviren Collection has been a particularly rich resource for Hoover. A
major portion, containing documentation on Turkish history and politics from the
period before Tanzimat until the 1950s and on various special subjects like Turkish
social life, religious and welfare organizations, national minorities, and Pan-Slavism,
is housed in the archives. Two hundred fifteen brief monographs and pamphlets, sep-
arated from these dossiers in the archives, form the Dağdeviren Pamphlet Collection
in the Tower stacks. This collection is a richly revealing cross section of Ottoman
history at the end of the empire. In it may be found the text of the *fetva* outlawing
Mustafa Kemal (Ataturk) and his movement and a manifesto of the Society for the
Revival of Islam issued in 1920 to convince the populace that the Nationalists were
nothing but a front for the former Party of Union and Progress.

Holdings of Turkish monographs are especially good for the periods 1923 to 1945
and 1950 to 1963. For the latter period, the Hoover collections stress holdings of
pro-government materials (for the Bayar period) and publications of the military
government. The collection is now acquiring currently published books on Turkish
history and politics, including materials on the period of terrorism, Turkey's role in
NATO, and Turkey as a Middle Eastern and Islamic state.

The collection makes available to readers encyclopedias and dictionaries, for both Ottoman and Modern Turkish, as well as materials like *Türkiye Bibliyografyası* and *Türkiye Makaleler Bibliyografyası*.

PERSIAN COLLECTION

The Persian Collection is the smallest component of Hoover's Middle East Collection. It nonetheless contains many useful and important materials. It provides valuable documentation on the Tudeh Party (the pro-Soviet Iranian communist party) and on revolutionary movements in Azerbaijan and Kurdistan after World War II. This includes materials on 51 Iranian communist leaders tried and jailed in 1937, then released in 1941 when the Allied invasion of Iran led to an amnesty of political prisoners. The collection contains considerable material relating to the Tudeh Party. A number of issues, but not complete sets, are held of its monthlies *Mardom* and *Razm*, along with various other party publications from Tehran and France, traditional refuge of Iranian dissidents. Some of the works of Marx, Engels, Lenin, Stalin, and other communist theoreticians are available in Persian translation. Articles on the Tudeh Party published in the newspaper *Shahid* and reissued in book form are also available. In addition, publications of political opponents of Tudeh are represented.

The collection has a fairly extensive set of materials on the Iranian oil industry and the nationalization of the Anglo-Iranian Oil Company in 1951, including speeches and writings of Mohammed Mossadegh. Holdings on other subjects of interest include materials on the Barazani tribe of Kurds in Iran and Iraq; Iran's ties with the Persian Gulf, particularly its former claim to Bahrain; and the question of Azerbaijan, the northwestern region of Iran, which borders on Turkey and the Soviet Union.

Revolutionary Iran is, of course, of great interest to an American library. At present, the Hoover's coverage of this crucial period is strongest in its Western-language collections, and the impact of Khomeini and of fundamentalist or resurgent Islam on the Middle East as a whole is well represented in the Arabic Collection. The Hoover is endeavoring to build up its holdings in Farsi on the Islamic Republic, holdings that now include writings of Ayatollah Khomeini, Mahdi Bazargan, and of Marxists in exile, and a growing set of the so-called "Documents from the American Spy-Den," papers seized by the Muslim Students Following the Line of the Imam, during the seizure of the U.S. Embassy.

WESTERN-LANGUAGE COLLECTION

The Middle East Collection includes not only materials in Arabic, Persian, and Turkish, but in Western languages also. These materials are shelved with the other Western-language holdings, which form the greater part of the Hoover Library. The Hoover's Western-language holdings on the Middle East are exceptionally rich. Coverage of modern history—of the Middle East (approximately 2,300 titles), the Jews (approximately 3,600 titles), the Arab world and Iran (approximately 1,000 titles), and Egypt and North Africa (approximately 3,000 titles)—is especially strong.

The Hoover Institution currently receives over 120 Western-language serials from and about the Middle East, as well as the newspapers of record of Europe, East Europe, and North America, certain of which, like *Le Monde*, are known for exceptional coverage of the Middle East.

The richness of Hoover's Western-language collections is exemplified by a collection of 800 bound volumes of French periodicals acquired in the early 1960s. Published in Europe, Morocco, Algeria, and Tunisia, these periodicals included long

From the T. E. Lawrence file (Hoover Institution Archives)   British anti-Nasser propaganda leaflets, 1956 Suez War

runs of journals like *Revue africaine, L'Asie française*, and *Revue algérienne, tunisienne, et marocaine de jurisprudence*. This acquisition, when added to the mass of French-language serials and newspapers already at Hoover, established virtually a library within a library, a massive record of the latter period of French colonialism in North Africa, France's relations with its dependencies in Africa and Asia, World War II in North Africa, and especially the movements for national independence of Morocco, Algeria, and Tunisia, and the Algerian War in particular.

The Hoover's holdings of materials in English, German, and other languages are equally strong.

ARCHIVAL HOLDINGS   Archival holdings, while housed in and administered by the Hoover Archives rather than the Middle East Collection, are nevertheless a major component of the collection. The Hoover Archives contains more than a hundred archival units, or collections, relating to the Middle East. These include papers and other materials of individuals famous in the modern history of the Middle East, like James Heyworth-Dunne, H. St. John Philby, Chaim Weizmann, T. E. Lawrence, Ahmed Emin Yalman, and even General "Chinese" Gordon. The last years of the Ottoman Empire, military operations in Turkey in World War I, postwar relief work, and the establishment of the Turkish Republic are documented in the collections of Luella Hall, Ruth Parmelee, E. Carl Wallen, Evgeniĭ Vasil'evich Maslovskiĭ, M. J. W. Pike, Benton Clark Decker, Ernest Wilson Riggs, Eliot Mears, Eleanor Bisbee, Hidayet Dağdeviren, Mary Mills Patrick, Kerim Key, Stanley E. Kerr, Anna V. S. Mitchell, Baron Petr Nikolaevich Vrangel', Tarik Z. Tunaya, and others. A unique perspective on Turkish affairs is given by the papers of Michal Sokolnicki, Polish ambassador to Turkey between the World Wars. Papers of the Inquiry (more technically, Paris Peace Conference, 1919. U.S. Division of Territorial, Economic and Political Intelligence) and of the Lausanne Conference, 1922–1923, illuminate the history of the establishment of the Turkish Republic.

North African history, from the latter part of the nineteenth century through World War II, is recorded in the papers of James Rives Childs, Horace H. Herr, Cuthbert P. Stearns, Douglas E. Ashford, Walter J. Muller, P. A. Bourget, and Robert Louis Delavignette. The attempted coup by the Organisation Armée Secrète (OAS) is living history in the archive of Yves Jean Antoine Noël Godard, a colonel in the French Army, director of police in Algeria, 1958–1960, and an organizer of the OAS.

Hoover has a file of Lebanese political leaflets from 1943 to 1957 and of anti-Nasser propaganda leaflets dropped on Egypt by the British in November 1956 during the Sinai war. Many of Hoover's Middle East archives contain photographs of political personalities, of relief operations, and of general conditions in the area. Mention has been made previously of the Richard P. Mitchell Collection on the Muslim Brotherhood as a major deposit of materials on that crucially important organization.

Finally, this highly selective survey of Hoover's archival holdings on the Middle East notes a few collections dealing with oil. Important in this area are the papers of Philip C. McConnell, former vice-president of ARAMCO, and of Harley C. Stevens, former vice-president of the American Independent Oil Company. The latter file includes the texts of agreements between various oil companies and the governments of the Middle East, relating to oil concessions. They and the Georg Spies file on efforts by Deutsche Bank in 1904–1906 to gain oil concessions in Romania, Bulgaria, and Turkey are a reminder of the pioneering days of the oil industry in the Middle East.

9 | THE LATIN AMERICAN COLLECTION

Joseph W. Bingaman
Curator

Joseph W. Bingaman, Curator, Latin and North American Collections

The Latin American Collection originated in 1919 at the Paris Peace Conference. The collectors of delegation propaganda at the conference obtained 36 items from representatives of the governments of Argentina, Bolivia, Chile, Costa Rica, Panama, and Peru. Additional materials were later received at Stanford University from nine Latin American states and four British colonies in the Caribbean. A number of Latin American delegates in Paris promised Stanford history professor E. D. Adams, organizer and, along with Ralph H. Lutz, an original director of the Hoover War History Collection, that their governments would send their publications free of charge to the library. The flow of material increased considerably after Professor Adams visited Latin American envoys in Washington in the fall of 1921.

The scholars directing the acquisitions program of the Hoover War Library decided that the participation of Latin America in World War I was to be documented adequately. In March 1920, Professor Percy A. Martin, who held the chair of South American history at the University, made a comprehensive list of Latin American publications on the war. Brentano's in New York was instructed to secure the works and bind them as rapidly as possible. Since few books on the war were published in South America, the library decided to acquire virtually everything being published in the field. Within the next year, 60 titles were received under this arrangement.

Professor Martin, who became one of the most distinguished Latin Americanists in the United States, had come to Stanford University in 1912 as professor of history. He became a favorite of Stanford President John Casper Branner, whose great interest was Brazil and who encouraged Martin immensely in his Brazilian studies. Branner had first visited Brazil in 1874 as a Cornell undergraduate and was to return several times before his death in March 1922. His collecting in that country laid the foundation for Stanford's pre-eminent collection on Brazil.

In May 1925, the Committee of Policy of the library recommended that collecting trips be made by special representatives. In 1924, Dr. Graham H. Stuart, associate professor of political science and a newly appointed member of the library directorate, had gone on a collecting trip to South America, the first of many such trips during the next 25 years. Professor Stuart returned with a valuable collection of Peruvian government documents in 1925. While in South America in 1926, Alfred Coester, professor of Spanish American literature, secured important collections of government documents, newspapers, and periodicals from Brazil, Argentina, and Uruguay. Professor of history Harley Lutz collected significant Chilean materials that same year. By 1928, Dr. Adams had completed the collection of documentary publications begun in 1920 and had acquired materials from every South and Central American government. Dr. Percy Martin made three trips to South America—in 1913 (with University President Casper Branner), 1925/26, and 1937. Mr. Nathan van Patten, then director of the University Library, collected in Mexico in 1928 and again in 1930. In 1941, Eliot G. Mears, professor of geography and trade, and Graham Stuart returned with publications from trips to South America.

The Policy Committee, in its 1925 statement, also recommended the use of resident agents abroad in those countries where the book trade was poorly organized. In May 1928, the directors of the Hoover War Library appointed as curator of the Mexican and Central American collections Rafael Heliodoro Valle, then the editor of the newspaper *Excelsior* and chief of the Bibliographical Section of the Library Department of the Mexican Ministry of Education. He later was appointed Honduran ambassador to the United States. In 1940, he presented to the library his extensive collection of books and pamphlets as a memorial to Señora Valle, and until 1947, when his association with the library ceased, Valle's efforts continued to enrich the Latin American collection. In 1947, Fedor Nemirovsky joined the staff of the Hoover Institution as special representative outside the United States for Argentina. For several years after 1947, Felipe Gil, secretary general of the University of Montevideo, represented the library in Uruguay.

Several important special collections were acquired during the 1920s. *The Inquiry Papers* consists of a fairly extensive set of documents of the group of American scholars and experts popularly known as the House Inquiry in honor of its head, Col. E. M. House. This organization prepared reports for the American plenipotentiaries on questions likely to come before the Peace Conference. Dr. Bailey Willis, head of the Latin American Section of the Inquiry, presented the materials on Latin America to the library. The *Papers of the Sixth International Conference of American States* (Havana, 1928) consists of the complete documentation of the Committee on Intellectual Cooperation of the conference and was presented by Stanford President Ray Lyman Wilbur, a delegate to the conference and member of the committee. The *Documents of the Special Neutrality Commission of the Pan-American Union* comprises minutes of meetings, reports, memorandums of the commission, and notes from the governments of the various delegates. The commission was established to study problems of international law arising from World War I and included the secretary of state of the United States and the ambassadors or ministers to the United States from Argentina, Chile, Brazil, Uruguay, Peru, Honduras, Ecuador, and Cuba. The first meeting of the commission was held on December 16, 1914, and the last on December 16, 1915. Dr. L. S. Rowe, director-general of the Pan-American Union, presented the *Documents* to the library.

Professor Ralph H. Lutz, second chairman of directors, whose collecting trips laid the foundation for the German and Central European collections, once noted that the teaching of Latin American history at the undergraduate level at Stanford in the 1920s was based on scarce English-language material existing in the Hoover War Collection. By the mid-1930s the library possessed a significant Latin American collection, and the first master's theses on Latin America written at Stanford were based on Hoover materials. The number of Latin American students, particularly from Mexico, grew in the late 1930s after study in Europe became impossible.

On July 1, 1941, as a contribution by Stanford University to hemispheric solidarity, the Office of Inter-American Relations was opened in the Hoover Library on War, Revolution and Peace, and Mrs. Maria McCormack Hoge was appointed curator and research associate in charge. The immediate objective was to prove the value of an agency on the Pacific Coast devoted to the task of implementing President Franklin Roosevelt's Good Neighbor policy. In developing the original program, the fundamental idea was to mold the public opinion of the Americas, not yet crystallized, in active, permanent support of inter-American cooperation. The office provided information service to students and faculty members, as well as to the general public, and broadcast a series of shortwave radio programs to Latin American countries. In general, most inquiries received by the office were from students writing term papers or theses on Latin America, from individuals planning trips to or wishing to study in the other Americas, and from elementary and secondary school teachers. The office sponsored lectures by prominent Latin Americans, most of them visiting this country at the invitation of the Department of State. It prepared radio scripts for two programs aired over the Columbia network and sponsored by the Foreign Trade Association of San Francisco and by the Inter-American Forum of the Air. The office acted as a clearinghouse for Stanford's Latin American students and furthered cooperation in Latin America by establishing contact with well-known editors, writers, poets, radio commentators, literary critics, and other intellectuals. It distributed quantities of materials covering broad fields of interest in inter-American affairs and provided assistance to people seeking employment in the inter-American field. During the three years that the Inter-American Office was in operation, it collaborated with the Pan-American Union, the Office of the Coordinator of Inter-American Affairs, the Institute of International Education, and the Division of Cultural Relations of the Department of State. Although the office was placed under direct University jurisdiction in 1942/43, it contributed, until its closing in June 1944, to a considerable strengthening of the Latin American holdings of the Hoover Library.

As the country became involved in World War II, interest and activity in Latin American studies at Stanford reached a low ebb. Budgetary and staff limitations resulted in further restriction of activities. The situation continued relatively unchanged until February 1954, when it was agreed that the University Library would be responsible for Latin American materials and the Hoover Library for Chinese-, Japanese-, and Korean-language materials. Hoover transferred its nonbook materials on Latin America to the University Library but retained materials on Spain published by Spanish émigré groups in Latin America and propaganda materials from European or Asian political groups published in Latin America.

This arrangement remained in effect until early 1962, when the Hoover Institution resumed its collecting activities for Latin America in a modest way. The impact of Castro's Cuba on the United States and on the other countries of the Western Hemisphere emphasized the necessity of documenting the political changes taking place in Latin America. The first step was the acquisition of all available Soviet publications on Latin America, the number of which had begun to grow considerably. English-language publications, particularly those on Cuba and communism in Latin America, were also acquired. A generous gift from the New York–based Calder Foundation enabled the Institution to proceed with its objective. More help came indirectly from a Ford Foundation grant to Stanford University for Latin American studies.

In order to centralize Latin American acquisitions, Joseph W. Bingaman, the assistant librarian, was asked to take over the curatorship of the collection in March

"Songs of the Cuban Revolution." Photograph on the jacket of a French phonograph record showing Fidel Castro at the head of a band of Cuban revolutionaries. Sung in Spanish, the songs have such titles as "Venceremos" ("We shall conquer"), "Yo si tumbo cana" ("Yes, I cut sugar cane"—a cha-cha), and "Viva el socialismo."

1963. Mr. Bingaman undertook a trip to South America in February 1964 in order to establish relations with major libraries and bookdealers in key cities. A second trip to South America in February 1967 and a visit to the Central American republics and Panama in February 1972 strengthened these contacts and established new ones. During these and later collecting trips, Mr. Bingaman visited every country in Latin America and acquired a significant amount of research material. An earlier trip to Mexico by Professor Witold S. Sworakowski, associate director of the Hoover Institution, had resulted in the acquisition of the Ricardo Heredia Alvarez Collection of periodicals, which numbered over 6,000 issues and included many rare revolutionary ephemera.

During 1965/66, with the aid of a Ford Foundation grant, normal collecting activity resumed. The earlier limitation to Soviet books and English-language publications dealing only with Cuba and communism in Latin America was expanded to include general works on problems of political, social, and economic change—a policy similar to those applying to the other major geographical area collections in the Institution. The growth of the Latin American collection is illustrated by the increase in the number of paid subscriptions to newspapers and periodicals from 10 in June 1964 to 170 in June 1970.

In 1963, Philip Ray, a specialist in economic relations between Latin American countries and the United States, was appointed research fellow at the Institution. The acquisitions program was greatly enhanced through his contacts with prominent persons in Latin America. In September 1964, Theodore Draper, another scholar and writer on Latin American affairs, joined the staff. With his cooperation, the Institution was able to obtain not only valuable material published in the Dominican Republic and in Cuba but also important personal accounts from close collaborators of Fidel Castro about the revolution and the takeover of Cuba.

Mr. Draper organized one collection as background material for the preparation of two books and many articles written about events taking place in Cuba between 1959 and 1966. A second collection donated by Mr. Draper documents the Dominican Republic crises of 1963–1966, with an emphasis on the U.S. involvement. In addition to these special collections, Mr. Draper donated his library on Cuba of almost 700 books and pamphlets, over 1,000 issues of periodicals, and 72 reels of microfilm of hard-to-obtain books and newspapers. In the spring of 1971, Col. Thomas L. Crystal, a scholar on Panama, turned over to Hoover his large research collection on twentieth-century Panama, which he had amassed over the preceding 25 years.

A substantial collection of books, pamphlets, newspapers, and archival materials was transferred from Bolivar House to the Hoover Institution Library when publication of the *Hispanic American Report* was suspended and Professor Ronald Hilton's Institute of Hispanic-American and Luso-Brazilian Studies dissolved in the fall of 1964 (the program continued as the Center for Latin American Studies). These extensive archives consist of materials collected from a wide range of Hispanic-American periodicals and newspapers and other sources. They cover the period January 1954 through December 1964, when the institute was publishing its *Report*, and help to fill the gaps that occurred when the Hoover Institution curtailed its acquisitions program.

SCOPE OF THE COLLECTION

The primary purpose of the collection is to document twentieth-century political, economic, and social developments in this geographic area. The Hoover Institution defines Latin America as the area between the U.S.-Mexican border and Antarctica, including the islands of the Caribbean and the Falkland Islands. This definition is identical to that accepted by the Stanford University Libraries. Within this area the subject division is more important than the country division, with the result that certain countries receive greater emphasis than others at a given time. Castro's Cuba, Allende's Chile, and Peron's Argentina are outstanding examples. The Institution's aim is to document change and new areas of interest, and thus it pursues an acquisitions policy that is responsive and flexible. The Hoover has collected in subject areas with which the University was not concerned in the past. For these reasons and also because of its responsibility to a wider clientele, its collecting extends beyond the needs of Stanford faculty and students. The collection serves teaching and research programs offered by the various departments of the University; it also serves a national and international clientele of graduate students and scholars who use its unique materials.

Collecting concentrates on the ideology, organization, and activities of communist, socialist, Trotskyist, and other Marxist-Leninist political parties and organizations; urban and rural guerrilla organizations; anti-U.S. national liberation movements; anti-Castro refugee organizations; pro-Castro groups; and foreign relations, particularly those of the United States, Cuba, China, and the USSR. On a more selective basis, the Hoover Institution collects on the ideology, organization, and activities of parties of the right, the democratic left, the radical left, and the Christian left; radical student movements; trade union movements; foreign relations, with an emphasis on border disputes; and antileftist groups.

Fields outside the collecting scope are philosophy, religion, linguistics, pure and applied science, geography, literature, arts, children's books, and recreation. Those publications falling partially or even wholly within any of these categories that have some bearing upon the subject interests of the Institution are, however, acquired.

Collecting focuses on the years following the outbreak of World War II. Selective collecting is carried on for the period between the two world wars, and limited collecting of background material for the earlier years of the twentieth century. Exceptions include documentation on U.S.-Panamanian relations, which extends from the early part of the century, and on U.S.-Cuban affairs, which dates even further back.

The principal languages of the materials are Spanish, Portuguese, and English. To a lesser degree, materials in Russian, French, German, and Dutch are acquired. Some preference is given to the original language of publication. When available, English translations are acquired for key documents.

Materials consist of books, pamphlets, periodicals, newspapers, microfilms, ephemeral publications, special collections, manuscripts, and archival material. Also acquired are posters, photographs, phonograph records, moving picture and television films, and tape recordings.

THE COLLECTION

The Latin American Collection comprises some 30,000 volumes of books and approximately 1,900 periodicals and newspaper titles, of which 170 titles from 33 countries of Europe and the Americas are presently being received. Materials are classified according to the Library of Congress subject headings. Since 1977, the library has made a concerted effort to obtain positive microfilm prints of Latin American newspaper titles. Between 1977 and 1984, it acquired some 5,600 reels representing 63 titles, 18 of which are current subscriptions. In its own microfilm program, the Institution films for resale four Cuban serials, one newspaper from Cuba, and one from Argentina. As of mid-1984, a total of 18 Latin American serial and newspaper titles on microfilm could be purchased from the Hoover Institution.

The Argentine section, the largest in the collection, contains almost 3,000 cataloged monographs and over 200 serial titles. It is strong on the period 1916 to 1930, when the Radical Party ruled the country. It contains an outstanding range of published materials covering the political, social, and economic aspects of the Perón regimes, especially the writings and speeches of Juan and Eva Perón. The Falkland Islands war is covered in depth from both the Argentine and the British perspective. The library has a complete file of *Mundo Peronista* and holdings of the socialist paper *La Vanguardia*, the communist party publications *Nuestra Palabra* and *Nueva Era*, and the Trotskyist paper *Voz Proletaria*. The last three were suppressed by the government in the 1960s. Currently received are the monthly publications *Extra*, *Política*, *Economía y Sociedad*, and *Véritas*, the dailies *La Razón* and *El Clarín*, and the weeklies *Confirmado*, *La Nación*, *La Prensa*, and *La Vanguardia*. Important microfilm holdings are *Buenos Aires Herald* (1900–1978), *El Clarín* (1962–1982), *La Nación* (1939–1950), *La Razón* (1962–1982), and *La Vanguardia* (1944–1980).

Some 800 books on Bolivia document the Chaco War of 1932–1935, the National Revolutionary Movement in the early 1940s, the revolution of 1952, the succession of coups and regimes since the presidency of Paz Estenssoro (1960–1964), the Debray and Guevara guerrilla episodes in the mid-1960s, and the struggle for a corridor to the sea.

The accomplishments of Getulio Vargas, the activities of Brazil in World War II, the coup of 1964, and succeeding military governments are covered. The library contains extensive material dealing with the literacy training program (*conscientización*, *conscientização*) developed by the famous Brazilian educator Paulo Freire to support the political activity of newly literate persons in Brazil and Chile. The communist

Eva Perón addressing the nation, with President Juan Perón and Buenos Aires governor Domingo Mercante to her right. Vice-President Dr. Juan Hortensio Quijano is in the foreground. The photograph is one of a large number in the Perón collection in the archives.

press is represented by the weekly *Folha da Semana*, now suppressed. Currently received dailies are *O Estado de São Paulo*, *O Globo*, and *Journal do Brasil*. On microfilm the collection possesses *Diario de Noticias* (1971–1976), *O Estado de São Paulo* (1940–1956), *O Globo* (1962–1983), and *Imprensa Popular* (1951–1958).

Over a thousand books cover recent events in Chile, especially the Frei, Allende, and Pinochet administrations. Also available are works on Christian democracy, recent political and economic history, and relations with Argentina and Bolivia. The collection houses files of the former Chilean Communist Party bimonthly *Principios*, its daily newspaper *El Siglo*, and the weekly *Vistazo*, in addition to nearly complete runs of the Socialist Party publication *Arauco*, the leftist *Punto Final*, and the pro-communist *Plan*. Currently received are the monthlies *Mensaje* (of Jesuit Robert Vekemans), *Estudios Sociales*, and *Realidad*, the weeklies *Ercilla*, *Qué Pasa*, *Vea*, and *El Mercurio* (airmail edition), and the dailies *La Nación*, *La Segunda*, and *La Tercera de la Hora*. Important microfilm files include *El Mercurio* (1960–1979), *La Nación* (1939–1973), and *Noticias de Última Hora* (1962–1964).

Works on Colombia number some one thousand titles, covering politics since the 1930s, especially guerrilla terrorism and the activities of the revolutionary Catholic priest Camilo Torres. The collection's file of the Jesuit monthly publication, *Revista Javeriana*, is current and starts with 1960. Also currently received are the bimonthlies *Desarrollo*, *Documentos Políticos*, and *El Espectador*, the weekly *Voz Proletaria*, and the dailies *El Siglo* and *El Tiempo*. A run of *El Siglo* for the period 1962–1982 is available on microfilm.

The 2,600 titles on contemporary Cuba, together with holdings of Cuban serials and newspapers, constitute the most important section of the Latin America collection. Included are works dealing with the revolution of 1895–1898, the political, social, and economic history of twentieth-century Cuba, and the writings of José Martí. Intensive collecting is carried on for works covering the Castro period, especially the writings and speeches of Castro and Guevara, making this part of the collection one of the most significant such holdings in the United States.

Of special interest is the documentation on the Cuban government's literacy campaign announced at the United Nations in October 1960 by Fidel Castro. Working with groups of 25 to 50 illiterates, some 280,000 teachers were trained in the use of the basic teaching manual. The Cuban government asserted by the end of the campaign that the illiteracy rate had been reduced to 3.9 percent, the lowest in the world.

The collection contains holdings of 172 Cuban periodical and newspaper titles, of which 48 are currently received. Complete or virtually complete sets are owned of *Cuba Socialista*, the Castro regime's theoretical monthly; *Verde Olivo*, the official journal of the Cuban Revolutionary Armed Forces; *Bohemia*, one of the most important general interest weekly magazines in Cuba; *Juventud Rebelde*, a daily published by the Union of Young Communists; *Nuestra Industria—Revista Económica* of the Ministry of Industry; and *Casa de las Américas*, a bimonthly political magazine aimed at the "revolutionary intellectual." (Positive microfilm copies of these titles are available from the Institution.) Other holdings include a set of the defunct *Obra Revolucionaria* and *El Orientador*, which contain speeches of government leaders, and titles covering cultural, economic, political, and social affairs. The current newspaper collection contains virtually complete sets of *Granma*, both the daily and weekly English-language editions and the daily Spanish-language edition. The file of *Trabajadores* extends from 1966. Microfilm holdings include the *Gaceta Oficial* (1964–1969), *Girón* (Matanzas, 1975–1979), *Havana Post* (1913–1960), *La Lucha* (1902–1913), *El Mundo* (1948–1969), *Noticias de Hoy* (1959–1965), *Revolución* (1959–1965), and *Diario de la Marina* (1949–1952, 1960).

Of the Latin American periodical titles published in the United States to be found in the collection, over fifty are sponsored by Cuban refugee groups. Many of these publications appeared for only one or a few issues. Currently received are the *Boletín* of the Comité Católico Cubano in New York and *RECE*, the journal of the Representación Cubana del Exilio in Miami. In addition to these current subscriptions, the library has several complete or significant files of Cuban refugee publications, including *Human Rights* and *Derechos Humanos*, both issued by the Committee of Cuban Youth Organizations in Exile, *Informe Sobre Cuba*, *Cuban Information Service*, the newspaper *Patria*, and *Latin American Report* (formerly *Free Cuba News*), issued by the Citizens Committee for a Free Cuba (all published in Miami). The Institution Archives house 58 manuscript boxes of records of the Citizens Committee for a Free Cuba, covering the period 1963–1974.

Documentation on the Dominican Republic includes significant coverage of the 31-year Trujillo era of violence and dissension. Current Dominican serials include the daily *El Nacional de Ahora*, dating from the first issue in September 1966, the daily *El Caribe* from 1976, and the weekly *Ahora* from 1965. *El Caribe* is available on microfilm for the years 1948–1973, as is the daily *Listín Diario* for the period 1964–1973.

The weekly publication of the Communist Party of Guadeloupe, *L'Etincelle*, and that of the Communist Party of Martinique, *Justice*, have both been received since the middle of 1964.

The recent repression in Guatemala is being carefully documented. *El Imparcial*, a daily from Guatemala City, is received on microfilm (379 reels covering the period since 1961). The collection also holds *Diario de Centroamérica* for 1956–1972.

The Institution's holdings of Guyanese serials include the *Daily Argosy* (1912–1941), *Guyana Graphic* (1966–1972, 1974–1975), *Guyana Chronicle* (1975–1977), and the *Evening Post* (1961, 1971–1973). The file of *Thunder*, the organ of

Only known copy of Fidel Castro biography by Luis Conte Agüero, who was commissioned by Castro to write an account of his life and work leading up to the Cuban Revolution. The book, although approved for publication by the Cuban leader, apparently displeased him on its release. Immediately after it appeared, the police were ordered to seize and destroy the plates and all copies.

Cheddi Jagan's People's Progressive Party, dates from 1964. In 1968 that publication changed from a weekly to a quarterly journal. Both the Jagan and the Burnham Marxist governments are documented by the collection, as is the 140-year-old border dispute with Venezuela.

The collection contains considerable material on modern Haiti, including the serials *Le Jour* (1962, 1964–1973), and *La Nation* (1946–1950). For Honduras, the library currently receives the daily *El Día* (59 reels of microfilm, 1961–). Jamaica is represented by *Jamaican Daily News* and *Struggle*, both currently received; the Bahamas by the *Nassau Daily Tribune* (1962, 1963–1966); and Bermuda by the *Royal Gazette* (1962–1968).

The Institution possesses about a thousand books on recent Mexican history, covering such subjects as the activities of revolutionary figures from Francisco Villa to Lázaro Cardenas, and battles, ideologies, and events of the Revolution. The current Mexican press is represented by the dailies *El Día* (1963–) and *Excelsior*. Issues of the latter dating since 1918 have been acquired on microfilm (some 950 reels). Currently received weeklies are *Oposición*, *Proceso*, and *Así es*, a publication of the Unified Socialist Party of Mexico. The library has a complete set of *Panoramas*, edited for three years by Victor Alba before it ceased publication in 1966.

Material on Nicaragua covers the Somoza and Sandinista regimes and includes the dailies *El Nuevo Diario* (1980–), *La Noticia* (1962–1966), and *Novedades* (1962–1978), the weekly *Barricada* (1983–), and the monthly *Patria Libre* (1980–).

U.S.-Panamanian relations are well covered as are the early history of the canal and the negotiations leading to the new canal treaties. Microfilm newspaper holdings include *La Estrella de Panamá* (1956–1972), *Matutino* (1975–), *El Panamá América* (1963–1970), and *Star and Herald* (1919–1929, 1940–1951, 1958–1964, 1975–). The Canal Zone supplies *Daily Digest*, *Panama Canal Review*, and *Panama Canal Spillway*.

There is a small collection on the Stroessner regime and Paraguay's participation in the Chaco War. Serial holdings include the dailies *ABC* (1976–), *Patria* (1962–1969), and *Última Hora* (1975–).

Daily newspapers from Peru are *La Prensa* (1962–) and *Tribuna* (1962 to 1970, when it ceased publication). The organ of the Peruvian Communist Party, *Unidad*, has been received since 1964. Other current serials are *Caretas* (1964–) and *Oiga* (1962–).

Material on Puerto Rico covers the period since 1898, when the island was ceded to the United States. Documentation of special interest covers the question of maintaining commonwealth status or of becoming a state of the United States. The daily newspaper *El Mundo*, from San Juan, has been received since 1962.

Of the 84 newspaper and serial titles from Uruguay in the collection, 17 are currently being received. Newspapers from that country include *El Popular* (1965 to October 1973, when it was suspended by the government) and *Época* (1962–1967). *El Socialista* (1911–1918), and its successor, *Justicia* (1919–1920), were organs of the Socialist Party of Uruguay. They cover the formative years of the Socialist Party and the communist party-to-be and are not known to be in any other library in the United States. Also received is a daily from Paysandú, *El Telégrafo* (1964–). Weeklies include the socialist *El Sol* (1945–1959, 1965–1966), and a complete file of *Marcha* (1939–1974), one of the most significant leftist publications in the hemisphere. The collection also has complete files of the monthlies *Oiga* (1964–1966) and *Estudios* (1956–1973), published by the Communist Party of Uruguay.

10 | THE NORTH AMERICAN AND INTERNATIONAL COLLECTIONS

Peter Duignan
Sara and Ira Lilick Curator

Although a major part of the library's acquisition effort focuses on foreign and regional materials, some of the most important collections have, since shortly after the founding of the Hoover War Library, been from and about North America, international organizations, and both public and private organizations devoted to the search for peace.

THE UNITED STATES

The United States Collection contains approximately 20,000 volumes of books, 2,500 periodical files, and 150 newspaper titles. In its development, the chief emphasis has been on the history of the United States during the two world wars, the Korean and Vietnam wars, and its foreign policy and relations with other world powers throughout the twentieth century. Domestic issues are also well documented.

The materials concerning the activities of the United States in World War I are voluminous. Public prosecution of the war on the home front is documented by such materials as the Edwin F. Gay Collection of letters, memorandums, and documents relating to the activities of the War Industries Board; the Alonzo E. Taylor Collection of materials concerning the activities of the War Trade Board, 1917–1919; and the dockets and records of the executive sessions of the National War Labor Board, 1918–1919. Books and pamphlets dealing with the U.S. military participation in World War I number approximately 2,200. These are complemented by manuscript reports and records concerning the activities of the American Expeditionary Forces in 1918, by many personal narratives by American combatants, and by official histories. American participation on the diplomatic front is dealt with in the papers of George D. Herron, unofficial adviser to President Wilson in 1917–1919, in the form of correspondence and interviews with leaders and statesmen of the United States and Europe on such subjects as the founding of the League of Nations, the Austrian and German peace moves, the civil war in Russia, and the establishment of the new governments in Europe; in the diary of Vance C. McCormick, a member of the American War Mission to the Inter-Allied Conference in London and Paris in 1917 and an adviser to President Wilson at the Paris Peace Conference in 1919; and in David Hunter

Peter Duignan, Senior Fellow

General Joseph Stilwell's private
notebooks, with his revealing and
caustic comments on men and
war, 1941–1944

Miller's *My Diary at the Conference of Paris, with Documents,* a 21-volume set containing minutes of the various councils and committees at the conference. The Hoover Institution copy is "No. 2" of a restricted edition of 40 copies.

The archives also holds seven manuscript boxes of materials prepared by the Division of Territorial, Economic and Political Intelligence (the House Inquiry), which prepared background information for the U.S. Delegation to the Paris Peace Conference.

The Institution's resources on the United States' participation in World War II include the papers of the late Joseph W. Stilwell, commanding general of U.S. forces in China, Burma, and India. This collection consists of more than 200 folders and contains diaries, a series of fifteen small notebooks for the period December 7, 1941, to December 5, 1944, and General Stilwell's "black and white" books, which contain his handwritten reflections on day-to-day events. The Robert D. Burhans Collection of documents, manuscripts, and maps delineates the activities of the First Special Service Force, 1941–1944. The papers of Maj. Gen. Frank S. Ross, former chief of transportation for the European Theater in World War II, treat the problem of logistics in the prosecution of the war. This collection contains a 21-volume "Historical

Report of the Transportation Corps in the European Theater of Operations" and 28 folio-sized sheets of executive minutes and personal correspondence. The Institution was also given the diaries of the late Professor Hubert G. Schenck, covering the years in which he served on General MacArthur's staff in Tokyo and as director of the Economic Cooperation Administration program in Taiwan. Civilian participation in the war is covered by the publications and records of political groups, committees, peace societies, relief organizations, churches, women's organizations, and business firms.

The archives of the America First Committee, acquired by the Hoover Institution in 1942 through the good offices of Gen. Robert E. Wood, consist of 124 cartons of administrative and financial records. These are extremely valuable records of the attitudes of U.S. citizens toward the participation of their country in World War II. The problem of the Japanese population on the Pacific Coast at the outbreak of World War II and its transfer to relocation centers is documented in the records of the War Relocation Authority, in correspondence carried on with the internees, in the files of newspapers published in eighteen relocation centers, and in collections donated by F. B. Duveneck, Alice Hays, Carey McWilliams, Henry W. Maier, Grace Nichols Pearson, Crane Rosenbaum, Margaret C. Sowers, Nathan van Patten, and Henriette B. Von Blon.

The methods of U.S. psychological warfare are illustrated by many collections of propaganda leaflets directed to enemy troops in both the Pacific and European theaters of war. The Hoover Institution owns a complete set of the over 400 pieces of propaganda produced in the Bern Office of the U.S. Office War Information.

The New Left Collection deserves special mention. In 1968, the Hoover Institution began collecting political research data on the American New Left movement in a joint effort with the Stanford University Libraries. The latter concentrated primarily on literary and cultural affairs, while Hoover, exercising the major collecting responsibility, stressed the acquisition of material dealing with other affairs of the movement and made a systematic effort to include in its collecting the position papers, policy statements, newspaper publications, and journals that best reflected the movement's history and development from 1960 to the present. The public catalog lists New Left under a large number of subject headings, such as "College students—political activity"; "Radicalism"; "Right and Left (Political Science)"; and the names of groups, such as "Student Non-Violent Coordinating Committee," "Students for a Democratic Society," and "Venceremos Brigade."

Not embraced within this New Left definition are associations—such as Progressive Labor, Young Socialist Alliance, and the DuBois Clubs—that function as extensions of traditional communist and Trotskyite parties. Although information in print, on film, and on tape is considerably more voluminous for the Left, the Hoover Institution has not confined itself to this extreme of radical politics, but is also collecting on the fringes of the Right. Here again, one criterion for acquisition is a particular organization's or movement's attitude toward actual revolution. The difficulty of such categorizing becomes daily more apparent, however, as self-styled anarchist and/or "libertarian" groups attempt a synthesis of rightist and leftist social criticism.

Canadian holdings cover both wars, relations with the United States, antigovernment activities and leftist movements. Materials on the Quebec independence movement are included within the Western European Collection because of its close ties with France.

As a depository library for League of Nations publications, the Hoover Library possesses nearly complete runs of major series such as the *Official Journal* (1920–1940), and the Records of the Plenary Meetings (1920–1940), and the Council Sessions (1920–1939), the *Annuaire de la Société des nations* (1920–1938), the Records of the Permanent Mandates Commission, and the Treaty Series (1920–1946) (all of which were taken over by the United Nations).

The monthly journal of the League, *Société des nations revue mensuelle documentaire* (1920–1926) can be consulted as can a special collection on the Saar plebiscite of 1934–1935 (see the Hartigan Collection in the archives).

The League documents also include complete documentation for the World Court, beginning with the *Procès verbaux* (1920) of the League Advisory Committee of Jurists on the Permanent Court of International Justice. The Hoover Institution holds only a small United Nations collection since Green Library is the official depository. The most important section consists of a full documentation of the San Francisco Conference of 1945. The Hoover holdings also include the continuation of the League of Nations Treaty Series now under United Nations auspices, and full records of the International Court of Justice.

The North American Collections include significant groups of material by and about pacifist organizations and other groups opposed to war. Three major peace collections are the library of Alfred Fried, Austrian jurist and pacificist, which consists of 2,500 books, pamphlets, and serial publications covering the first quarter of the twentieth century; the David Starr Jordan Collection, which includes not only correspondence and manuscript reports, but also 500 books and pamphlets relating to peace and peace organizations; and the Alice Park Collection. Mrs. Park was a delegate to the Peace Conference in the Hague in 1913 and a member of the Ford Peace Ship Expedition. Important materials in the Park Collection deal with con-

Herbert Hoover examining materials in the Paris Peace Conference Collection, which he personally assembled in Versailles as President Wilson's chief adviser on food relief and economic reconstruction of post–World War I Europe.

scientious objectors during World War I. Current collecting emphases in the North American Collection include communism and anticommunism, socialism in the United States, U.S. foreign relations, military policy, the CIA, and retrospective literature on military history, the internment of Japanese Americans in 1942, both world wars, the Korean and Vietnam wars, and the New Left. Regional organizations like the Council of Europe are represented by the agenda, minutes, and documents of their activities. (See Chapter 5 for description of this material.)

THE HERBERT HOOVER ARCHIVES

The Herbert Hoover Archives has an excellent assortment of papers from several organizations with which Mr. Hoover was affiliated. Among these are WWI relief agencies such as the Commission for Relief in Belgium and the American Relief Administration and several WWII groups created to promote relief for war victims. The papers of Mr. Hoover when he was secretary of commerce (1921–1928) and president of the United States (1929–1933) are at the Herbert Hoover Presidential Library in West Branch, Iowa, but photocopies of selected records are here at Stanford.

INTERNATIONAL ORGANIZATIONS

Among the earliest major international acquisitions were records of the Inter-Allied Food Council, which came to the library as a part of the record of Mr. Hoover's responsibilities as U.S. representative to the council; as chairman of the Supreme Economic Council, the American Relief Administration, and the Commission for Relief in Belgium; and as director general of relief in Europe.

The records of these relief organizations, many of them manuscript archives now in the Hoover Institution Archives, were the early nucleus of the library's collections of documents from international organizations. The biggest early international collection is of the documents produced for and by the Paris Peace Conference from January to September 1919. The Paris Peace Conference Collection includes minutes of the plenary sessions, the Supreme Council, the Council of Ten, the Council of Five, and the Council of Heads of Delegations, as well as several thousand supporting documents, including delegation propaganda published by the 53 national delegations to the conference.

The Commission for Relief in Belgium (CRB) was organized in October 1914, under the chairmanship of Mr. Hoover, to purchase, transport, and supervise the distribution of food and other commodities for the relief of the population of those regions of Belgium and northern France occupied by the German armies. The CRB was disbanded in 1919.

The CRB archives contain the files of its offices in Antwerp, Brussels, London, New York, Paris, Rotterdam, and Washington, D.C., and include the commission's diplomatic correspondence with governments; the reports of field workers; its shipping, accounting, and administrative records; and its general reports on conditions in Belgium and northern France.

The American Relief Administration (ARA) was designated by President Wilson in 1919 to administer relief abroad after the armistice of World War I. The ARA administered relief in 24 countries, including Soviet Russia. During the period of its activity, 1919–1923, ARA offices were established in Paris, London, New York, Washington, Rotterdam, Hamburg, Stockholm, Copenhagen, Danzig, Belgrade, Trieste, Saloniki, and Constantinople; relief missions were set up in Finland, Estonia, Latvia, Lithuania, Poland, Czechoslovakia, Germany, Austria, Hungary, Romania, Yugoslavia, Turkey, and Soviet Russia—where district missions were maintained in the capitals of most of the provinces of the Russian Socialist Federated Soviet Republic, the Ukraine, the Crimea, and the North Caucasus.

The ARA files consist of the reports, the correspondence, and the financial, commodity, and other records of its various offices and missions; these deal chiefly with food, economic matters, transport, public health, and finance.

The Hoover also holds records of closely connected organizations such as the European Coal Commission, European Technical Advisers, and the Supreme Economic Council. The Supreme Economic Council, established in February 1919, had representatives of ministerial rank from France, Italy, Great Britain, the United States, and, somewhat later, Belgium; it was authorized to replace existing inter-Allied bodies and to handle economic and relief questions of the principal Allied and associated powers.

The U.S. Food Administration was created in August 1917, with Herbert Hoover as food administrator, to provide for the supply, distribution, and conservation of food within the total war effort. Although the major part of its records are in the National Archives in Washington, D.C., the papers of Mr. Hoover and many of the officials of the Food Administration are in the Hoover Archives. Included are the final report on the Food Administration, in three volumes, and documents of the Allied Provisions Export Commission.

Reports on food conditions in Germany in 1914–1916 and materials of the French Ministère du Ravitaillement and the British Ministry of Food and auxiliary bodies are preserved in the Hoover archives. Papers of other WWI relief organizations of the war period are also in the archives. These include the files of the American National Red Cross and some papers of the Near East Relief Committee.

Records of several organizations created to promote relief for famine-stricken populations during and after World War II are also in the Hoover Archives. These include reports of the Finnish Relief Fund, the Polish Relief Commission, and the National Committee on Food for the Small Democracies.

In 1946 President Truman asked Mr. Hoover to advise on means of coping with the famine created by World War II. Mr. Hoover visited the principal nations affected to evaluate their minimum needs and to discover possible additional food resources. The Hoover Archives' files contain memorandums, diaries, and notes written by Mr. Hoover and several people who accompanied him on this trip to 38 countries between March and June of 1946 and a trip to Germany and Austria in 1947.

Mr. Hoover's papers relating to his work in world relief and on the reorganization of the U.S. government (done by the Hoover Commissions of 1947–1949 and of 1953–1955) are in the archives. Correspondence, interoffice memorandums, and reports are included in the collection of the Hoover Commissions.

In addition to the beautiful treasures housed in the Lou Henry Hoover Memorial Room, the archives have Mrs. Hoover's correspondence for the period of the Hoovers' White House residency.

Many individuals who have worked with or admired Mr. Hoover have given their papers to the Hoover Archives. There is not room enough to list the 150 individuals who have made such contributions, but mention of a selected few may indicate the breadth of material contained in these personal collections:

> Hugh Gibson. Mr. Gibson was U.S. minister to Poland in 1919–1924 and to Switzerland in 1924–1927. He was also ambassador to Belgium in 1927–1933 and in 1937–1938 and ambassador to Brazil in 1933–1937. His papers were opened in 1971.

These embroidered flour sacks are by-products of the World War I work of the Commission for Relief in Belgium, headed by Herbert Hoover. From empty flour sacks, Belgian women created lampshade covers, pillow cases, and countless other articles to be sold to raise money for relief work. Many of the sacks show the original printing of American flour manufacturers as well as notes of thanks to the American people, from whom most of the relief came. In gratitude for shipments of food, Belgian women embroidered the original printing on the flour sacks.

Robert A. Theobald. Admiral Theobald was chief of staff, U.S. Pacific Fleet, 1939. The collection contains correspondence about his controversial book, *The Final Secret of Pearl Harbor*, and classified material that is in a restricted category.

Payson J. Treat. Mr. Treat was professor of history at Stanford. The collection contains, among other items, articles, manuscripts, letters, and typescripts of diplomatic correspondence dealing primarily with China and Japan in the last half of the nineteenth century.

Ray Lyman Wilbur. Stanford's third president served as secretary of the interior in President Hoover's Cabinet from 1929 to 1933. His papers as secretary of the interior are housed in the archives.

Woodrow Wilson. There is an important and highly significant collection of correspondence between Mr. Hoover and Mr. Wilson covering the years 1914–1920.

For descriptions of more recent gifts of archival materials, for example, the papers of President Ronald Reagan, George P. Shultz, Caspar W. Weinberger, Jay Lovestone, and Sidney Hook, see Chapter 11.

11 | THE ARCHIVES

Charles G. Palm
Archivist

Charles G. Palm, Archivist

Over the past half-century, the Hoover Institution developed—hand in hand with its world-renowned library for advanced research—one of the largest collections of archival materials on twentieth-century social, political, and economic change held by any private organization in the world. The 3,723 archival and manuscript collections, consisting of 32 million items, include portrait paintings of Catherine the Great and Emperor Alexander I of Russia, tsarist secret police reports on Russian revolutionaries, motion picture film of Leo Tolstoy in 1907, drafts of Franklin D. Roosevelt's 1932 presidential campaign speeches, letters by Winston Churchill, 68,000 revolutionary and wartime propaganda posters, underground literature, photographs of Mao Tse-tung in 1937, Heinrich Himmler's diaries, and other priceless historical documents.

The archival and manuscript holdings cover most geographical areas, including North America, Eastern Europe and Russia, Western Europe, East and Southeast Asia, Latin America, Africa, and the Middle East. There are records of organizations, papers of individuals, special collections, manuscripts accessioned as single units, and audiovisual materials, as well as microfilm and other copies of collections held privately or located at other repositories. In general, they document the causes of war, propaganda, and military history; wartime dislocation and relief; underground resistance movements and governments-in-exile; political ideologies, especially communism, fascism, and nazism; revolutionary movements and liberation groups; colonialism; international organizations, conferences, and diplomacy; peace negotiations and pacifism; education; and political, economic, and social change in numerous countries.

Holdings vary by geographical area. Three areas—Western Europe, Eastern Europe and Russia/USSR, and North America (primarily the United States)—account for about 25 percent of the total each. Materials on East and Southeast Asia constitute 8 percent of the total; on Africa and international organizations, 5 percent each; and on Latin America and the Middle East, 2 percent each.

Materials on the United States dominate the North American section. They relate to politics and government since 1919; diplomacy; military involvement in both world wars, Korea, and Vietnam; communism and internal subversion; journalism and public opinion; and economic and social problems.

Invaluable materials on U.S. politics and government are abundantly present in the collections. Foremost among these are the papers of President Herbert Hoover, including records of the Hoover Commission on the Organization of the Executive Branch of Government, 1947–1949 and 1953–1955. The papers of Raymond Moley (editor of *Newsweek*), who served as political adviser to Franklin D. Roosevelt and who coined the phrase "New Deal," provide substantial documentation on the 1932 campaign and origins of New Deal policies. Papers of other prominent political and government leaders include those of George P. Shultz (secretary of labor, 1969–1970; director of the Office of Management and Budget, 1970–1972; secretary of the treasury, 1972–1974; and secretary of state, 1982–), Caspar W. Weinberger (secretary of health, education and welfare, 1973–1975; secretary of defense, 1981–), Carla A. Hills (secretary of housing and urban development, 1975–1977), Dixy Lee Ray (chairman of the Atomic Energy Commission, 1973–1975; and governor of the State of Washington, 1977–1981), Denison Kitchel (general director of the Republican Presidential Campaign, 1964), Congressman Paul N. McCloskey, Senator S. I. Hayakawa, and California Governor George Deukmejian, during the period that he served as state assemblyman and senator (1963–1979), and attorney general of California (1979–1983).

The gubernatorial papers of President Ronald Reagan constitute the single largest collection in the archives. More than a year before he left office as governor of California, efforts were made to organize his papers and collect material from key staff members as well as copies of records of state agencies. The Reagan papers include legislative bill files, cabinet minutes and memorandums, correspondence, budget and financial records, speeches, press conference transcripts, press releases, sound recordings, films, and videotapes. The collection documents many of the fundamental problems that have beset California and the United States since the mid-1960s and governmental policy responses to them. Future scholars will find in-depth coverage of such issues as campus unrest, welfare reform, crime and law enforcement, drug abuse, economy in government, tax reform, federal-state relations, and environmental concerns. New materials are continually being added to the gubernatorial files. Among the most significant additions are the oral history interviews on the Reagan gubernatorial period produced by the Bancroft Library Regional Oral History Office at the University of California at Berkeley with assistance from the Hoover Institution.

The Reagan Collection also contains papers of the 1976 and 1980 presidential campaigns, as well as records of the Office of the President Elect. The 1980 campaign and transition files occupy some 500 linear feet of shelf space. Steps were taken during the campaign to save materials for the Reagan Collection at the Hoover Institution, and all campaign officials were asked to set aside their papers for the collection. One campaign worker was assigned to accompany the candidate at all public appearances and to record all of his formal and informal remarks. The result is a comprehensive file of hundreds of sound recordings of President Reagan's speeches and comments. In addition to the records of the Reagan/Bush Campaign Committee Headquarters, the Hoover Institution was successful in acquiring materials from related organizations, including Campaign '80 (the public relations firm for the cam-

UNITED STATES

Memorandum by Raymond Moley, one of Franklin D. Roosevelt's "brain trust," in which the phrase "New Deal" first appeared. The memo was written at Hyde Park in May 1932 and outlines the major policies of Roosevelt's first term.

In preparing his 1981 Inaugural Address, President-elect Reagan was reminded by a friend of a quotation from a diary found on the body of a young soldier killed in World War I, Private Martin Treptow. Unable to verify the authenticity of the quotation, he was advised not to use it. Verification came from the Hoover Institution. Among the 68,000 posters in the archives was an original World War I Liberty Loan poster depicting Private Treptow and his pledge: "I will fight cheerfully and do my utmost as if the whole issue of the struggle depended on me alone." The concluding remarks of President Reagan's Inaugural Address included this quotation. (cont'd.)

A duplicate of the poster was presented to the president at a White House Cabinet meeting as a gift of the Hoover Institution. In congratulating the staff on this find, President Reagan said: "I have reason to know nothing is impossible to the Hoover Institution."

On September 3, 1941, Stanley K. Hornbeck, chief adviser in the Department of State on Far Eastern Affairs, wrote this report predicting that Japan would not attack the United States "within the next three months." He was right by four days. This original report is part of the Stanley Hornbeck Collection, totaling some 600 manuscript boxes of materials relating to American diplomacy in the Far East.

paign), the California headquarters of the Reagan/Bush Campaign Committee, Californians for Reagan (the state campaign organization), Decision Making Information (the private polling firm for the Reagan campaign), Citizens for the Republic, and the Presidential Inaugural Committee.

Holdings on U.S. diplomatic and military history are extensive. American activities in the Far East are especially well documented. The papers of Stanley K. Hornbeck (the chief adviser on the Far East in the Department of State, 1928–1944) contain over 350,000 items covering nearly two decades of U.S. foreign policy in the Pacific. Additional U.S. diplomatic files on the Far East are those of Julean H. Arnold (commercial attaché in China, 1919–1940), Eugene H. Dooman (assistant secretary of state for Far Eastern affairs, 1944–1945), R. Allen Griffin (deputy chief of the Economic Cooperation Administration China Aid Mission, 1948–1949), Maxwell Hamilton (chief of the Division of Far Eastern Affairs, 1937–1943), and Jay Calvin Huston (consul in China, 1917–1932). Important periods of Indonesian history are recorded in the papers of Howard P. Jones (ambassador to Indonesia, 1958–1965), whose term included the abortive communist coup of 1965, and Guy Pauker (RAND Corporation specialist on Indonesia).

Coverage of World War II military action in the Far East is comprehensive. In her book, *Stilwell and the American Experience in China*, Barbara Tuchman relied heavily on the Joseph W. Stilwell Collection. General Albert C. Wedemeyer, who replaced Stilwell as commanding general of the China-Burma-India theater in 1944, donated his extensive collection to the Hoover Institution. These papers cover Wedemeyer's entire career, including his service as a war planner on the Army General Staff (1941–1943), as assistant chief of staff to Admiral Lord Mountbatten in the Southeast Asia Command (1943–1944), and as commanding general of U.S. forces in China and chief of staff to Generalissimo Chiang Kai-shek (1944–1946).

Other U.S. military figures who served in key positions in the Far East and whose papers the archives houses include Lt. Gen. Claire Lee Chennault (head of the Flying Tiger volunteer group in China and adviser to Chiang Kai-shek), Adm. Charles M. Cooke (deputy chief of naval operations, 1944–1945), Adm. Raymond A. Spruance (commander in chief of the Pacific fleet, 1945–1946), and Gen. Robert C. Richardson (commanding general of U.S. Army forces in the Pacific, 1943–1946).

Both the Korean and Vietnam wars are extensively covered. The papers of Adm. Charles Turner Joy (chief U.N. negotiator at the Korean military armistice talks at Panmunjom) contain a three-volume diary detailing his strategies and frustrations while negotiating the end of the Korean War. The diary was published by the Hoover Institution as a volume in Hoover Archival Documentaries series with a foreword by Gen. Matthew B. Ridgway.

Maj. Gen. Edward G. Lansdale's papers document the early period of the war in Vietnam. An OSS officer during World War II, Lansdale was a leader after the war in developing tactics to counter communist insurgency. His papers, including diaries, confidential reports, and prisoner interrogations, relate to his role as head of a secret 1954–1955 U.S. military intelligence mission in Vietnam to assist anticommunists after the fall of Dien Bien Phu, as special envoy of President Eisenhower during the rise to power of Ngo Dinh Diem in 1954–1956, as adviser to Defense Secretary Robert S. McNamara during the creation of a U.S. counterinsurgency capability in Vietnam, and as special assistant to Ambassadors Lodge and Bunker in Vietnam during the 1960s.

American diplomatic and military papers on other areas of the world are equally impressive. Among the diplomatic holdings are the collections of Vance C. McCormick (adviser to President Wilson at the Paris Peace Conference), Hugh Gibson (ambassador to Poland, and chairman of the 1930 London Naval Conference), Joseph E. Jacobs (ambassador to Czechoslovakia, 1948–1949, and Poland, 1955–1957), Robert D. Murphy (deputy undersecretary of state, 1953–1959), Warren R. Burgess (ambassador to the North Atlantic Treaty Organization, 1957–1961), Robert C. Hill (ambassador to Costa Rica, El Salvador, Mexico, Spain, and Argentina), James B. Donovan (U.S. negotiator of both the Rudolf Abel–Gary Powers exchange with the USSR, 1962–1964, and the Cuban prisoner exchange following the Bay of Pigs invasion), Philip D. Sprouse (ambassador to Cambodia, 1962–1964), and William R. Kintner (president, Foreign Policy Research Institute, 1976–).

Other U.S. military holdings include the papers of William S. Graves (commander of the American Expeditionary Forces in Siberia, 1918–1920), Truman Smith (U.S. military attaché to Germany, 1935–1939, who warned U.S. officials of the German military buildup during the 1930s), Frederick L. Anderson (deputy commander of operations, Strategic Air Forces in Europe, 1944–1945), Robert T. Frederick (commanding general of First Special Service Force during World War II), M. Preston Goodfellow (deputy director, Office of Strategic Services, 1942–1946), Walter C. Short (commanding general of the Hawaiian Department, 1941), David M. Shoup (commandant, Marine Corps, 1960–1963), John R. Chaisson (chief of staff of the U.S. Marine Corps, 1971–1972), and Lloyd M. Bucher (commander of the USS *Pueblo* when it was captured by the North Koreans).

More than sixty collections of journalistic papers provide substantial documentation on U.S. public opinion and intellectual history. These include the papers of Mark Sullivan (columnist for the *New York Herald-Tribune*, 1923–1952, and author of *Our Times*), Herbert Solow (editor of *Fortune*, 1945–1964), Lewis H. Lapham (managing editor and editor, *Harper's Magazine*, 1971–1981), John C. O'Laughlin (publisher of the *Army-Naval Journal*, 1933–1948), Frederick C. Nossal (Far East correspondent who opened the first Western newsbureau in mainland China), Karl H. von Wiegand (Hearst newspaper foreign correspondent who had exclusive interviews with many nazi leaders during the 1930s), and Gerald Lee Warren (deputy press secretary to Presidents Nixon and Ford).

No treatment of American intellectual life since the end of World War II would be complete without reference to Nobel Laureate Milton Friedman and one of the world's most distinguished physicists, Edward Teller, both of whose collections are in the Hoover Institution Archives.

In addition to Milton Friedman, papers of other major American economists in the archives include Fritz Machlup, Benjamin S. Rogge, Dan Throop Smith, Murray L. Weidenbaum, Roger A. Freeman, and William A. Niskanen. The Hoover Institution Archives is also the repository for the files of the Mont Pelerin Society, an international organization of economists, public figures, and journalists for the study of free-market economics.

Documentation on American radicalism is equally extensive and includes the papers of Jay Lovestone and Bertram D. Wolfe (among the founders of the communist party in the United States) and Benjamin Gitlow (cofounder of the Communist Labor Party). The papers of Lovestone, Wolfe, and socialists Sidney Hook and Joseph Freeman (editor of *New Masses* and *Partisan Review*) are also rich sources for materials on the undercurrents of U.S. intellectual history throughout this past half-century. More recently, the Hoover Institution has developed a voluminous New Left collection, focusing on the student disorders of the late 1960s and the anti–Vietnam War protests.

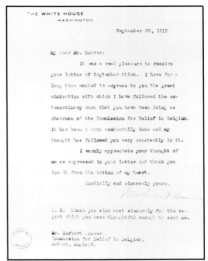

Letter of appreciation from President Woodrow Wilson to Herbert Hoover for his relief work in Belgium. Some 107 original Wilson letters are contained in the Hoover Papers.

WESTERN EUROPE

When the Russians occupied Berlin in 1945, they went through the official German archives, emptying papers on the floor and shipping to Russia the steel filing cabinets that had contained them. What they left behind, among other records, were the diaries of Joseph Goebbels, minister of propaganda for the Third Reich. The 7,100 pages of diaries were retrieved from the rubble by an amateur junk collector and sold as scrap paper. After passing through several hands, they came into the possession of Frank E. Mason, a correspondent and friend of Herbert Hoover. At Mr. Hoover's request, the original diaries were placed at the Hoover Institution. Covering the period 1942–1943, the Goebbels diaries document the major events and policy decisions of the Third Reich and constitute an invaluable source for the study of wartime Germany.

In the West European section, holdings are strongest for Germany, France, Belgium, Spain, and Italy. German subjects covered include the 1918–1919 revolution, the rise of nazism, the Third Reich and its leaders, anti-nazi resistance, and the Allied occupation after World War II. The French collections emphasize interwar diplomacy, the Vichy regime, World War II resistance, trade unionism, the Fifth Republic, the Algerian war, and the 1968 student revolt. Additional subject areas within the West European Collection are war propaganda, relief operations in Belgium, the German occupation of Belgium in both world wars, the Spanish Civil War, Italian fascism, the rise of the British Labour Party, and the Irish revolutionary movement.

The letters and diaries of Rosa Luxemburg, a leader of the German Social Democratic Party and cofounder of the German Communist Party, document the radical revolutionary movements in Europe during the first two decades of the twentieth century. Holdings on Germany during the Third Reich are particularly strong and include original diaries of Joseph Goebbels (minister of propaganda), the diaries and personal photo album of Heinrich Himmler (chief of the SS), the personal photo album of Foreign Minister Joachim von Ribbentrop, as well as one of the only existing complete copies of the Gestapo arrest list for Great Britain, containing the names of all those in England whom the Gestapo intended to arrest following a successful German invasion. The archives also holds over 300 motion picture films of German newsreels for the period 1939–1942.

Resistance to the nazi government is documented in the papers of Christopher T. Emmet (founder of the Christian Committee to Boycott Nazi Germany), Karl B. Frank (socialist and anti-nazi leader), Kurt R. Grossman (anti-nazi author and journalist), and Franz Schoenberner (editor of *Simplicissimus*, 1929–1933). There are substantial holdings of materials on various underground resistance movements in most of the occupied countries. The René de Chambrun Collection concerns the French government of Marshal Pétain and Pierre Laval during the German occupation.

The archives also include the papers of many diplomatic, political, and military

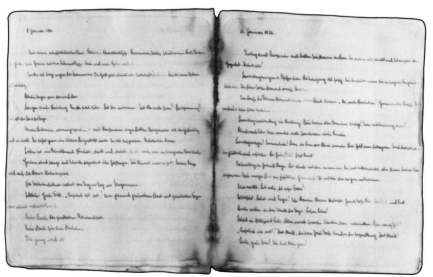
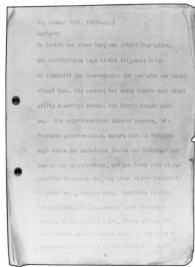

Diaries of nazi propaganda chief Joseph Goebbels

Calendar diary of Rosa Luxemburg, German revolutionary and leader of the communist insurrection that briefly took over Germany at the end of World War I. The calendar entries were written during her wartime imprisonment and contain many personal notes, some of which have not been deciphered.

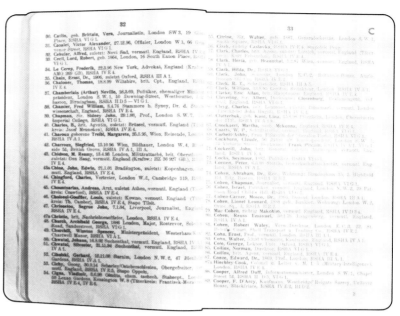

One of the few remaining copies of the "Gestapo Arrest List," showing the names of British and European émigré leaders slated for arrest by the Nazis after the expected invasion of England; names include Winston Churchill and Neville Chamberlain. There are blank pages for adding more names.

leaders from Western Europe. The papers of Louis Loucheur (French minister of commerce, 1922–1924), Gaston Bergery (French ambassador to the USSR, 1941), and Yves Godard (director of police in Algeria, 1958–1960, an organizer of the anti-Gaullist Secret Army Organization, 1961–1962), are particularly noteworthy. The papers of Gen. Pierre Gallois, a leading French military expert, deputy to NATO Commander Lauris Norstad (1954–1957), and General de Gaulle's closest military adviser, constitute a major new collection on postwar strategic defense of Western Europe.

Some of the main currents of European intellectual history can be traced through the diaries of Henri Barbé (leading official of the French Communist Party, 1920–1934), papers of Stéphane J. V. Lauzanne (editor of *Le Matin*, 1920–1940), the Georges Lefranc papers (prominent member of the French trade union movement, 1930–1973), diaries of British journalist and intellectual Malcolm Muggeridge, and the original World Wars I and II cartoons and drawings of Dutch artist Louis Raemaekers.

Leaflets, proclamations, pamphlets, and ephemera of all kinds have always been a strength of the Hoover Institution holdings, and this is especially true of the Western European collection. During revolutions and other periods of intense political agitation, Hoover collectors or their agents were on the scene gathering the fugitive materials that appear only briefly and in limited numbers. Subjects that are particularly well documented are the occupation of Belgium during World War I, Berlin during and immediately after the 1918–1919 revolution, the German elections following World War I, communism and socialism in Great Britain during the 1930s, World Wars I and II propaganda on both sides, the French Fifth Republic, and the French and German student revolts of 1968.

The Hoover Institution's collection of Spanish Civil War materials is perhaps the largest of its kind in the United States. The core of this collection consists of the Burnett and Gladys Bolloten archives and printed materials. Bolloten started collecting sources while working as a United Press correspondent during the war. After leaving Spain in 1938, Bolloten moved to Mexico, where he began his lifelong commitment to the study of the Civil War. Over a period of several years, he and his wife, Gladys, managed to obtain documents from over a dozen countries, including Great Britain, France, Germany, and several Latin American republics (where thousands of Spaniards had taken refuge following the war), eventually amassing over 2,000 books and pamphlets, 12,000 bound newspapers, over 67 boxes of documents, ten large scrapbooks, and 60,000 frames of microfilm (made from hundreds of newspapers, journals, and political pamphlets).

In addition to the Bolloten collection, the archives holds several important collections relating to the Spanish Civil War, including those of Milly Bennett (an American correspondent who was in Spain between 1936 and 1937) and Joaquín Maurín (a founder-member of the controversial Partido Obrero de Unificación Marxista, POUM). Maurín's papers are a particularly valuable resource for the study of the Spanish communist movement during the 1920s and 1930s.

RUSSIA, THE SOVIET UNION, AND EASTERN EUROPE

Russian and East European materials are among the most significant of the archival holdings. They document the tsarist regime between 1880 and 1917 (especially diplomacy), revolution and counterrevolution, war relief, civil war, émigré movements, and the USSR. Holdings on Poland are also prominent, especially those concerning foreign affairs between the world wars and the World War II government-in-exile (London). Materials on other East European countries, notably Yugoslavia, Romania, Czechoslovakia, Hungary, Bulgaria, and the Baltic states, primarily concern the interwar, World War II, and immediate postwar periods.

The Hoover Institution Archives possesses over 250 individual archives on Imperial Russia and the Provisional Government period, constituting the most significant accumulation of documentation on pre-1917 Russia anywhere outside of that country. The Nicolas de Basily Room is the centerpiece of the collection. It is the result of the generosity of Mrs. Lascelle de Basily, who created this memorial to her husband, Nicolas de Basily, a Russian diplomat and statesman who left Russia after the revolution of 1917. The room contains his extraordinary collection of portraits of Russian emperors, courtiers, diplomats, and statesmen; landscape paintings; miniatures; and other works of art. Most remarkable are the portraits of reigning sovereigns: Empress Elizabeth, Empress Catherine II (Catherine the Great), her husband Peter III, their son Emperor Paul I, and Paul's son Emperor Alexander I.

Original manuscript materials on the Imperial Russian family are especially noteworthy. There are fifteen manuscript boxes of letters written by Mariia Feodorovna (empress-consort of Alexander III, emperor of Russia) to Alexandra (queen-consort of Edward VII, king of Great Britain), letters of Georgiĭ Mikhailovich (grand duke of Russia), and letters of Kseniia Aleksandrovna (grand duchess of Russia and sister of Nicholas II, emperor of Russia). Other nobility represented in the collection include Princess Barbara Dolgorouky, Baroness Maria F. Meiendorf, the Cherkasskiĭ family, and the Obolenskiĭ family. Vasili Romanov, nephew of Nicholas II and prince of Russia, is an honorary curator at the Hoover Institution.

Diplomatic and political papers on pre-1917 Russia are extensive. They include among others the records of the Russian embassies in Paris (1917–1924) and Wash-

At 3:00 in the afternoon of March 15, 1917, Tsar Nicholas II stepped to the window and looked out for a while at the snow-covered Russian landscape. Turning to his generals, he made the sign of the cross and declared that he had decided to abdicate. The abdication document, which his generals had just presented to him, was written by Nicolas A. de Basily, at the time chief of the Diplomatic Division at Army headquarters at Mogilev. Basily kept all of the drafts of this historic document, and after his death in 1963, Mrs. Lascelle de Basily, his widow, donated them to the Hoover Institution, together with a large collection of other archival materials.

An original holograph letter from Lenin, written in 1912 to a group of Russian social democrats in New York City claiming that he had not misspent the money they had contributed to the cause (from the Boris I. Nicolaevsky Collection)

ington, D.C. (1900–1933); records of the Russian consulates and legations in various German cities (1828–1914); the Paris files of the Imperial Russian secret police (Okhrana); as well as papers of numerous Imperial Russian and Provisional Government officials, such as Nicolas Alexandrovich de Basily (deputy director of the Chancellery of Foreign Affairs, 1911–1914; and member of the Council of the Ministry of Foreign Affairs, 1917), Sergeĭ Dmitrievich Sazonov (minister of foreign affairs, 1910–1916), Vasiliĭ Alekseevich Maklakov (ambassador of the Provisional Government to France, 1917–1924), Dimitriĭ Nikolaevich Liubimov (chief of staff of the Ministry of Interior, 1902–1906), Mikhaiľ Vasil'evich Alekseev (chief of staff of the Russian Imperial Army, 1915–1917), Sergeĭ Nikolaievich Pototskiĭ (major general, Russian Imperial Army), and Dimitriĭ Grigorevich Shcherbachev (general, Imperial Russian Army).

The tsarist secret police, known as the Okhrana, maintained an office at the Imperial Russian Embassy in Paris to monitor the activities of revolutionaries who were trying to topple the tsar. The files of this organization are a unique source on the internal operations of the revolution. Covering the period 1883 to 1917, the files include transcripts of intercepted letters from suspected revolutionaries, police photographs, code books, over 40,000 reports from 450 agents and informers operating in twelve countries, and dossiers on all of the major revolutionary figures.

Another extremely valuable collection on revolutionary Russia consists of rare materials assembled by Boris I. Nicolaevsky, who was a prominent Menshevik during the Russian Revolution. Following the revolution, he emigrated to Paris and was later described by Lenin's biographer Louis Fischer as "undoubtedly the greatest expert in the Western world on Soviet politics and Marx." His collection contains rich documentation about the party and prerevolutionary Russia, including letters and papers from Trotsky, Lenin, Bakunin, Herzen, Lavrov, Plekhanov, Akselrod, Martov, Tseretelli, and Chernov. In the Trotsky file are approximately three hundred letters exchanged between Leon Trotsky and Leon Sedov, Trotsky's son and closest political collaborator. The letters, which were recently added to the collection following the death of Nicolaevsky's widow, cover the period 1931–1938 and reflect Trotsky's thoughts and recollections during a crucial period of political upheaval in the Soviet Union, when Stalin purged the communist system of Trotsky's influence.

Because of the richness and value of its collections, the Hoover Institution was the first place visited by Alexander Solzhenitsyn during his first trip to the United States in 1975, following his exile from the Soviet Union. At that time he stated the following: "The documentation I have examined at the Hoover Institution is outstanding and, in many respects, unique. Materials dated prior to 1922 are especially well represented here. It is the kind of original source material that the Soviets, in order to rewrite history, either destroyed or refuse to make available to scholars. I look forward to utilizing your special collections and library materials for the rest of my life."

The Herman Axelbank Film Collection on Russia (1890–1970) contains 250,000 feet of film documenting activities of the tsar, his family, and his associates; the two Russian revolutions of 1917 and their leaders; the Provisional and Soviet governments; Soviet military forces in World War II; and Russian culture and economy. It includes film of the March 1921 Kronstadt mutiny, the first purge trials of Social Revolutionaries in June 1922, and many political figures of the time (Kerensky, Lenin, Trotsky, Zinoviev, Kamenev, Stalin). According to one film expert, it is "undoubtedly the largest and most valuable film collection devoted to the subject of revolutionary and prerevolutionary Russia in the Western hemisphere, and probably in the Western world."

The Russian Civil War period is well represented in the archives by the papers of Mikhail Nikolaevich de Giers (chief diplomatic representative of the Vrangel' Government), Pëtr Nikolaevich Vrangel' (commander of the White Russian Volunteer Army, 1920), Nikolai Nikolaevich Iudenich (commander of the White Russian Northwest Expedition, 1918–1920), Boris Vladimirovich Heroys (chief of the White Russian Military Mission to London), and Evgeniĭ Karlovich Miller (chief military representative of General Vrangel' in Paris).

Apart from the unique tsarist secret police files and the Axelbank film collection, the archives holds extensive documentation on the communist seizure of power in the countries of East Central Europe and the Baltic states after World War II. These materials include, for example, some 43,000 certificates issued to prisoners released from forced labor camps in the Gulag Archipelago.

The Institution's archival and curatorial staff continue to collect material on communist movements in all countries, including the Soviet Union. This primary source material is utilized by scholars from throughout the world and the contributors to the Institution's annual *Yearbook on International Communist Affairs*. These files also attract government officials, representatives of the media, and others who seek the kind of information that remains unavailable elsewhere.

Since 1980, the Hoover Institution has undertaken a major program to collect documentation on the Solidarity movement in Poland. The library now possesses one of the strongest collections in the country, with nearly 200 serial titles, dozens of monographs, and hundreds of pieces of organizational materials, minutes of meetings, communiqués, correspondence, and posters as well as a complete videotape of the 1980 Gdansk general strike negotiations between Solidarity and the Polish government.

Polish holdings in general constitute one of the major strengths of the archives. When the Soviet Union established a communist government in Poland after World War II, the Polish government-in-exile in London deposited over 500 linear feet of official records at the Hoover Institution, including files of its embassies in Paris, Moscow, Lisbon, and Washington, D.C. In addition, the archives obtained the papers of Ignacy Jan Paderewski (Polish premier, 1919, and internationally acclaimed pianist), Stansiław Mikołajczyk (Polish prime minister, London government-in-exile,

Photo from the personal album of German foreign minister Joachim von Ribbentrop, showing Stalin and Ribbentrop at the signing of the Russo-German Nonaggression Pact of 1939, which led to the German and Soviet invasion of Poland and to World War II

1943–1944), Władysław Anders (commander in chief of the Polish Armed Forces in the USSR), Leon Mitkiewicz (chief of intelligence of the Polish Army), August Zaleski (foreign minister, 1926–1932, and president, government-in-exile, 1947–1972), among others.

The other areas of Central and Eastern Europe are well covered. For the Baltic states region, many materials pertaining to Latvia, Lithuania, and Estonia between World Wars I and II were collected, including the papers of Jules Feldmans (Latvian delegate to the League of Nations, 1930), Felix Cielens (Latvian minister of foreign affairs, 1926–1928, and Minister to France, 1933–1940), Kaarel R. Pusta (Estonian minister of foreign affairs, 1924–1925), Vilis Sumans (Latvian minister to France, 1926–1934), Eduardas Turauskas (Lithuanian diplomat and journalist), as well as the files of the Latvian embassy in Stockholm, 1917–1939, and the Latvian Central Committee, the principal émigré organization during and after World War II.

Czechoslovakian holdings include the papers of Štefan Osuský (ambassador to Great Britain and France, 1918–1940), Juraj Slavik (ambassador to the United States, 1946–1949), Joseph Lettrich (president of the National Slovak Council and Slovak Democratic Party, 1945–1948), and Ladislav K. Feierabend (minister of finance for the government-in-exile in London, 1941–1945). For Romania and Hungary, there are the papers of Nicolas Titulescu (Romanian minister of foreign affairs, 1927–1928 and 1932–1936), Ion George Duca (Romanian minister of foreign affairs, 1922–1926), Constantin Visoianu (Romanian minister of foreign affairs, 1945–1946), Rusztem Vámbéry (Hungarian minister to the United States, 1946–1948), and files of the Hungarian embassies in Moscow, Madrid, and Bern.

Bulgaria and Yugoslavia are well covered in the papers of Georgi M. Dimitrov (president of the Bulgarian National Committee), Dimitri Stanchov (Bulgarian minister of foreign affairs, 1906–1908; minister to Paris, 1908–1915, and to London, 1920–1924), Božidar Purić (premier, Yugoslav government-in-exile, London, 1944), Dragiša Cvetković (prime minister of Yugoslavia, 1939–1941), Konstantin Fotić (Yugoslavian ambassador to Washington, D.C., 1935–1944), and Milan Gavrilović (Yugoslav ambassador to Moscow, 1940–1941; member of the government-in-exile, London, 1941–1943).

EAST ASIA

From the time they first met in 1901, Homer Lea became Sun Yat-sen's military adviser and chief of staff. Lea's cottage in Santa Monica, California, served as Dr. Sun Yat-sen's official headquarters during Sun's campaign over the next decade to marshal moral, financial, and military support for the liberation of China. In 1911, in London, after ascertaining that the time was ripe for revolution in China, Lea cabled Sun in America. Sun joined Lea in Europe and together they sailed for Canton. In Nanking in 1911, Lea saw Sun Yat-sen elected president of the new Chinese Republic. He was the only Westerner present at this occasion. The Homer Lea Collection in the archives contains correspondence with Sun Yat-sen, including a letter from Sun to Lea detailing the revolution's financial needs and Lea's 1909 estimate of the cost of a revolution in China.

The East Asian Collection is rich in archival holdings. The collection is especially strong on the Chinese Revolution of 1911, the Chinese Communist Party from 1921 to the present, the rise of the Kuomintang under Chiang Kai-shek, economic development since the 1920s, educational reform beginning with the Ch'ing regime, the Sino-Japanese War, operations in the China-Burma-India theater during World War II, the Chinese Civil War to 1949, and economic and political developments in both Taiwan and the mainland since 1949.

The papers of Homer Lea, military adviser to Sun Yat-sen, document the founding of the Republic of China in 1911. The history of the new republic is fully covered in the collections of Paul M. W. Linebarger (American lawyer and legal adviser to Sun Yat-sen, 1907–1925) and Arthur N. Young (chief financial adviser to the Chinese government, 1926–1947). The papers of Helen Foster Snow, first wife of Edgar Snow and one of the first journalists to interview Mao Tse-tung after the Long March, contain interviews and hundreds of photographs of the Chinese communist leaders in 1937 during their stay in Yenan.

Materials on China from the perspective of the Chinese themselves are abundant. Among the most prominent Chinese leaders represented in the archives are T. V. Soong (Chinese minister of finance, 1925–1933; minister of foreign affairs, 1941–1945), Huang Fu (minister of foreign affairs, 1928), Kia-ngau Chang (chairman of the Northeast Economic Commission, which negotiated with the Soviets for the return of Manchuria to Chinese control at the end of World War II), Hsin-ai Chang (ambassador to Czechoslovakia and Poland, 1934–1937), I-ch'i Mei (minister of education, 1958–1961), and W. W. Yen (ambassador to the USSR, 1933–1936).

Archival holdings on Japan relate primarily to the Japanese government in Korea, 1894–1910, and to the Allied occupation of Japan following World War II. The original records of the Japanese government in Korea were destroyed during World War II. Fortunately, photographic plates were made before the war and hidden from Japanese authorities. The Hoover Institution and the Korean National History Museum microfilmed these plates in 1948, and copies were placed in both repositories. They include records of the Japanese legation in Korea, 1894–1905, the Japanese residency general in Korea, 1906–1910, and the Japanese government-general in Korea, 1910.

Following World War II, the Allied occupation authorities attempted to transform the basic values and institutions of Japan. The papers of Joseph C. Trainor (deputy chief of the Civil Information and Education Section at SCAP Headquarters) contain a vast amount of documentation on educational reform. Other papers on the occupation include those of Hubert G. Schenck (chief of the Natural Resources Section at SCAP Headquarters), Clovis E. Byers (chief of staff, 8th Army), Crawford F. Sams (chief of the public health and welfare section at SCAP Headquarters, 1945–1951), John D. Montgomery (American political scientist who studied Japanese public opinion regarding the purge of wartime leaders), and Milo Rowell (military lawyer at SCAP Headquarters who helped to write the revised Japanese constitution).

African archival materials relate primarily to ethnography, colonialism and colonial administration, nationalism, and revolutionary movements. The most useful record groups are collections of ephemera on revolutionary movements and recent events in South Africa and papers of scholars who have studied modern Africa. Among the latter are Virginia Adloff (author of *Conflict in Chad*), Henry Bienen (professor of political science, Princeton University, and author of *Armies and Parties in Africa*), David W. Brokensha (author *of Social Change at Larteh, Ghana*), Peter Duignan (senior fellow, Hoover Institution, and author with Lewis Gann of *Burden of Empire*), Lewis H. Gann (senior fellow, Hoover Institution, and author of *History of Southern Rhodesia: Early Days to 1934*), George D. Jenkins (American political scientist and author of *The Price of Liberty: Personality and Politics in Colonial Nigeria*), Rene Lemarchand (director of the African Studies Center, University of Florida, and author of *Rwanda and Burundi*), Keith Middlemas (British historian and author of *Power and the Party: Changing Forces of European Communism since 1968*), Frederick Quinn (American anthropologist and author of *Changes in Beti Society, 1887–1960*), William H. Vatcher (American political scientist and author of *White Laager: The Rise of Afrikaner Nationalism*), and Herbert J. Weiss (professor of political science, Brooklyn College, and author of *History of Political Parties in Zaire*).

For the Middle East, some of the prominent collections are the papers of Louis Edgar Browne (correspondent in Turkey for the *Chicago Daily News* and associate of Mustafa Kemal), the Ahmed Emin Yalman papers (editor of the Turkish newspapers *Vakit*, 1917–1922; *Vatan*, 1922–1926, 1940–1961; and *Tan*, 1936–1939), the Hidayet Dağdeviren Collection on the Ottoman Empire and the first years of the Turkish Republic, the James Heyworth-Dunne papers (British arabist), and the Richard P. Mitchell Collection on the Muslim Brotherhood, the fanatical religious movement in Egypt that has had a major political impact throughout the Middle East. There are small collections of letters of T. E. Lawrence and Henry St. John Bridger Philby (British arabist and adviser to King Ibn Saud) as well as selected records of the Arabian American Oil Company.

Latin American archival holdings focus on boundary disputes, the Panama Canal, the Cuban revolution, and major political events throughout South America for the period 1954–1964. Of particular note are the records of the Citizens Committee for a Free Cuba, 1962–1974, the Theodore Draper Collection on Cuba and the Dominican Republic, and the vast clipping and pamphlet collection of the Institute of Hispanic-American and Luso-Brazilian Studies. The latter collection, organized by Professor Ronald Hilton, is a unique depository of source materials, primarily newspaper clippings, covering developments in Spain, Portugal, and Latin America during the period 1948 to 1964. They provided the basis for the monthly journal *Hispanic American Report* published under Hilton's editorship during that period.

In addition to archives of particular geographical areas, the archives has extensive holdings on international organizations and conferences. Those covered in depth include the 1919 Paris Peace Conference, the League of Nations, the reparations commissions of the 1920s, the 1930 London Naval Conference, the international military tribunals at Nuremberg and Tokyo, the founding conference of the United Nations at San Francisco, and numerous international relief organizations. Especially important collections include the records of the American Relief Administration, the Commission for Relief in Belgium, the International Rescue Committee, Aid Refugee Chinese Intellectuals (1952–1970), American Committee on United Europe (1949–1959), American Council of the Institute of Pacific Relations (1925–1960), League of Red

Cross Societies (1919–1922), National Committee on Food for Small Democracies (1939–1945), and the Atlantic Council (1955–1980).

SUBJECT COLLECTIONS   The archives holds strong subject collections that cut across all geographical areas. Foremost among these are the John D. Crummey Collection on Peace, the Paul and Jean Hanna Collection on the Role of Education, the Poster Collection, and the Herbert Hoover Collection.

When establishing the Hoover Institution, Herbert Hoover, a Quaker and a man who had known and experienced the ravages of war, emphasized the development of a strong peace collection. After more than six decades of collecting effort, the Hoover Institution has become one of the major documentary repositories in the world on twentieth-century peace movements, conferences, and related topics.

John D. Crummey Peace Collection

In 1977, the FMC Corporation gave a grant to the Hoover Institution to endow the peace collection, which is now named after John D. Crummey, the founder of the FMC Corporation. In addition to a vast number of books, periodicals, newspapers, and other published matter on peace, the John D. Crummey Collection contains over two million pages of archival documentation relating to peace, peace conferences, founding of the League of Nations and United Nations, pacifism, disarmament, isolationism, conscientious objectors, and antiwar activism.

Specific record groups among many others on peace include the files of the America First Committee (a private organization to promote U.S. nonintervention in World War II), Fellowship of Reconciliation (nondenominational religious pacifist organization in the United States), Alfred H. Fried (Austrian pacifist and cowinner of the Nobel Peace Prize, 1911), American Friends Service Committee, 1941–1945 (American Quaker organization), Kurt R. Grossman (president, German League for Human Rights, 1926–1933), David Starr Jordan (American educator and international pacifist leader), Ernest Lundeen (isolationist U.S. representative and senator from Minnesota), Alice Park (American pacifist, feminist, and socialist), Rosika Schwimmer (Hungarian feminist and pacifist), San Francisco Chapter of the United Nations Association of the U.S.A., the Stanford Draft Counseling Office, 1967–1973, as well as over 87 linear feet of materials collected by Herbert Hoover at the Paris Peace Conference, 1919.

Paul and Jean Hanna Collection

A second subject collection, the Paul and Jean Hanna Collection on the Role of Education, was founded in 1977. The objective of the Hanna Collection is to explore how education—both formal schooling and informal communications—operates as a powerful influence on the development of and interactions between societies throughout the world. This focus includes questions of creating and maintaining peace, preparing for war, and developing national resources and potential. The collection is described in a 250-page guide entitled *Guide to the Hanna Collection and Related Archival Materials at the Hoover Institution on War, Revolution and Peace on the Role of Education in Twentieth Century Society* (Hoover Institution Press, 1982), compiled by Fakhreddin Moussavi.

The Hanna Collection was made possible by a gift from Paul and Jean Hanna. Dr. Paul R. Hanna was for many years the Lee L. Jacks Professor of Child Education at Stanford University and is now senior research fellow at the Hoover Institution.

Mrs. Jean S. Hanna was a teacher of English for many years in the United States and overseas and is coauthor and editor with her husband of several widely acclaimed textbook series. Today the Hanna Collection is the most important collection of its kind in the United States, and its holdings will be of critical value for scholars in the decades to come. Included in the collection are the papers of Samuel Halperin (deputy assistant secretary of health, education and welfare for legislation, 1966–1969), James A. Perkins (chairman, International Council for Educational Development, 1970–), Oliver J. Caldwell (assistant commissioner of education for international education, 1952–1964), Franklin Moore (representative of the Ford Foundation to Asia and U.S. Agency for Development official), Earl J. McGrath (U.S. commissioner of education, 1949–1953), Samuel M. Brownell (U.S. commissioner of education, 1953–1956), Philip H. Coombs (U.S. assistant secretary of state for educational and cultural affairs, 1961–1962), William J. Platt (deputy assistant director general for education, UNESCO, 1970–1975), George D. Stoddard (chairman, U.S. Education Mission to Japan, 1946), William Carr (executive secretary, National Education Association, 1929–1967), and R. Freeman Butts (associate dean, Teachers College, Columbia University, 1961–1975). The International Council for Educational Development contributed over 200 linear feet of its records on international education and education in developing countries.

Poster Collection

As of mid-1984, the Poster Collection in the Hoover Institution Archives totals approximately 68,000 items: illustrated wall placards, official proclamations, propaganda of various types, and miscellaneous items in poster format. It constitutes the largest known collection of international political posters in the United States. Over half of the posters date from the era of World War I and the 1920s. About one-third date from the World War II era; the majority were created in the United States, Germany, Great Britain, France, and Russia. Of particular significance are about 1,600 posters issued in Russia during the revolutionary and Civil War period. There are also hundreds of posters from Latin America, the Middle East, Japan, and various Asian countries.

Herbert Hoover Collection

No description of the Hoover Institution Archives would be complete without a discussion of the Herbert Hoover Collection. Between 1919, when he founded the Hoover Institution, and his death in 1964, Herbert Hoover routinely deposited papers of historical value at the Hoover Institution. Today, the Herbert Hoover Papers in the Hoover Institution Archives cover the years from 1895 to 1976 and contain some 278,000 items (185 linear feet).

These materials relate to Mr. Hoover's relief activities during and after World War I and II, his relationship with President Woodrow Wilson, his political and personal philosophy, his post-presidential career, his public service activities, and his public reputation. The principal series include a biographical file; correspondence with Woodrow Wilson; speeches and writings; articles, clippings, press summaries, and press releases about him; analyses of editorial comment published during the Hoover administration; correspondence; subject and card files; as well as memorabilia, microfilms, motion picture films, sound recordings, and photographs. Selected materials on his service as secretary of commerce and president of the United States are also present.

In addition to Herbert Hoover's own papers, other materials on Mr. Hoover are available for research at the Hoover Institution Archives. The Herbert Hoover Oral

One of 68,000 political posters in the Hoover Institution Archives, one of the largest collections of political posters in the United States

the Civil War; the Soviet Union post-1923; Siberia; Turkey; the Ukraine; the U.S. military; and Yugoslavia. All but one are unpublished and may be obtained by writing to the archivist. A list on Imperial Russia, the Russian Revolution, and the Civil War is being compiled by Carol Leadenham and will be published by the Hoover Institution Press in 1985.

Other unpublished finding aids have been prepared for use in the Archives Reading Room. Of these, the most important is the card catalog, which provides an exhaustive and up-to-date coverage of all archival holdings at the Hoover Institution. There are also detailed folder-by-folder guides to some 400 individual collections. Three of these have been published: *Herbert Hoover: A Register of His Papers in the Hoover Institution Archives* (Hoover Institution Press, 1983), compiled by Elena S. Danielson and Charles G. Palm; *General Claire Lee Chennault: A Guide to His Papers in the Hoover Institution Archives* (Hoover Institution Press, 1983), edited by Robert Hessen and compiled by Dale Reed; and *Japanese Penetration of Korea, 1894–1910: A Checklist of Japanese Archives in the Hoover Institution* (Hoover Institution Press, 1959), compiled by A. C. Nahm. Another source for archival materials on Herbert Hoover is *Herbert Hoover—A Bibliography: His Writings and Addresses* (Hoover Institution Press, 1977) by Kathleen Tracey.

Hoover Institution archival holdings have been listed in a number of national archival guides. New acquisitions are periodically reported to and published in the *National Union Catalog of Manuscript Collections* (Washington, D.C.: Library of Congress). Other major reference works containing entries for Hoover Institution archives include Lee Ash's *Subject Collections* (5th ed.; New York & London: R. R. Bowker Company, 1978); *The Russian Empire and Soviet Union: A Guide to Manuscripts and Archival Materials in the United States*, compiled by Steven A. Grant and John H. Brown (Boston: G. K. Hall, 1981); and *Women's History Sources*, edited by Andrea Hinding (New York & London: R. R. Bowker Company, 1979).

12 | BIBLIOGRAPHICAL RESEARCH

S ince its founding in 1919, the Hoover Institution on War, Revolution and Peace has made available to scholars and students a total of 127 checklists, bibliographies, guides to its collections, and other research tools. Few libraries in the United States, with the exception of the Library of Congress, have produced as many bibliographies and research tools as has the Hoover Institution. These works have saved thousands of scholars and students valuable time in locating desired materials.

The great majority of these research tools were prepared by staff members of the Institution; outside scholars produced the remainder, usually at the initiative of staff members and always with their active cooperation. It was to a large degree thanks to the curatorial system of administering its area and topical collections that the Institution was able to accomplish so much bibliographic work. The curators—usually scholars or librarians with advanced degrees in various disciplines, knowledge of foreign languages, and competence in the area or subject of their specialization—understand the difficulties confronting scholars in locating sources for their projects. Curators have often carried on research for their own articles and books and as a result have a better understanding of scholars' needs.

The curators are responsible for acquisitions in their areas or fields and well acquainted with the collections entrusted to their care. They are consulted by the users of the library's resources and have the chance to gather firsthand information about the needs of scholars. These consultations are extremely helpful in establishing requirements and priorities for research tools. Furthermore, knowledge of the collections enables curators to direct scholars to strong holdings in neglected fields.

In the past some outsiders considered the Hoover's curatorial system of library operations unconventional. They criticized it as a luxury operation because curators' salaries had to be higher than librarians' salaries. The practice of having faculty

---

This essay is an adapted and expanded version of a bibliographical survey prepared in 1967 by Witold S. Sworakowski, associate director of the Institution. Dr. Sworakowski died in 1979. The editor, curators, and bibliographers covered the period since 1967.

members determine acquisition policies in college and university libraries remained strongly entrenched in American schools, and few librarians dared to challenge it. In recent years, however, the curatorial system has been introduced in the libraries of many universities with specialized institutes and teaching programs. Naturally, a curator must satisfy the needs of faculty members because faculty members are major users of the library. But the acquisition efforts of Hoover curators must be much broader because they are also expected to secure resources for future research projects.

The curatorial system of library operations as developed in the Hoover Institution helps explain why it is one of the leading producers of reference tools in the United States.

＊　　　＊　　　＊

The first of these tools, a checklist of the holdings of an exceptionally large and rare collection of "delegation propaganda" distributed by governments and pressure groups during the Paris Peace Conference of 1919, appeared in 1926 as the first item in the Bibliographical Series.[1] It does not bear the name of the compiler, but Miss Nina Almond, librarian of the Hoover War Library, prepared it under the supervision and with the cooperation of Professor Ephraim D. Adams, first chairman of the Directors of the Library (1920–1925), and Professor Ralph H. Lutz, one of the original collectors of the material in Europe, a close collaborator of Professor Adams's, and his successor as chairman (1925–1944). The checklist was intended to introduce this extraordinary collection and to encourage scholars and students to use it in their research on the Peace Conference.

From the very start, the library staff aimed at getting as many scholars and students as possible to use the growing collection. This was clearly their motivation when, in 1925, they started the Bibliographical Series, in which they hoped to "advertise" the valuable holdings of the library. However, their good intentions lacked the necessary financial backing. The staff was small and overloaded with the work of organizing the incoming material. Funds were modest, and acquisitions received priority over publications. Thus, the second item in the Bibliographical Series, a bibliography of documents, monographs, and memoirs on the Paris Peace Conference compiled by Miss Nina Almond and Professor Ralph H. Lutz, had to wait for publication funds until 1935.[2]

Meanwhile, the curator of the Slavic Collection, Dimitry M. Krassovsky, a historian and lawyer turned librarian, had begun to prepare badly needed reference tools in order to facilitate the use of the library's excellent Russian-language holdings. In the early 1920s, Professor Frank Golder, another untiring collector for the Hoover War Library, had acquired some 85,000 books, pamphlets, periodicals, and large runs of newspapers in Russia. The cataloging of this material proceeded slowly, but scholars' demand for it grew from day to day. In 1928, the directors created the Research Committee (later renamed Institute) for the History of the Russian Revolution as an adjunct to the library. This was the first research institute in the United States to specialize in Russian affairs. The Russian holdings of the Hoover War Library attracted young Ph.D. candidates from all parts of the United States to Stanford. Many of today's "older generation" of American specialists in Russian history and politics did their first research in the Hoover Library. Krassovsky, whose task it was to serve them, understood their needs.

His first effort was directed toward the preparation of a subject list of uncataloged pre-1914 Russian material in the Hoover Library.[3] This typewritten checklist (in

Cyrillic script), completed in 1931, was for many years a most useful source of information. After the material was cataloged, this checklist became obsolete. It stood out, however, as the first typewritten bibliographical reference tool for users of the Library.

Krassovsky's next work concerned the 1918 revolution in Germany. This again was a subject excellently covered by Hoover Library holdings, and it attracted scholars to the library. Krassovsky translated from Russian a bibliography on this revolution published in a Soviet periodical.[4] Then he returned to the Russian field and in 1934 prepared a dictionary of Russian pseudonyms and initial signatures, which was a much-needed key to revolutionary authors.[5] He continued to work on this list until 1947, when he left the Hoover Library and became Slavic librarian at the University of California at Los Angeles. This "dictionary," although superseded by similar postwar publications, is still much in use by scholars working at the Hoover.

In 1943, Krassovsky completed for use in the library the first part of a biographical index of prominent people in the Slavic world.[6] He continued to work on this major contribution to Slavic biography in Los Angeles after he left Stanford in 1947. Completed in 1954, the nine volumes (700 pages) were a much-needed biographical reference work. Krassovsky's last research tool produced for the users of the Hoover Library was a short guide to the transliteration of Russian names.[7]

Krassovsky's pioneering research and reference tools in the field of Russian studies were of particular value because nothing else was available at the time. The many similar reference and bibliographical works available in the Russian field today are all postwar publications. Unfortunately, the persistent lack of publication funds in the Hoover Library caused all these items to remain in typewritten form. Copies, however, found their way to many other libraries in the United States.

Just before the outbreak of World War II, another member of the library staff began preparing bibliographical reference tools. In 1939, Mrs. Ruth Perry, who later became reference librarian and then the first curator of the African Collection, chose for her master's thesis for the Library School at Berkeley the preparation of a checklist of clandestine WWI Belgian serials in the Hoover collections.[8]

Shortly after the outbreak of World War II, there appeared in print a much-needed listing of special collections and archival files in the Hoover Library—the result of painstaking work undertaken by Miss Nina Almond and Professor Harold H. Fisher, former curator of the American Relief Administration archives and later (1944–1952) chairman of the Board of Directors of the Library. This work appeared in 1940 as a separate print, outside the Bibliographical Series.[9] This guide to the uncataloged holdings of the library was for many years a valuable source of information for users of the library and its archives. However, the rapid growth of special collections and archival holdings during and after World War II, and the incorporation of printed material from special collections into the cataloged holdings of the library made this first guide obsolete.

During the war, two annotated bibliographies on industrial (labor) relations in Great Britain and Germany were prepared under the direction of Professor Waldo Chamberlin. They were the result of a project sponsored by the Division of Industrial Relations of the Graduate School of Business at Stanford University. The first volume, comprising books, pamphlets, periodicals, newspapers, and articles in periodicals dealing with labor relations in Great Britain during World War I, included only Hoover Library holdings.[10] The second volume dealt with the same problem in Germany, but over a much longer period—1914–1939—and listed materials in the Hoover Library and the Stanford University Library.[11] These volumes appeared in 1940 and 1942, respectively. Although the initiative and financing for the preparation of these two checklists came from outside, staff members of the library cooperated in their compilation and received due credit in the prefaces. Both volumes, based almost entirely on Hoover Library and Stanford University Library material, became standard bibliographical reference works in the field covered. The volume on Germany became especially important in view of the war with Germany.

As a result of wartime collecting activities, the flow of materials in the first five postwar years more than doubled the prewar holdings of the Hoover Library, which was renamed the Hoover Institute and Library on War, Revolution and Peace. A revival of research activities based on materials in the Hoover Tower that had gotten under way in the late 1920s with the research institutes on the German and Russian revolutions and abandoned for lack of funds during the Depression led to the addition of the word "institute." During the years of this high tide of incoming materials, several new area collections were added to the library. As a consequence of this expansion of the library, the staff increased considerably. By 1950, there were six area curators and several area assistants. And at the same time, the need for bibliographic aid became even more pressing.

The new collection on China created particular interest among students and scholars. Dr. Mary Wright, curator of the Chinese Collection, initiated and directed the preparation, by Miss Chao Kuo-chun, of a survey of Hoover materials on communism in China during the years 1927–1934.[12] This was the first bibliographical aid to the excellent collection on communism in China, which, in 1948 when this survey was completed, was not yet fully cataloged.

The collection on modern China attracted a growing number of scholars to the library. The Research Branch of the Committee for a Free Asia in San Francisco used the Hoover Library for its studies of political changes in China. A by-product of this use was a bibliography, prepared by staff researchers of the committee, of Mao Tsetung's writings in the library's holdings.[13] This list of Hoover Library holdings later became the basis for a more complete bibliography of Mao's writings published on the East Coast.

Also in 1948, the curator of the Polish Collection, Witold S. Sworakowski, produced a checklist of the large and exceptionally rare collection of illegal Polish publications that appeared in German-occupied Poland during World War II.[14] Until 1962, when the Polish Academy of Sciences published a cumulative list of Polish underground publications in major libraries in Poland, this checklist remained the only reference tool on Polish underground publications.

In 1950 and 1951, the Hoover collecting organizations in Belgium and Japan published complete lists of the material collected by them for the Hoover Institute and Library. In 1950, the Belgian-American Educational Foundation published an "inventory" of the 39 large crates of material collected for the Hoover Library during the war.[15] As the Belgian material was processed and cataloged in the library, the inventory lost its practical value. Nevertheless, it still is a good general reference source for wartime publications on Belgium.

Upon concluding its activities, the Tokyo Office of the library, formed after World War II, printed a detailed list of the 1,468 cases of material that it had collected and shipped to Stanford.[16] This list was very useful during the first years, but lost its importance after the material was cataloged in the Hoover Library. Both the Belgian and the Japanese lists, however, will remain as signposts of the development of these two collections and a testimonial to the men and women who contributed to their growth.

In 1951, Mrs. Helena Sworakowski prepared a checklist of Hoover Library holdings of serials published in Germany and Austria shortly after World War II by Belorussian, Russian, and Ukrainian displaced persons.[17] This ephemeral material was listed at the request of a scholar on the East Coast, and a carbon copy of the checklist remained in the library for the use of interested scholars.

Interest in the collection on Southeast Asia prompted the Department of Far Eastern Studies at Cornell University to commission Miss Giok Po Oey to prepare, in 1952, a survey of the material on this area in the Hoover Library.[18] Miss Oey was assisted in her work by the staff members of the library, and the library still retains a copy of the survey as a valuable guide to this material.

By 1952, the curators and principal librarians of the Hoover Library had begun to hold regular meetings that undertook a broad survey and discussion of the extent of coverage and quality of particular area collections. This study aimed at detecting weak spots and gaps that demanded additions and improvements. One of the results of these "curators' meetings" was the decision to prepare and publish short surveys of particular area collections to inform students and scholars about the holdings of the Hoover Library and their strengths and weaknesses. It was hoped such surveys would encourage scholars to undertake research projects for which the library had adequate resources. Three surveys in the new Survey Series fulfilled this task.

The first of the Survey Series, published in 1954, dealt with the collection on Russia.[19] It was prepared by Professor Witold S. Sworakowski, who had in the meantime become curator of the Eastern European collections. The second survey, published in 1955, described the collection on Germany and was prepared by the curator of the German Collection, the late Hildegard R. Boeninger.[20] The third survey, prepared by Dr. Nobutaka Ike, curator of the Japanese Collection, and published in 1958, described the collection on Japan.[21] All three surveys included selective lists of the more important periodicals and newspapers in the collection. These surveys were well received by scholars and librarians, and it was necessary to reprint the surveys on Russia and Germany. Publication of this useful series stopped temporarily, owing to financial difficulties.

While the collection surveys were being written, work on other bibliographical tools proceeded. In 1953, a checklist of Indonesian-language publications available in the Hoover Library was put in the hands of users.[22] In 1954, an annotated bibliography on Japanese-sponsored governments in China during the years 1937–1945, based exclusively on Hoover Library holdings, appeared in print.[23] The author, Dr. Frederick W. Mote, prepared this bibliography as a first stage in his work on a historical study of Japanese-sponsored puppet regimes in China. His was a great contribution to research on the contemporary Far East, and at the same time its publication as the third number in the Bibliographical Series revived that series. Following the publication of the Mote bibliography, interest in bibliographical work in the Hoover Library grew at a steady pace.

In 1953, the Mid-European Studies Center in New York planned a research project on federation plans in Central and Eastern Europe during World War II. The little-known initiative of the governments-in-exile of Czechoslovakia, Poland, Greece, and Yugoslavia was to be the subject of this project. As a preparatory step, the center asked the Hoover Institute and Library to prepare a bibliography on this subject, based on materials available in its holdings. A team of scholars under the direction of Witold S. Sworakowski prepared the bibliography. The result was two checklists: the first one including books, pamphlets, and articles in periodicals on those federation plans,[24] and the second listing pertinent archival material in the Hoover Library.[25] They were completed in 1954 and reproduced in limited editions.

In 1954, the former reference librarian in the Hoover Library, Mrs. Ruth Perry, became curator of the new collection on Africa and immediately proceeded to prepare bibliographical aids for the use of the collection. In 1955, after a trip to Nigeria, she compiled a modest checklist of new sources for research in Nigerian history available at the Hoover Library.[26] The following year she published a bibliography on nationalism in Nigeria.[27] Her premature death in Lagos, while on a collecting trip for the library, interrupted her broadly planned bibliographical work on Africa.

During academic year 1955–56, the Hoover Institute and Library undertook on behalf of the United States International Cooperation Administration a training program on overseas development, which was designed to prepare American university personnel for fieldwork in Asia. The lecturers and consultants conducting this program prepared individual reading lists on thirteen Asian and Southeast Asian countries for use by the participants.[28] The lists included books, pamphlets, government documents, and articles in periodicals available in the Hoover Library and in the Stanford University Library. Although at present outdated, these checklists are still useful for information on these countries.

Also in 1955, Professor Witold S. Sworakowski produced a bibliography of law journals published in Eastern Europe.[29] Although now obsolete, it was much in demand by law libraries in the United States at the time of its publication.

In 1956, Eugene Wu, librarian on the staff of the Chinese Collection, compiled an annotated bibliography of selected Chinese biographical works in the Hoover Library.[30] This was the fourth bibliographical reference work prepared on the basis of the holdings of the Chinese collection in the library and also the first English-language bibliography of biographies on modern China.

In 1958, Professor Witold S. Sworakowski compiled a checklist of all periodicals and newspapers published in Eastern Europe, or published elsewhere but dealing with that area, that were received regularly by the library of the Hoover Institution.[31] Although this list was chiefly intended to aid users of the library in the Hoover Tower, many other libraries requested copies for their own reference purposes.

With finances at an all-time low and a vacancy in the directorship for nine months, 1959 was a year of crisis for the Hoover Institution. Nevertheless, with some outside assistance, it was possible to publish three reference tools in the Bibliographical Series. Andrew C. Nahm, a Stanford Ph.D. candidate and part-time employee of the Japanese Collection, prepared a detailed descriptive listing and index to the archive of the Japanese legation in Korea and of the Japanese residency-general in that country during the crucial years 1894–1910.[32] The photographic copies of this vast archive were the result of a dramatic rescue operation by the Hoover Institution, and its use by historians depended on a listing and indexing of its contents.

The next item to appear in the series was a bibliographical essay on the Chinese student movement, based on resources in the Hoover Institution.[33] This study was written by John Israel, who based his doctoral dissertation for Harvard University on materials in the Chinese Collection of the Institution. His survey included a list of the more important books and periodicals available in the Institution's holdings.

The broad problem of Chinese settlements outside China was the object of a prolonged study based on Hoover Institution materials undertaken by Naosaku Uchida, professor of Oriental economic history at Seijo University in Tokyo. During his work at the Hoover, Professor Uchida prepared a bibliographical essay on Chinese and Japanese sources for the study of this subject and shared with interested scholars his experiences in handling these sources. Eugene Wu and Chün-tu Hsüeh, both from the staff of the Hoover Institution, added two appendixes to this enlightening essay: the first containing a table of variant romanizations of personal, place, and organization names; the second listing 679 items (books, pamphlets, periodicals, newspapers, and articles in periodicals) on the subject available at the Hoover Institution.[34]

During the same year, two bibliographical aids listing Hoover Institution holdings also appeared. The curator of the African Collection, Dr. John Cudd Brown, prepared a reading list on Africa south of the Sahara as an aid to the growing number of students at Stanford interested in African affairs.[35] At the time, when decolonization in Africa was beginning to get under way and scholarly interest in the continent was growing, reference works on Africa were scarce; hence Brown's work, though now obsolete, became a useful reference tool.

The second such publication was a preliminary survey of foreign statistical documents in Stanford libraries, including the holdings of the Hoover Institution.[36] It was prepared by Miss Minna Stillmann, an employee of the Stanford University Library. (Early in 1967 an updated edition of this list appeared.)

The material on communism in China continued to attract the growing attention of American and foreign scholars, and the preparation of a guide to this material became a pressing need. As the Institution was short of funds in 1958–1959, the Stanford Committee on East Asia Studies financed the preparation by Dr. Chün-tu Hsüeh of an annotated checklist of these materials. The first part of his work included the material published during the years 1921–1937;[37] it appeared in 1960. The second part covered publications that appeared during the years 1937–1949;[38] it was published in 1962.

In 1962, a checklist of materials in the Hoover Library and the Stanford University Libraries on Madagascar (the Malagasy Republic), prepared by the curator of the African Collection, Dr. Peter Duignan, was published.[39] This was the first of several bibliographical reference tools on Africa initiated, prepared, or edited by Dr. Duignan. Although dealing with a comparatively small area, it became the model for specialized bibliographies on individual new states in Africa. Dr. Duignan, as head of the revised research program, initiated numerous bibliographic studies published by the Hoover Press. The 1960s became one of the most productive decades for bibliographies in the Hoover's history.

The newly appointed curator of the East European collection, Mr. Karol Maichel, in 1962 started the publication of a series of guides to Russian reference books. This was much needed for the growing number of students and libraries interested in Russian studies. The first volume of this guide, a list of general Russian bibliographies and reference books, appeared in 1962.[40] The second volume, listing Russian reference books in the fields of history, ethnography, and geography appeared in 1964.[41]

In 1962, the first of four volumes of a detailed listing of the files and microfilms of the German Foreign Ministry archives for the years 1920–1945 appeared.[42] This volume was the outcome of a joint publications project of the Hoover Institution and the U.S. Department of State. The files (400 tons of them) of the German Ministry of Foreign Affairs were captured by the Allies in 1945 and brought to England where a team of American, British, and French historians microfilmed some of them and undertook to publish selected documents in several multivolume series. A large part of this archive was microfilmed by the three governments, and additional microfilming was done by several American universities. These microfilms amount to a staggering total of over 5,000 reels. Copies were easily obtained, but in order to make the contents accessible to scholars and students, users required a listing of the entire archive and its microfilmed parts. The Department of State prepared this listing but was unable to obtain funds for printing. In 1961, the State Department and the Hoover Institution entered into an agreement by which the Institution undertook the printing and distribution of the entire listing prepared by the department. The product of this agreement is the four volumes of the *Catalog*, totaling close to 4,000 pages. The initial work on this *Catalog* was done by a team of scholars and State Department officials. Dr. George O. Kent, an official of the Historical Office of the Department of State, was entrusted with the editing of the material and supervision of the production of the final text. The Institution agreed to publish this important and costly reference work as a service to scholars.

Also in 1962, Professor Witold S. Sworakowski prepared a short survey of the collection on Armenia in the Hoover Institution.[43] It outlined the events and subjects covered by this small but quite rare collection.

In 1962, an especially fruitful year for the Institution's bibliographical work, three items in the Bibliographical Series, one large volume of the *Catalog* of the German Foreign Ministry archives, and one mimeographed collection survey were published. Work on these items was started and successfully completed thanks to the improved financial situation of the Institution. The printing of the more than 800-page *Catalog*, in particular, demanded a considerable financial investment, which could hardly be fully recovered from sales. From 1962 on, the bibliographical work of the Institution and its staff has shown steady progress. The world of scholarship owes a debt for this improvement to Dr. W. Glenn Campbell, who in 1960 became the director of the Institution and greatly encouraged and supported the preparation and publication of bibliographical reference tools. Work was no longer confined only to listing materials held by the Institution; in addition general reference tools were also prepared.

Further bibliographies on Africa prepared by Dr. Peter Duignan and his associates on the staff of the African Collection, as well as by outside scholars, appeared in 1963. The first was a guide to American missionary archives and manuscript collections prepared by Drs. Duignan and Robert Collins.[44] This survey facilitated the study of the libraries and archives of American religious missions beginning in the 1820s.

It was followed by a checklist of the very valuable serials for African studies located in the library of the Hoover Institution and in the Stanford University Libraries, prepared jointly by Dr. Duignan and Dr. Kenneth M. Glazier, deputy curator of the African Collection.[45] Although this checklist included serials available on the Stanford campus only, it served other libraries as a reference tool in compiling want lists for their acquisitions and also identified important serial publications. College libraries in Africa and the United States, in particular, made much use of the publication.

The next bibliography on Africa published by the Institution was especially important because it began a systematic, annual list of books, pamphlets, and articles in periodicals on Africa south of the Sahara published in the United States and Canada. The first list of this kind was published by the Library of Congress and covered the year 1960. The material for the first six months of 1961 was compiled by the Library of Congress, and the listing for the last six months was completed by Miss Hilary Sims from the Hoover Institution staff. By an arrangement with the African Section of the Library of Congress, the Hoover Institution assumed the responsibility for preparing and publishing the bibliography for 1961 and the following years. Dr. Duignan assumed the editorship of the volumes, and a member of his curatorial staff assisted in the bibliographic work. The bibliography for 1961, compiled by Miss Hilary Sims, appeared in 1963.[46] This was followed in 1964 by the bibliography for 1962, also compiled by Miss Sims,[47] and a year later by the bibliography for 1963, compiled by Miss Liselotte Hofmann.[48] The edition for 1964 was published in late 1966.[49] It also was compiled by Miss Hofmann. These volumes, all containing an average of 1,300–1,500 entries yearly and organized topically as well as by regions and countries, have become the standard bibliography for publications on Black Africa in the United States and Canada. The series was discontinued after the 1966 annual; costs of compilation and production proved too high.[50-51] But the model stimulated the production of national bibliographies on writings on Africa in Great Britain, France, and West Germany.

The fiftieth bibliographical item prepared and/or published by the Hoover Institution was a select and annotated bibliography on Africa south of the Sahara, covering publications that appeared during 1958–1963.[52] Prepared by Dr. Kenneth M. Glazier, it was selected in 1965 by the American Library Association as one of the "outstanding reference books of the past year." (It was followed in 1969 by a companion volume for 1964–1968.)[53]

The next item published in the series was a guide to the central archive (*Hauptarchiv*) of the Nazi Party (NSDAP) prepared by Mrs. Agnes F. Peterson, curator of the Western European Collection, and Mrs. Grete Heinz.[54] The Hoover Institution received permission to microfilm this entire archive before U.S. authorities turned it over to the German federal government. The bulk of the 155 reels of microfilm consists of the papers of the NSDAP proper. The remainder consists of files from the Streicher archive and the entire Himmler archive. These last two archives were not part of the NSDAP archives but were added during the microfilming. The guide contains a detailed listing of each of the nearly 2,000 folders, with a description of the contents and explanatory annotations. This reference work serves as a key to this massive archive.

In 1965, the Institution published four items in its Bibliographical Series in addition to the bibliography of U.S. and Canadian publications on Africa for 1964 discussed above. A by-product of Dr. Jon Bridgman's work on a doctoral dissertation dealing with German history was a select and annotated bibliography of books, pamphlets, government documents, periodicals, and other material on German Africa available in the Hoover Library. Later revised and edited by Dr. David E. Clarke, it was published early in 1965.[55] Besides material originating in Germany and other countries, it includes a listing of British confidential prints dealing with the German colonies.

The Hoover Institution's holdings on international communism were known to be particularly strong. Until Professor Sworakowski prepared a research guide and checklist of holdings in 44 American and 4 leading European libraries on the Communist International and six of its most active front organizations, however, it was uncertain which library had the best holdings. In 1965, Hoover published this listing of over 2,300 books and pamphlets in many Western and Slavic languages.[56] It was the first bibliographical reference work on these organizations of international communism and indicates pertinent titles and the libraries in which each title may be located. The study showed that the Hoover Institution's library holdings on international communism were then twice as large as the holdings of any other library in the United States and Western Europe.

The annotated bibliography by Dr. Walter C. Clemens, Jr., on Soviet disarmament policy during the years 1917–1963 was another welcome research tool for the study of a little-known aspect of Soviet foreign policy.[57] It lists government documents, books, pamphlets, and articles in periodicals on the subject, most of which are available in the Hoover Library.

The last item to be published in 1965 was a detailed guide to the so-called treason trials in South Africa (1956–1961), which stirred so much interest among American and foreign scholars.[58] It was prepared by Dr. Thomas Karis, who had done extensive research on these trials and was well qualified to handle this complicated material. His work was based on a microfilm of selected trial documents acquired by the Hoover Institution and facilitates the use of the 24 reels of microfilm.

There are also various typescript inventories of special microfilm collections, such as K. M. Glazier, "Index to South Africa Materials, 1902–1963," 15 reels; "The Herbert Weiss Collection on the Belgian Congo," 13 reels; "Index of Microfilms of the Grand Conseil de l'Afrique Occidentale Française," 15 reels; and "Inventory of the A. B. Xuma Papers," 10 reels. See also Ms. Karen Fung, "Index to 'Portraits' in *West Africa*," later published as an article in *African Studies Bulletin* (December 1966). There is also an index and concordance to the 156 reels of microfilm of the Confidential Prints of the Colonial and Foreign offices of Great Britain.

The African Studies Association undertook a survey of library resources on Africa in the United States whose findings were to be published in its *Bulletin*. Dr. Peter Duignan prepared a survey of the African collections in the libraries of Stanford University for the association. This survey was published in the September 1966 issue of the *African Studies Bulletin* and is also available in reprint form.[59] It traces the history of the African Collection in the Hoover Institution, evaluates strengths, and lists its most important holdings for particular colonies, regions, and recently established countries, as well as archival material available on microfilm.

The next item to appear in the Bibliographical Series was Karol Maichel's catalog of Russian newspapers in the Hoover Institution.[60] A survey of the Russian holdings in all the libraries of the United States revealed that the Hoover Institution had the largest holdings of Russian newspapers in this country. Maichel's *Catalog* lists these holdings and includes references to similar catalogs prepared earlier by the Library of Congress and the library of Columbia University. It was welcomed by scholars and students as a useful guide to the Institution's newspaper resources.

The curator of the African Collection, Dr. Peter Duignan, encouraged by the Library Committee of the African Studies Association, had begun publication of the *Africana Newsletter*, meant to provide scholars and students with "information on research projects, library, bibliographic, and archival material dealing with Africa south of the Sahara." The *Newsletter* became a periodical publication of the Hoover Institution. The first issue appeared in October 1962, and in 1965, after six issues had appeared (last issue: 2, no. 2, December 1964), the *Newsletter* was merged with the *African Studies Bulletin*, the official organ of the African Studies Association. In 1965 and 1966, the Institution published the *Bulletin* for the African Studies Committee, with Professor David W. Brokensha of the University of California at Berkeley and Dr. Duignan as joint editors.

Both the *Newsletter* and the *Bulletin* contained a wealth of bibliographical information. Surveys of the African holdings of several American libraries, bibliographical essays, bibliographies of various kinds, and other information on research resources on Africa made up the contents of the *Newsletter* and later filled more than half of the *Bulletin*. Both were major contributions by the Hoover Institution toward the dissemination of bibliographical reference information to scholars, students, and librarians.

Between 1966 and 1968, the Hoover Institution prepared and published eleven bibliographical tools of varying kinds, thereby enlarging the Institution's service to the users of its library and to scholars at large.

In the wake of a large-scale transfer of worldwide statistical documentation from the Hoover Institution to the reorganized Documents Division of the Stanford University Library, Mrs. Joyce Ball was encouraged to edit a reference guide to major runs of foreign statistical documents.[61] At the same time, the then-curator of the German area collection at the University Library was interested in producing a checklist of German-language serials and series available in all of the libraries of the University. At that time no computer checking was possible; hence the list was put together painstakingly by hand by Gabor Erdelyi.[62] Also in 1967 appeared the Berton-Wu guide to contemporary China that John Fairbank, the doyen of sinology and a history professor at Harvard University, called a minor masterpiece.[63]

The year 1968 saw the publication of two valuable bibliographies in the Russian area. The first, a guide to the Menshevik movement, was compiled by longtime Hoover staff member, Anna M. Bourguina.[64] Her many years' work with Boris I. Nicolaevsky, a leader of the Russian Social Democratic Party, allowed her to create a truly comprehensive bibliography, based heavily on his vast collection of sources. A second publication was a bibliography dealing with the Imperial Russian Army and the history of its various regiments, produced by M. Lyons.[65] Edward Smith, a former U.S. foreign service officer, prepared a bilbiography of the Okhrana, the Russian secret police, which Hoover published in 1967.[66]

As a labor of love, Philip T. McLean, soon after retiring as librarian of the Institution, pulled together in two volumes of typescript a listing of archival, manuscript, and special collections.[67] (These volumes were eventually superseded by a guide to the archives published in 1980.) In 1970, the first of a series of new area surveys was issued as a guide to the collections. Agnes F. Peterson's *Western Europe* began the series.[68]

The curator of the Central and Western European Collection had invested a great deal of effort in documenting the establishment and consolidation of the French Fifth Republic and the war in Algeria. An annotated and carefully indexed bibliography for the period 1958–1965 was published in 1970,[69] followed by a second volume covering the years 1966–1970 to the end of the first phase of the Fifth Republic and de Gaulle's resignation.[70]

In 1970 Ronald Chilcote, a professor at the University of California at Riverside, assembled a massive two-volume bibliography on revolution and change in Latin America.[71]

A major guide (7,935 listings), *International Organization: An Interdisciplinary Bibliography*, was compiled by Dr. Michael Hass and published in 1971.[72] The study successively deals with international organizations in their historical context from antiquity to the present century, the League of Nations, the United Nations, regional organizations of an international kind, and proposals for world government, all with detailed thematic subdivisions.

A guide to resources for African studies in the United States, prepared by Peter Duignan, was the first handbook on this particular topic to be published in this country. The guide concentrates on material in the National Archives and describes the holdings of 95 library and missionary collections, 108 church and missionary archives, and 95 art and ethnographic collections. It also provides details on the size, location, founding dates, and other organizational data for each of these bodies.[73]

Ronald Chilcote's bibliography on emerging nationalism in Portuguese Africa appeared at a time when guerrilla movements had launched a general assault on the Portuguese empire in Africa and covers the birth of these movements up to 1965, as reflected in a wealth of ephemeral publications. The bibliography formed part of a wider project to collect, translate, and edit a volume of documents issued by the Portuguese African nationalist movements. The bibliography is divided by geographical areas, with special sections on particular bodies.[74]

The largest extant guide on African studies appeared in 1971. Edited and largely compiled by Peter Duignan and Helen Conover, the book lists 3,127 entries, each one annotated.[75] Its first section covers research organizations, libraries, archives, and the book trade, subdivided by geographical areas. The second part deals with general African bibliographies, and the third with specific subjects—history, politics, arts. The fourth provides data on each region, as a colony power and as an independent country. Also in 1971, the Institution published a bibliography compiled by historians at UCLA on Southern African history before 1900.[76]

Publication of Robert Hess and Dalvin Coger's bibliography of primary sources covering Africa before the completion of the European conquest proved a difficult task as more than 3,700 white travelers had visited Africa and left a significant record of their activities. The authors' approach was therefore selective; still the study includes 7,732 entries.[77]

During the same period, the Hoover published an annotated bibliography on the history of Ethiopia and the Horn of Africa by Harold G. Marcus, again the first of its kind in this field. Over 2,000 entries cover books and journal articles in English, French, Italian, German, Russian, and other languages. The author especially stressed geographical journals since in the nineteenth century these publications were the most important sources and contained much information on related disciplines.[78]

Russell H. Bartley and Stuart L. Wagner's 1972 survey of American library resources for Latin American studies included Hoover's collections.[79]

A bibliography on colonialism in modern Africa, prepared by Peter Duignan and Lewis H. Gann, appeared in 1973. It is the most comprehensive survey of its kind and was the last volume of their standard five-volume work, *Colonialism in Africa*, published by Cambridge University Press. Containing 2,516 annotated entries and describing works in six different languages, the guide constitutes a general introduction to colonial research and research institutions concerned with Africa. The authors discuss the various publications of leading centers, institutions, libraries, and archives in Western Europe, the United States, and Africa (complete with institutional descriptions), followed by a subject guide for Africa in general and area guides for each colonial power, subdivided into regions, and particular colonies.[80]

A Ghanian librarian, J. O. Asamani, compiled *Index Africanus*, a catalog of articles in Western languages dealing with Africa, published between 1885 and 1965 in periodicals, *Festschriften*, symposia, and conference proceedings. The first section covers Africa in general, subdivided by particular disciplines. Subsequent sections deal with particular regions, again subdivided by countries, and then by topics.[81]

Overall, the bibliographical work done by the Hoover Institution was at the time the most extensive of its kind, approached both in quality and quantity only by the Library of Congress.

The 1970s also were a very productive decade for the bibliographies of Western European and Eastern European collections. The vast avalanche of books on World War II had slowed somewhat, and it became feasible for Janet Ziegler, senior reference librarian at UCLA, to concentrate on a list of books in English on the war.[82]

In 1951, George Tanham had written his dissertation on the Belgian underground and incidentally produced a checklist of Belgian underground publications at Hoover. In 1971, his thesis was translated into French and published, making the information available to a wider scholarly audience.[83] Similarly Werner Warmbrunn's dissertation on the Netherlands under German occupation provided a guide to Hoover materials on the Dutch underground.[84]

In 1971, the Museum of Art at Stanford organized an exhibit of propaganda posters and produced a catalog utilizing the pictorial riches of a vast but underused

Hoover collection.[85] A reference tool for the use of the newly founded Consortium of Western Universities and Colleges was also prepared—a list of materials on microfilm available for circulation among consortium members.[86]

Of particular interest to scholars in British history was a new, updated edition of Carl F. Brand's *History of the British Labour Party*,[87] which also gave an overview of the riches of Hoover holdings on the Labour Party.

The Institution has traditionally been interested in youth movements, particularly in the German Youth Movement, which was dissolved in 1933 and of which individual strands were incorporated into the Hitler Youth in nazi times. From the old youth movement headquarters in Jugendburg Ludwigstein, the Hoover managed to acquire a large number of serial publications, as well as books and pamphlets. In 1974, a checklist was prepared of all the various materials in the collection.[88]

Ralph H. Lutz played an important part in the establishment of the Hoover Library and in the development of the Central and Western European Collections, and a biographical study and affectionate description of his association with the Institution was put together by his son-in-law, Dr. Charles Burdick. The account of the early growth of the collections is particularly interesting.[89]

In the 1970s, the need for detailed bibliographical overviews of selected countries became obvious. No survey, for example, had ever been made of the Hoover's holdings on Great Britain. This overview now became particularly important since the Government Document Department in the University Library had built up a fine collection of microfilms, particularly from the Foreign and the Cabinet offices.[90] Surveys were also made by the curator of the Central and Western European collections for the German collections.[91] This complemented some earlier lists that had been made informally as the need arose, such as a bibliography on German National Socialism,[92] a list of periodicals issued by the German Communist Party in factories in the 1920s and early 1930s,[93] a preliminary bibliography on European unification movements,[94] and a description by James Robertson of the Institution's German working-class collection.[95]

A list of French parliamentary papers at Hoover and at the Stanford University Library was made in 1964,[96] and a new extensive overview of the French collection in 1976.[97] Surveys of holdings on Ireland,[98] Portugal,[99] and Austria[100] were also put together. A detailed survey of the Austrian collections for the period 1886–1918 appeared in a newsletter.[101]

Unfortunately, no extensive survey of the Italian collections exists, and only a mimeographed list of fascist serials is available.[102]

Since the Spanish Civil War material collected and donated to the library by Burnett Bolloten had a large newspaper component, a list of those papers was made and is available at the reference librarian's desk,[103] as are all the other lists.

Recently scholarly and popular interest in the subject of the Holocaust has risen. To meet the demand for information on archival materials available at Hoover on this subject, Agnes F. Peterson compiled an annotated list.[104]

During the 1970s, the Hoover Institution Press published half a dozen bibliographies and reference guides in the Soviet and East European field. Two of these dealt with individuals: Sidney Heitman's bibliography on Bukharin,[105] and Louis Sinclair's bibliography on Trotsky.[106] Three others covered the study of various East European nations in differing periods of history: Ivan Volgyes's work on the Hungarian Soviet Republic of 1919,[107] published in 1970; Elemer Bako's monumental two-volume guide to Hungarian studies,[108] issued in 1973; and C. M. Nowak's annotated bibliography on Czechoslovak-Polish relations in the 1918–1939 period.[109] Another reference work published in 1970 was a listing of Western sources for the study of the Soviet armed forces, compiled by Michael Parrish.[110] Senior Fellow Martin Anderson edited an annotated bibliography on the question of conscription in the United States (1976).[111]

Since 1970, the Hoover Institution has also published a number of important bibliographies based on the holdings of the East Asian Collection. Two critical surveys of Hoover's Chinese-language holdings came out in 1975 and 1981, respectively. The first is a survey of materials on the 1911 Chinese Revolution by Winston Hsieh,[112] and the second is a study by Ming Chan of source materials on the Chinese labor movement during the 55 years before the establishment of the communist government.[113] The Hoover Press issued a concise general survey of the East Asian Collection's holdings prepared by then-curator John T. Ma.[114] Bibliographies of two kinds of Chinese serial publications, one government serials and the other academic serials, were prepared by Julia Tung, the Chinese bibliographer, and published in 1979 and 1982, respectively.[115–16] In 1981, a listing by Michiko Kiyohara, the Japanese bibliographer, of monographs and periodicals on the Japanese colonial expansion to Sakhalin, Korea, Taiwan, and Micronesia was published.[117] A small but very important listing is the *Asian Supplement* to the Hoover Press microfilm catalog. Collected in this list are materials on communist base areas during the Chinese Civil War of 1945–1949.[118]

The Hoover's East Asian Collection and the East Asiatic Library of the University of California at Berkeley issued four checklists. Compiled jointly by the two libraries, these checklists surveyed the strengths of the combined library holdings of two of the outstanding East Asian libraries in selected fields and are useful tools for cooperative library development and services. The three lists of Japanese-language materials in local histories, company histories, and newspapers were all published in 1978 with a grant from the Japan–United States Friendship Commission.[119–121] The Chinese local histories list was published in 1980.[122] Compilations of joint checklists of the Chinese newspapers and Japanese government documents are currently in process.

Printing orders for the volumes in the Bibliographic Series published before 1960 ran from 200 to 750 copies. Later the print runs were increased to 1,000 copies, and recently some items for which larger demand could be expected were printed in quantities of 3,000 copies. It was also necessary to reprint a few of the items because of unexpected demand. From a financial point of view, the cost of production of these bibliographical reference tools is greater than income from their sale, and only a few items in recent years have approached the break-even point. The Institution covers the deficit from generous donations of individuals and corporations.

Once the G. K. Hall *Catalog* of the Institution's holdings was published (1969–1972), the need for surveys of Hoover holdings lessened. Financial support for general reference tools declined, and so fewer bibliographies have appeared in recent years. Between 1969 and 1972 the curatorial staff did, however, produce a series of brief and inexpensive paperback surveys of their holdings. (See *Africa and the Middle East*; *East Asia*; *Western Europe*; and *Latin America*.)

In 1980, the Hoover Press published two major survey guides. The first was a comprehensive guide to the holdings of the Hoover Institution Archives,[123] compiled by Charles G. Palm and Dale Reed. (See Chapter 11 for a full description of archival finding aids.) It is an annotated listing of the 3,569 individual collections held in 1978. Its detailed index facilitates location of materials according to subject. The second work, edited by Joseph D. Dwyer, is a narrative survey, country by country, of the entire holdings of the Hoover Institution dealing with Russia, the Soviet Union, and Eastern Europe.[124] It stresses published materials held in the library, but also gives an overview of the most important relevant archival collections. The archives also compiled a genealogy of the Hoover family and a bibliography of his writings and addresses.[125–26]

Since 1978 the Hoover Institution's Soviet and East European Collection has been making a concerted effort to gather and preserve all possible uncensored and clandestine publications emanating from Eastern Europe, particularly Poland. The Solidarity period in Poland produced an especially great amount of documents. In 1982 Joseph D. Dwyer compiled a guide to the Institution's nearly one thousand items of this type.[127]

These achievements in the field of bibliographical reference work must be credited largely to the area curators and to scholars dedicated to library research. It was their initiative and work that produced these results. They were greatly aided by the librarians in the reference and cataloging departments and other staff. Without their team work, the results would not have been as good as scholarly users and critical reviewers have found them. This bibliographic research may be among the most important and long lasting of Hoover's many services to scholarship.

NOTES

1. A *Catalogue of Paris Peace Conference Delegation Propaganda in the Hoover War Library*. Stanford: Stanford University Press, 1926. 96 p. (Hoover Institution Bibliographical Series 1.) (The full name of this series changed several times. In this essay, for consistency, it will be called the "Hoover Institution Bibliographical Series," its present name.)

2. Almond, Nina, and Lutz, Ralph Haswell, comps. *An Introduction to a Bibliography of the Paris Peace Conference: Collections of Sources, Archive Publications, and Source Books*. Stanford: Stanford University Press, 1935. 32 p. (Hoover Institution Bibliographical Series 2.)

3. Krassovsky, Dimitry M. "Subject List of Pre-war Russian Material in the Hoover Library." Stanford, 1931. 85 p. Typewritten in Russian.

4. Rainov, T. I., comp. *November Revolution of 1918 in Germany: An Annotated Bibliography*. Translated by Dimitry Krassovsky from *Istorik marksist*, 1933, no. 5 (33): 170–207, and no. 6 (34): 159–62. Stanford, 1938. 72 p.

5. Krassovsky, Dimitry M. "Russian Pseudonyms, Initials, etc.: Materials for the Dictionary." Compiled at Hoover Library, Stanford University, and University of California at Los Angeles, 1934–1948. Los Angeles, 1951. 307 p. Typewritten. (Includes "Supplement" [l:180–96] and "Index to the Real Names" [l:197–307].)

6. Krassovsky, Dimitry M. "Biographical Index of Slavic Men and Women of Letters, Science, Art, Politics, Army, Navy, Etc." Stanford, 1934–1954. 9 vols. Typewritten.

7. Krassovsky, Dimitry M. "Transliteration of Russian Names." Stanford, 1944. 6 p. Typewritten.

8. Perry, Ruth M. "Clandestine Publications Issued in Belgium During the German Occupation, 1914–1918: With a Checklist of Clandestine Serials in the Hoover Library on War, Revolution and Peace . . . May 1939." M.A. thesis, University of California at Berkeley, 1939. 67 p. Typewritten.

9. Almond, Nina, and Fisher, Harold H. *Special Collections in the Hoover Library on War, Revolution and Peace*. Stanford, 1940. 111 p.

10. Chamberlin, Waldo, comp. *Industrial Relations in Wartime Great Britain, 1914–1918: Annotated Bibliography of Materials in the Hoover Library on War, Revolution and Peace*. Prepared under the direction of the Division of Industrial Relations, Graduate School of Business, Stanford University. Stanford: Stanford University Press; and London: H. Milford and Oxford University Press, 1940. 239 p. Reproduced from typescript.

11. Chamberlin, Waldo, comp. *Industrial Relations in Germany, 1914–1939: Annotated Bibliography of Materials in the Hoover Library on War, Revolution and Peace and the Stanford University Library.* Prepared under the direction of the Division of Industrial Relations, Graduate School of Business, Stanford University. Stanford: Stanford University Press; and London: H. Milford and Oxford University Press, 1942. 403 p. Reproduced from typescript.

12. Chao, Kuo-chun. "Draft Survey of Materials Relating to Communism in China, 1927–1934" (collected by Harold R. Isaacs). Stanford, 1948. 57 p. Dittoed.

13. Committee for a Free Asia. Historical Research Branch. "List of the Writings of Mao Tse-tung Found in the Hoover Library at Stanford University." Stanford, 1951. 25 p. Dittoed.

14. Sworakowski, Witold S. "List of the Polish Underground Collection in the Hoover Library, 1939–1945." Stanford, 1948. 18 p. Mimeographed.

15. van der Belen, Jacques. *Inventaire de la collection consacrée à la Belgique dans la deuxième guerre mondiale réunie par les soins de la Belgian American Educational Foundation, Inc., à l'intention de la Hoover Library on War, Revolution and Peace, Stanford University, California.* Brussels: Les Presses Tilbury, 1950. 128 p.

16. Higashiuchi, Yoshio. *Literature on Contemporary Japan: Based on Materials Collected by the Tokyo Office, the Hoover Institute and Library on War, Revolution and Peace.* Stanford and Tokyo, 1951. 138 p.

17. Sworakowski, Helena. "List of Periodical Publications Published by Belorussian, Russian, and Ukrainian DP's, 1945–1951: Holdings of the Hoover Library." Stanford, 1951. 134 p. Typewritten.

18. Oey, Giok Po. "Survey of Chinese-Language Materials on Southeast Asia in the Hoover Institute and Library." Prepared for Southeast Asia Program, Department of Far Eastern Studies, Cornell University, with the assistance of the staff of the Hoover Library. First draft. Annotated. Stanford, 1952. 71 p. Dittoed.

19. Sworakowski, Witold S. *The Hoover Library Collection on Russia.* Stanford: Stanford University Press, 1954. 42 p. (Collection Survey, no. 1.)

20. Boeninger, Hildegard R. *The Hoover Library Collection on Germany.* Stanford: Stanford University Press, 1955. 56 p. (Collection Survey, no. 2.)

21. Ike, Nobutaka. *The Hoover Institution Collection on Japan.* Stanford: Hoover Institution, 1958. 63 p. (Collection Survey, no. 3.)

22. "Indonesian-Language Publications in the Hoover Library." Stanford: 1953. 21 p. Dittoed.

23. Mote, Frederick W. *Japanese-Sponsored Governments in China, 1937–1945: An Annotated Bibliography Compiled from Materials in the Chinese Collection of the Hoover Library.* Stanford: Stanford University Press, 1954. 68 p. (Hoover Institution Bibliographical Series 3.)

24. Sworakowski, Witold S., ed. "Bibliography of Books, Pamphlets and Articles in Periodicals Dealing with Federation Plans for Central and Eastern Europe Developed During the Second World War." Stanford, 1954. 86 p. Dittoed.

25. Sworakowski, Witold S., ed. "List of Archive Material Dealing with Federation Plans for Central and Eastern Europe Developed During the Second World War." Stanford, 1954. 30 p. Dittoed.

26. Perry, Ruth M. *New Sources for Research in Nigerian History.* London: International African Institute, 1955. 3 p.

27. Perry, Ruth M. "A Preliminary Bibliography of the Literature of Nationalism in Nigeria." London: International African Institute, 1956. 38 p. Mimeographed.

28. Hoover Institute and Library. "Reading Checklists on Asian and Southeast Asian Countries: Selected Items in Western Languages in the Hoover Library and in the Stanford University Library; Prepared for Use of Participants in the Program for Overseas Development in the Hoover Institute and Library." Stanford, 1955–1956. 14 separately paginated parts. Total 248 pages. Dittoed or mimeographed.

29. Sworakowski, Witold S. "Bibliography of Law Journals Currently Published in Eastern Europe." Stanford: Hoover Institute and Library, 1955. 9 p. Mimeographed.

30. Wu, Eugene. *Leaders of Twentieth-Century China: An Annotated Bibliography of Selected Chinese Biographical Works in the Hoover Library.* Stanford: Stanford University Press, 1956. 106 p. (Hoover Institution Bibliographical Series 4.)

31. Sworakowski, Witold S. "Periodicals and Newspapers Concerning East-Central and East Europe in the Library of the Hoover Institution: A Checklist." Stanford, 1958. 22 p. Mimeographed.

32. Nahm, Andrew C., comp. *Japanese Penetration of Korea, 1894–1910: A Checklist of Japanese Archives in the Hoover Institution.* Compiled under the direction of Peter A. Berton. Stanford: Hoover Institution, 1959. 103 p. (Hoover Institution Bibliographical Series 5.)

33. Israel, John. *The Chinese Student Movement, 1927–1937: A Bibliographical Essay Based on the Resources of the Hoover Institution.* Stanford: Hoover Institution, 1959. 29 p. (Hoover Institution Bibliographical Series 6.)

34. Uchida, Naosaku. *The Overseas Chinese: A Bibliographical Essay Based on the Resources of the Hoover Institution.* Stanford: Hoover Institution, 1959. 134 p. (Hoover Institution Bibliographical Series 7.)

35. Brown, John C. "A Reading List on Africa South of the Sahara." Stanford: Hoover Institution, 1959. 19 p. Duplicated.

36. Stillmann, Minna. "Foreign Statistical Documents in Stanford Libraries: A Preliminary Survey of Holdings Published by Approximately 198 Countries and Dependent Territories in Collections of the Document Library of the Stanford University Libraries, the Food Research Institute Library and the Hoover Institution." Stanford: 1959. 164 p. Mimeographed.

37. Hsüeh, Chün-tu. *The Chinese Communist Movement, 1921–1937: An Annotated Bibliography of Selected Materials in the Chinese Collection of the Hoover Institution on War, Revolution and Peace.* Stanford: Hoover Institution, 1960. 131 p. (Hoover Institution Bibliographical Series 8.)

38. Hsüeh, Chün-tu. *The Chinese Communist Movement, 1937–1949: An Annotated Bibliography of Selected Materials in the Chinese Collection of the Hoover Institution on War, Revolution and Peace.* Stanford: Hoover Institution, 1962. 312 p. (Hoover Institution Bibliographical Series 11.)

39. Duignan, Peter. *Madagascar (the Malagasy Republic): A List of Materials in the African Collection of Stanford University and the Hoover Institution on War, Revolution and Peace.* Stanford: Hoover Institution, 1962. 25 p. (Hoover Institution Bibliographical Series 9.)

40. Maichel, Karol. *Guide to Russian Reference Books,* Vol. 1, *General Bibliographies and Reference Books.* Edited by J. S. G. Simmons. Stanford: Hoover Institution, 1962. 92 p. (Hoover Institution Bibliographical Series 10.)

41. Maichel, Karol. *Guide to Russian Reference Books,* Vol. 2, *History, Auxiliary Historical Sciences, Ethnography, and Geography.* Edited by J. S. G. Simmons. Stanford: Hoover Institution, 1964. 297 p. (Hoover Institution Bibliographical Series 18.)

42. Kent, George O., comp. *A Catalog of Files and Microfilms of the German Foreign Ministry Archives, 1920–1945.* Stanford: Hoover Institution, 1962–1972. 4 vols. (Hoover Institution Publications 29.)

43. Sworakowski, Witold S. "A Survey of the Collection on Armenia in the Hoover Institution on War, Revolution and Peace." Stanford: 1962. 6 p. Photocopy of typescript.

44. Collins, Robert, and Duignan, Peter. *Americans in Africa: A Preliminary Guide to American Missionary Archives and Library Manuscript Collections on Africa.* Stanford: Hoover Institution, 1963. vii, 96 p. (Hoover Institution Bibliographical Series 12.)

45. Duignan, Peter, and Glazier, Kenneth M. *A Checklist of Serials for African Studies: Based*

on the Libraries of the Hoover Institution and Stanford University. Stanford: Hoover Institution, 1963. 104 p. (Hoover Institution Bibliographical Series 13.)

46. Duignan, Peter, ed. *United States and Canadian Publications on Africa in 1961.* Stanford: Hoover Institution, 1963. 114 p. (Hoover Institution Bibliographical Series 14.)

47. Duignan, Peter, ed., and Sims, Hilary, comp. *United States and Canadian Publications on Africa in 1962.* Stanford: Hoover Institution, 1964. 104 p. (Hoover Institution Bibliographical Series 15.)

48. Duignan, Peter, ed., and Hofmann, Liselotte, comp. *United States and Canadian Publications on Africa in 1963.* Stanford: Hoover Institution, 1965. 136 p. (Hoover Institution Bibliographical Series 20.)

49. Hofmann, Liselotte, comp. *United States and Canadian Publications on Africa in 1964.* Stanford: Hoover Institution, 1966. 180 p. (Hoover Institution Bibliographical Series 25.)

50. Hofmann, Liselotte, comp. *United States and Canadian Publications on Africa in 1965.* Stanford: Hoover Institution, 1967. 227 p. (Hoover Institution Bibliographical Series 34.)

51. Hofmann, Liselotte, comp. *United States and Canadian Publications on Africa in 1966.* Stanford: Hoover Institution, 1970. 300 p. (Hoover Institution Bibliographical Series 38.)

52. Glazier, Kenneth M. *Africa South of the Sahara: A Select and Annotated Bibliography, 1958–1963.* Stanford: Hoover Institution, 1964. 65 p. (Hoover Institution Bibliographical Series 16.)

53. Glazier, Kenneth M. *Africa South of the Sahara: A Select and Annotated Bibliography, 1964–1968.* Stanford: Hoover Institution Press, 1969. 139 p. (Hoover Institution Bibliographical Series 42.)

54. Heinz, Grete, and Peterson, Agnes F. *NSDAP Hauptarchiv: Guide to the Hoover Institution Microfilm Collection.* Stanford: Hoover Institution, 1964. 175 p. (Hoover Institution Bibliographical Series 17.)

55. Bridgman, Jon, and Clarke, David E. *German Africa: A Select Annotated Bibliography.* Stanford: Hoover Institution, 1965. 120 p. (Hoover Institution Bibliographical Series 19.)

56. Sworakowski, Witold S. *The Communist International and Its Front Organizations: A Research Guide and Checklist of Holdings in American and European Libraries.* Stanford: Hoover Institution, 1965. 493 p. (Hoover Institution Bibliographical Series 21.)

57. Clemens, Walter C., Jr. *Soviet Disarmament Policy, 1917–1963: An Annotated Bibliography of Soviet and Western Sources.* Stanford: Hoover Institution, 1965. 151 p. (Hoover Institution Bibliographical Series 22.)

58. Karis, Thomas. *The Treason Trial in South Africa: A Guide to the Microfilm Record of the Trial.* Stanford: Hoover Institution, 1965. 124 p. (Hoover Institution Bibliographical Series 23.)

59. Duignan, Peter. "The African Collections at Stanford University." Stanford, 1966. 17 p. Mimeographed. (The text of the above item, with slight changes, was printed in *African Studies Bulletin* 9, no. 2 [September 1966]: 25–34.)

60. Maichel, Karol. *Soviet and Russian Newspapers at the Hoover Institution: A Catalog.* Stanford: Hoover Institution, 1966. 235 p. (Hoover Institution Bibliographical Series 24.)

61. Ball, Joyce, ed. *Foreign Statistical Documents: A Bibliography of General, International Trade and Agricultural Statistics, Including Holdings of the Stanford University Libraries.* Stanford: Hoover Institution Press, 1967. 173 p.

62. Erdelyi, Gabor, ed. *German Periodical Publications: A Checklist of German Language Serials and Series Currently Received in the Stanford University Libraries.* Prepared in collaboration with Agnes F. Peterson. Stanford: Hoover Institution Press, 1967. 175 p. (Hoover Institution Bibliographical Series 27.)

63. Berton, Peter, and Wu, Eugene. *Contemporary China: A Research Guide.* Stanford: Hoover Institution, 1967. 695 p. (Hoover Institution Bibliographical Series 31.)

64. Bourguina, Anna M., comp. *Russian Social Democracy, The Menshevik Movement: A*

Bibliography. Stanford: Hoover Institution Press, 1968. 391 p. (Hoover Institution Bibliographical Series 36.)

65. Lyons, M., comp. *The Russian Imperial Army: A Bibliography of Regimental Histories and Related Works*. Stanford: Hoover Institution Press, 1968. 188 p. (Hoover Institution Bibliographical Series 35.)

66. Smith, Edward Ellis. *"The Okhrana," the Russian Department of Police*. Stanford: Hoover Institution Press, 1967. 280 p. (Hoover Institution Bibliographical Series 33.)

67. McLean, Philip T. "Archival, Manuscript and Special Collections in the General Library of the Hoover Institution." 1968. 2 vols. Typewritten.

68. Peterson, Agnes F. *Western Europe: A Survey of Holdings at the Hoover Institution on War, Revolution and Peace*. Stanford: Hoover Institution Press, 1970. 60 p. (Hoover Institution Survey of Holdings 1.)

69. Heinz, Grete, and Peterson, Agnes F. *The French Fifth Republic: Establishment and Consolidation (1958–1965). An Annotated Bibliography of the Holdings at the Hoover Institution*. Stanford: Hoover Institution Press, 1970. 170 p. (Hoover Institution Bibliographical Series 44.)

70. Heinz, Grete, and Peterson, Agnes F. *The French Fifth Republic: Continuity and Change, 1966–1970. An Annotated Bibliography*. Stanford: Hoover Institution Press, 1974. 125 p. (Hoover Institution Bibliographical Series 54.)

71. Chilcote, Ronald H. *Revolution and Structural Change in Latin America: A Bibliography on Ideology, Development and the Radical Left (1930–1965)*. 2 vols. Stanford: Hoover Institution Press, 1970. (Hoover Institution Bibliographical Series 40.)

72. Hass, Michael, comp. *International Organization: An Interdisciplinary Bibliography*. Stanford: Hoover Institution Press, 1971. 944 p. (Hoover Institution Bibliographical Series 41.)

73. Duignan, Peter. *Handbook of American Resources for African Studies*. Stanford: Hoover Institution, 1967. 218 p. (Hoover Institution Bibliographical Series 29.)

74. Chilcote, Ronald H. *Emerging Nationalism in Portuguese Africa: A Bibliography of Documentary Ephemera Through 1965*. Stanford: Hoover Institution, 1969. 114 p. (Hoover Institution Bibliographical Series 39.)

75. Duignan, Peter, ed.; and Conover, Helen F., and Duignan, Peter, comps.; with the assistance of Evelyn Boyce, Liselotte Hofmann, and Karen Fung. *Guide to Research and Reference Works on Sub-Saharan Africa*. Stanford: Hoover Institution Press, 1971. 1102 p. (Hoover Institution Bibliographical Series 46.)

76. Thompson, Leonard; Elphick, Richard; and Jarick, Inez, comps. *Southern African History Before 1900: A Select Bibliography of Articles*. Stanford: Hoover Institution Press, 1971. 102 p. (Hoover Institution Bibliographical Series 49.)

77. Hess, Robert L., and Coger, Dalvan M. *Semper ex Africa . . . A Bibliography of Primary Sources for Nineteenth-Century Tropical Africa as Recorded by Explorers, Missionaries, Traders, Travelers, Administrators, Military Men, Adventurers, and Others*. Stanford: Hoover Institution, 1972. 800 p. (Hoover Institution Bibliographical Series 47.)

78. Marcus, Harold G. *The Modern History of Ethiopia and the Horn of Africa: A Select and Annotated Bibliography*. Stanford: Hoover Institution Press, 1972. 639 p. (Hoover Institution Bibliographical Series 56.)

79. See Bartley, Russell H., and Wagner, Stuart L. *Latin America in Basic Historical Collections: A Working Guide*. Stanford: Hoover Institution Press, 1972. 212 p. (Hoover Institution Bibliographical Series 17.)

80. Duignan, Peter, and Gann, Lewis H. *Colonialism in Africa, 1870–1979*, Vol. 5, *A Bibliographical Guide to Colonialism in Sub-Saharan Africa*. Cambridge, Eng.: Cambridge University Press, 1973. 552 p.

81. Asamani, J. O. *Index Africanus*. Stanford: Hoover Institution Press, 1975. 659 p. (Hoover Institution Bibliographical Series 53.)

82. Ziegler, Janet, comp. *World War II: Books in English, 1945–1965*. Stanford: Hoover Institution Press, 1971. 194 p. (Hoover Institution Bibliographical Series 45.)

83. Tanham, George Kilpatrick. "The Belgian Underground Movement, 1940–1944." Ph.D. thesis, Stanford University, 1951. 398 p. Bibliography, pp. 387–98. (Later published as *Contribution à l'histoire de la résistance belge, 1940–1944*. Brussels: Presses Universitaires, 1971. 204 p.)

84. Warmbrunn, Werner. "The Netherlands Under German Occupation, 1940–1945." Ph.D. thesis, Stanford University, 1955. 369 p. Bibliography, pp. 353–67. (Published as *The Dutch Under German Occupation, 1940–1945*. Stanford: Stanford University Press, 1963. 338 p.)

85. Stanford University. Museum of Art. *War, Revolution and Peace: Propaganda Posters from the Hoover Institution Archives, 1914–1945*. An Exhibition Organized by Paula Harper and Marcia Cohn Growdon. Catalog by Paula Harper. Stanford: Stanford University Press, 1971. 72 p.

86. Consortium of Western Universities and Colleges. *List of Microfilms and Non-circulating Items in the Holdings of the Hoover Institution Available to Members of the Consortium*. Stanford: Hoover Institution, 1971. 21 p.

87. Brand, Carl F. *The British Labour Party: A Short History*. Stanford: Hoover Institution Press, 1974. 424 p. (Hoover Institution Publications 136.)

88. "German Youth Movement Collection: List of Materials in the Special Collection on Floor 6 of Hoover Tower and of Materials Sent to the Archives." Stanford, 1974. 100 p. Typewritten.

89. Burdick, Charles Burton. *Ralph H. Lutz and the Hoover Institution*. Stanford: Hoover Institution Press, 1974. 185 p. (Hoover Institution Publications 131.)

90. "Survey of Hoover Institution Holdings on Great Britain." Stanford, 1976. 34 p. Typewritten.

91. "Survey of the German Collection at the Hoover Institution." Stanford, 1970. 110 p. Typewritten.

92. "German National Socialism: A Bibliography Prepared Under the Direction of Mr. Edrich—for Professor Ralph H. Lutz in 1939." N.p., 1939. 120 p. Typewritten in German.

93. "Kommunistische Partei Deutschlands: Betriebs- und Fabrik-Zeitungen, 1929–1931" [List of periodicals issued by communist groups in factories in Germany]. Stanford, 1948. 28 p. Typewritten.

94. Deutsche Gesellschaft für Auswärtige Politik. Forschungsinstitut, Frankfurt am Main. "Publikationen der Europäischen Bewegung, 1947 bis 1. Juli 1953: Eine vorläufige Bibliographie, zusammengestellt vom Institut für Europäische Politik und Wirtschaft, Frankfurt am Main, in Verbindung mit dem Hoover Institute and Library on War, Revolution and Peace, Stanford University." Frankfurt am Main, 1953. 42 p. Typewritten.

95. Robertson, James. "The Hoover Institution's German Working Class Collection." *International Labor and Working Class History*, no. 12 (November 1977): 10–18.

96. "French Parliamentary Papers in the Hoover Institution and the Stanford Library." Stanford, 1964. 3 p. Typewritten.

97. "Survey of the French Collections at the Hoover Institution." Stanford, 1976. 75 p. Typewritten.

98. "Survey of Hoover Institution Holdings on Ireland." Stanford, 1976. 6 p. Typewritten.

99. "Survey of Hoover Institution Holdings on Portugal." Stanford, 1976. 10 p. Typewritten.

100. "Survey of Hoover Institution Holdings on Austria." Stanford, 1976. 16 p. Typewritten.

101. "Austro-Hungarian Material, 1867–1918, at the Hoover Institution, Stanford University." *Austrian History Newsletter*, no. 2 (1961): 25–32.

102. "Italian Fascist Serials." Stanford, 1948. 39 p. Mimeographed.

103. "List of Newspapers Integrated in the Newspaper Collection from the Bolloten Collection." Stanford, 1979. 50 p. Photocopied list of cards.

104. Peterson, Agnes F. "Annotated List of Archival Materials Relating to the Holocaust at the Hoover Institution Archives." Stanford, 1980. 45 p. Typewritten.

105. Heitman, Sidney, ed. and comp. *Nikolai I. Bukharin: A Bibliography.* Stanford: Hoover Institution Press, 1969. 181 p. (Hoover Institution Bibliographical Series 37.)

106. Sinclair, Louis, comp. *Leon Trotsky: A Bibliography.* Stanford: Hoover Institution Press, 1972. 1089 p. (Hoover Institution Bibliographical Series 50.)

107. Volgyes, Ivan. *The Hungarian Soviet Republic, 1919: An Evaluation and a Bibliography.* Stanford: Hoover Institution Press, 1970. 90 p. (Hoover Institution Bibliographical Series 43.)

108. Elemer Bako, comp. *Guide to Hungarian Studies.* Stanford: Hoover Institution Press, 1973. 2 vols. (Hoover Institution Bibliographical Series 52.)

109. Nowak, C. M., comp. *Czechoslovak-Polish Relations, 1918–1939: A Selected and Annotated Bibliography.* Stanford: Hoover Institution Press, 1975. 218 p. (Hoover Institution Bibliographical Series 55.)

110. Parrish, Michael, comp. *Soviet Armed Forces: Books in English, 1950–1967.* Stanford: Hoover Institution Press, 1970. 128 p. (Hoover Institution Bibliographical Series 48.)

111. Anderson, Martin, ed. *Conscription: A Select and Annotated Bibliography.* Stanford: Hoover Institution Press, 1976. 472 p. (Hoover Institution Bibliographical Series 57.)

112. Hsieh, Winston. *Chinese Historiography on the Revolution of 1911: A Critical Survey and a Selected Bibliography.* Stanford: Hoover Institution Press, 1975. 165 p. (Hoover Institution Studies, 34.)

113. Chan, Ming K. *Historiography of the Chinese Labor Movement, 1895–1949: A Critical Survey and Bibliography of Selected Chinese Source Materials at the Hoover Institution.* Stanford: Hoover Institution Press, 1981. 232 p. (Hoover Institution Bibliographical Series 60.)

114. Ma, John T. *East Asia: A Survey of Holdings at the Hoover Institution on War, Revolution and Peace.* Stanford: Hoover Institution Press, 1971. 24 p. (Hoover Institution Survey of Holdings 2.)

115. Tung, Julia, comp. *Bibliography of Chinese Government Serials, 1880–1949: Materials in Hoover Institution on War, Revolution and Peace.* Stanford: Hoover Institution East Asian Collection, 1979. 136 p.

116. Tung, Julia, comp. *Bibliography of Chinese Academic Serials, Pre-1949: Materials in Hoover Institution on War, Revolution and Peace.* Stanford: Hoover Institution East Asian Collection, 1982. 107 p.

117. Kiyohara, Michiko, comp. *A Checklist of Monographs and Periodicals on the Japanese Colonial Empire in the East Asian Collection, Hoover Institution on War, Revolution and Peace.* Stanford: Hoover Institution Press, 1981. 334 p.

118. *Hoover Institution Microfilms: Asian Supplement.* Stanford: Hoover Institution Press, 1977. 13 p.

119. *A Checklist of Japanese Local Histories.* Study sponsored by Japan–United States Friendship Commission. East Asiatic Library, University of California at Berkeley, and East Asian Collection, Hoover Institution, Stanford University, 1978. 312 p. (East Asia Library Series 1.)

120. *A Checklist of Japanese Company Histories.* Study sponsored by Japan–United States Friendship Commission. East Asiatic Library, University of California at Berkeley, and East Asian Collection, Hoover Institution, Stanford University, 1978. 92 p. (East Asian Library Series 2.)

121. *A Checklist of Japanese Newspapers.* Study sponsored by Japan–United States Friendship Commission. East Asiatic Library, University of California at Berkeley, and East

Asian Collection, Hoover Institution, Stanford University, 1978. 22 p. (East Asia Library Series, 3.)

122. *A Checklist of Chinese Local Histories*. Stanford-Berkeley Joint East Asia Center, 1980. 470 p. (East Asia Library Series 4.)

123. Palm, Charles G., and Reed, Dale, comps. *Guide to the Hoover Institution Archives*. Stanford: Hoover Institution Press, 1980. 418 p. (Bibliographical Series 59.)

124. Dwyer, Joseph D., ed. *Russia, the Soviet Union, and Eastern Europe: A Survey of Holdings at the Hoover Institution on War, Revolution and Peace*. Stanford: Hoover Institution Press, 1980. 233 p. (Collection Survey 6.)

125. McLean, Hulda Hoover, comp. *Genealogy of the Herbert Hoover Family*. Stanford: Hoover Institution Press, 1977. 486 p. (Hoover Institution Bibliographical Series 58.)

126. Tracey, Kathleen H. *Herbert Hoover: A Bibliography of His Writings and Addresses*. Stanford: Hoover Institution Press, 1977. 216 p. (Hoover Institution Bibliographical Series 58.)

127. Dwyer, Joseph D., comp. "Solidarność—The Polish Uncensored Press, 1977–1982: Holdings of the Hoover Institution." Stanford: Hoover Institution Library, 1982. 48 p. Photocopied.

BIBLIOGRAPHY

UNPUBLISHED
MANUSCRIPTS

Adams, Ephraim Douglas. "Early Letters on the Hoover War Library: Also Containing a Letter from Mr. Hoover Relative to the Lusitania." Stanford: Hoover Institution Archives, n.d.

Golder, Frank A. "Correspondence, 1919–1929." (A variety of letters, notes, and articles written by and about Golder from Dr. Charles Burdick's collection.)

———. "Letters of Frank A. Golder, 1917–1926." Stanford: Hoover Institution Archives, n.d. (Two folders of unpublished manuscripts.)

Lutz, Ralph Haswell. "Correspondence, 1919–1944." (A miscellaneous collection of letters, reports, etc., from the private library of Ralph H. Lutz. These valuable materials are in the possession of Dr. Charles B. Burdick of Santa Cruz, California, and may be consulted upon permission.)

———. "Correspondence and Memoranda Between the Chairman of the Hoover War Library and the Director of University Libraries, January 8, 1925 to August 22, 1929." Palo Alto, Calif.: privately bound, n.d. (Bound copy of all notes recorded between the parties indicated, as compiled by Dr. Ralph H. Lutz, in the Burdick collection, in Santa Cruz, California.)

Paul, Gary Norman. "The Development of the Hoover Institution on War, Revolution and Peace Library, 1919–1944." Doctoral dissertation. University of California, Berkeley, 1979.

Stanford University. Librarian's Correspondence from 1891. Stanford: Stanford University Archives, 1919– .

Stanford University. Presidents' Office Documents. Stanford: Stanford University Archives, n.d.

———. Ray Lyman Wilbur Papers, Presidential and Personal. Stanford: Stanford University Archives, n.d. (The papers of all subsequent Stanford presidents also should be consulted.)

PUBLISHED REPORTS

Adams, Ephraim Douglas. *The Hoover War Collection at Stanford University, California: A Report and an Analysis.* Palo Alto, Calif.: Stanford University Press, 1921. (Major analysis of the origin and content of the early collections gathered by the Hoover War Library. Dr. Adams includes names and dates for important events in the initial organization of the collection.)

Annual Report of the Chairman, Hoover War Library. Stanford: Stanford University Press, 1929/30–1944/45.

Annual Report of the Director of Stanford University Libraries. Stanford: Stanford University Press, 1927– .

Hoover Institution on War, Revolution and Peace. Palo Alto, Calif.: Stanford University Press, 1963. (This brochure was designed to give "a brief account of the origin, development, and present status of this great scholarly resource, as well as to outline current activities and future plans.")

———. Hoover Institution on War, Revolution and Peace. *Report, 1963–1966*. Stanford: Stanford University Press, 1966.

———. *Report, 1966–1969*. Stanford: Stanford University Press, 1966.

———. *Report, 1969–1972*. Stanford: n.p., 1972.

———. *Report, 1975*. Stanford: n.p., 1976.

———. *Report, 1977*. Stanford: Hoover Press, 1978– . (Annual hereafter.)

MONOGRAPHS

Burdick, Charles Burton. *Ralph H. Lutz and the Hoover Institution*. Stanford: Hoover Institution Press, 1974.

Fisher, Harold Henry. *A Tower to Peace: The Story of the Hoover Library on War, Revolution and Peace*. Stanford: Stanford University Press, 1945. (A brief discussion of the library, history, content, research publications, construction, building, and staff by the director of the library.)

Robinson, Edgar E., and Edwards, Paul C., eds. *The Memoirs of Ray Lyman Wilbur, 1875–1949*. Stanford: Stanford University Press, 1960.

Stanford University. *Dedication of the Hoover Library on War, Revolution and Peace*. Stanford: Stanford University Press, 1941. (Transcript of the dedication ceremonies at Stanford University, including the various addresses, etc.)

Wilson, Neill Compton. *Saving Just Yesterday for Tomorrow: The Story of the Great Hoover War Library at Stanford University*. Stanford: Stanford Associates, 1935.

HOOVER INSTITUTION STAFF

Director / W. Glenn Campbell

Associate Directors / Dennis L. Bark, Richard T. Burress, John B. Dunlop, Thomas H. Henriksen, John H. Moore

Budget and Finance Officer / Sally Vanders

Public Affairs Coordinator / Julie Jordan

Assistant Directors / Joseph Kladko, Laverne M. Rabinowitz

RESEARCH

Honorary Fellows / Friedrich A. Hayek, Ronald W. Reagan, Alexander Solzhenitsyn

Senior Fellows / Richard V. Allen (by courtesy), Martin Anderson, Kenneth Arrow (by courtesy), Dennis L. Bark, Joseph Berger (by courtesy), Michael Boskin (by courtesy), Richard T. Burress, Gerald A. Dorfman, Milorad M. Drachkovitch, Peter J. Duignan, John B. Dunlop, Heinz Eulau (by courtesy), Roger A. Freeman (emeritus), Lewis H. Gann, William J. Goode (by courtesy), Robert E. Hall, Alex Inkeles, Bobby R. Inman (by courtesy), Melvyn B. Krauss, Seymour Martin Lipset, Charles E. McLure, Jr., James G. March, John H. Moore, Thomas G. Moore, Ramon H. Myers, Stefan T. Possony (emeritus), Alvin Rabushka, Rita Ricardo-Campbell, Giovanni Sartori (by courtesy), Thomas Sowell, Richard F. Staar, Nancy B. Tuma (by courtesy), Robert E. Ward (by courtesy)

Consultant / Yuan-li Wu

Senior Research Fellows / Annelise Anderson, William C. Bark, Mikhail Bernstam, John H. Bunzel, John F. Cogan, Robert Conquest, Kingsley Davis, Aaron Director, John Ferejohn, Milton Friedman, Philip C. Habib, Paul R. Hanna, Robert T. Hartmann, Thomas H. Henriksen, Robert Hessen, Walter E. Hoadley, Sidney Hook, George Lenczowski, Thomas E. MaCurdy, George Marotta, Chiaki Nishiyama, Paul Craig Roberts, Sherwin Rosen, Henry S. Rowen, William Schneider,

Kenneth E. Scott, Pablo Spiller, James B. Stockdale, Edward Teller, Darrell M. Trent, William R. Van Cleave, Eric Voegelin, Carolyn Weaver, Robert Wesson, Albert Wohlstetter

Research Fellows / Fu-mei C. Chen, Constantin Galskoy, Julie Jordan, Stephen Jurika, Jr., Sig Mickelson, William E. Ratliff, Paul B. Ryan, Pauline Ryan, Molly Tuthill

LIBRARY AND ARCHIVES

Associate Director for Library and Archives / John B. Dunlop

Secretary / Beverley Kuerner

TECHNICAL SERVICES

Assistant Director for Technical Services / Joseph Kladko

Catalog Department

Librarians / William Boreysza, Paul Thomas

Associate Librarians / Laszlo Horvath, Irene Mischkinis

Group Supervisor / Barbara Lasarev

Library Specialists / Diane Hill, Natalie Koretsky, Michael Truesdale, Joanne Fraysse

Acquisitions Department

Group Supervisor / Riva Richards

Library Specialists / Eugenia Von Salza, Bernice Ares, Marguerite Moravcsik

Conservation Officer / Judith Fortson-Jones

Library Specialist / Irene Jones

READERS' SERVICES

Head / David W. Heron

Reference

Librarian / Hilja Kukk

Associate Librarian / Linda Ann Wheeler

Circulation

Group Supervisor / Natascha Gass

Library Specialists / Galena Dotsenko, Andre Pierce

Interlibrary Loan / Andre Pierce

Photography / Helene Pashin

Serials Records

Group Supervisor / Ellen Leung

Library Specialists / Maria Quinonez, Benny Tsan, Jean Andrews, Lia Borshchevsky

CURATORSHIPS

East Asian Collection

Curator / Ramon H. Myers

Research Fellow / Fu-mei C. Chen

Deputy Curators / Emiko Moffitt, Mark Tam

Librarians / Michiko Kiyohara, Julia Tung

Associate Librarian / T. Y. Wu

Library Specialists / Akiko Grubaugh, Yu-Ching Hu, Kathy Chazan, Miyako I. Sueyoshi, Jeanne Szeto, Ito Barker, Naomi Findley, Elsie Lung, Kyoko Muecke, Mayumi Peterson

Secretary / Maxine Douglas

Africa and Middle East Collection

Curator / Peter Duignan

Deputy Curators / Lewis Gann, Karen Fung

Middle East Bibliographer / Edward Jajko

Secretary / Patricia Ortega

Russian, Soviet, and East European Collection

Curator / Robert Conquest

Deputy Curator / Joseph D. Dwyer

Library Specialists / Maciej Siekierski, Lia Borshchevsky

Secretary / Amy B. Desai

Latin and North American Collections

Curator / Joseph W. Bingaman

Library Specialist / Anna Fernicola

West European Collections

Curator / Agnes F. Peterson

Library Specialist / Helen Berman

Hanna Education Collection

Curator / Gerald A. Dorfman

Secretary / Aurelia Klipper

British Labour Collection

Honorary Curator / Peter Stansky

Imperial Russian Collection

Honorary Curator / Vasili Romanov

Spanish Archival Collection

Honorary Curator / Burnett Bolloten

Hoover Institution Archives

Archivist / Charles G. Palm

International Associate / Weldon B. Gibson

European Field Representative / Francis de Tarr

Special Representative / Franz G. Lassner

Deputy Archivist / Robert Hessen

Assistant Archivists / Elena Danielson, Dale Reed

Archival Specialists / Ronald Bulatoff, Linda Bernard, Michael Jakobson, Carol Leadenham, Robert E. Tompkins

Office Assistants / Dana Harris, Nada Stoy

Secretaries / Gailynne Bouret, Elisabeth Tatarinoff